CW00485811

XVI.—*On the Hieratic Papyrus of Nesi-Amsu,*[a] *a scribe in the Temple of Amen-Rā at Thebes, about* B.C. 305. *By* E. A. WALLIS BUDGE, *M.A., F.S.A.*

Read January 30th, 1890.

THE papyrus which is transcribed and translated in the following pages is preserved in the collection of Egyptian antiquities in the British Museum, where it bears the number 10188. It was found at Thebes in the year 1860, and was purchased by the late Mr. A. H. Rhind;[b] in 1865 it was sold to the trustees of the British Museum by Mr. David Bremner, together with a number of other papyri collected by Mr. Rhind. A few years later its existence was pointed out by Dr. Birch to Dr. Pleyte, who wrote a short article upon it,[c] in which he gave a description of the chapters and translated some passages principally from the first work written on the papyrus. In November, 1886, a further account of it was given by me,[d] together with hieroglyphic transcripts of some important passages in it.

The papyrus is about 19 feet long by 9½ inches wide, and is very fine in texture; it contains thirty-three columns, or 940 lines, of well-written hieratic.

[a] The sign  is commonly but erroneously read Khem. The variants of the name are 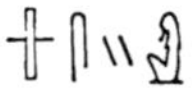 and 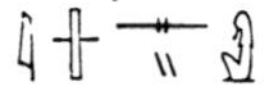 Renouf, *Transactions of the Society of Biblical Archaeology*, vol. viii. p. 204, note 2.

[b] The late Dr. Birch informed me that Mr. Rhind had found this papyrus during the excavations which he made at Thebes in 1861. I have searched in Mr. Rhind's *Thebes, its Tombs and their Tenants*, London, 1862, and in his *Account of the Tombs in which the Papyri and Tesserae were found* (printed in Birch, *Facsimiles of two Papyri found in a Tomb at Thebes*, London, 1863, pp. 18-29), for particulars, but no mention of this papyrus appears to exist there. Its registration mark is 2$\frac{6}{4}$518.

[c] In *Recueil de Travaux*, t. iii. pp. 57-64.

[d] In the *Proceedings of the Society of Biblical Archaeology*, 1886-87, pp. 11-26.

The beginnings of some of the lines in the first column, and parts of the foot lines of the first four columns, are broken away; here and there small breaks in the text occur, but the text as a whole is wonderfully perfect, and nearly all the missing parts can be restored from parallel passages. The bottom edge of the papyrus is stained with bitumen.

The titles of the books, the first words of each paragraph, the directions for reciting the verses and for performing the various parts of the service for the destruction of Apepi, the names of his companion fiends and devils, and certain words are throughout written in red; in my transcript these are represented by a black line printed over the hieroglyphics so written. The handwriting is small and neat, and is of interest to the palaeographer because it exhibits the forms of many of the characters in the transition state between the ordinary hieratic and demotic scripts.

This papyrus seems to have formed one of a number kept in stock by a person who made it his business to supply funereal papyri to be placed in the tombs by relatives of the dead: it was not written expressly for Nesi-Àmsu, as we may see by comparing the carelessly written colophon with the careful hand in which a part of the papyrus is written. Traces of two or three handwritings appear in the work. The date when the papyrus was purchased and the titles of the deceased are set forth in the two columns of very cursive writing which occur between the first and second and the second and third compositions written on it. They read: "Written in the fourth month[a] of the sowing season, in the twelfth year of Alexander,[b] the son of Alexandèr, for Nesi-Àmsu,[c] son of Petâ-Àmen-

[a] The Egyptian , Coptic ϪΟΙΑΚ=November 27—December 26.

[b] Alexander IV. son of Alexander the Great, reigned, according to the canon of Ptolemy, about twelve years. He began to reign about B.C. 317, but was murdered six years after; in B.C. 305 his successor Ptolemy Soter began to reign. The scribe appears to have added the six years of the interregnum to those of the actual reign of Alexander IV. Dr. Brugsch has published a decree of this king dated in the "first month of the sowing season of the seventh year," (*Aeg. Zeitschrift*, 1871, p. 1) and M. Revillout has published the texts of monuments dated in the thirteenth year of his reign (*Revue Égypt.* 1880, pp. 8, 15). See also Lepsius, *Königsbuch*, Synoptische Tafeln, p. 9; and *Ueber einige Ergebnisse der Aeg. Denkmäler für die Kenntniss der Ptolemaer-Geschichte*, p. 8. Ptolemy Soter became Macedonian governor of Egypt B.C. 322, and assumed the title of king B.C. 305.

The prenomen of Alexander II. was  *Hāā-àb-Àmen-setep-en-Rā.*

[c] *i.e.* "belonging to Amsu." The ithyphallic god Amsu was a form of Amen-Rā, the sun-god, and represented the generative power in nature. He is called "Amsu-Amen, bull of his mother," "Amsu, son of Isis," and "Amsu, engendered of Rā." He was worshipped particularly at Panopolis, the modern اخميم

suten taiu[a] the prophet, and Ta-shere, a sistrum bearer of Ȧmen-Rā, daughter of Nesti-Tûra[b] . . " His titles and offices were as follows: "Prophet of the temple of Het,[c] scribe of Amen of the third order, first divine father and prophet of Amen-Rā, king of the gods; prophet of Horus-Rā, the great and mighty first-born son of Ra-Amen; prophet of Amen the two-horned;[d] prophet of Chensu within Benenet;[e] prophet of Osiris, the great god of the 'persea trees;'[f] prophet of Osiris, the dweller in Asher;[g] prophet of Amen (may his throne be exalted!) the dweller in Apt;[h] first priest of Ra in the temple of Amen of the second order; inspector and scribe of Amen of the second order; vicar of Amen of the second and fourth orders; prophet of Nefer-hetep[i] the great and prophet of

[a] *i.e.* "the gift of Amen, king of the world."

[b] I am not certain about the reading of this name.

[c] A name of the metropolis of the seventh nome of Upper Egypt (*Diospolis parva*).

[d] *Sept ābu*, literally "provided with two horns," is the original form of the title which Alexander the Great gave to himself as the son of Amen. The Greeks translated it by κερασφόρος, the Arabs by ذو القرنين and the Ethiopians by ዘክልኤ፡አቅርንቲሁ፡

[e] *Benenet*, or *Benbenet*, was a tract of land which surrounded the temple of Chensu at Karnak. See Brugsch, *Dict. Géog.* p. 195.

[f] Name of a part of Thebes.

[g] Asher was the name given to a part of Thebes which lay to the south of the great temple at Amen at Karnak, on the right bank of the river. It was the seat of the goddess Mut, the wife of Amen. See Brugsch, *Dict. Géog.* p. 74.

[h] Apt is the name given in the Egyptian monuments to the part of Thebes which lies on the east bank of the river, and which is represented to-day by the ruins at Karnak and Luxor (El-ukṣûr); it was surrounded by a wall and was called the "fortress of Ap," and "Ap of the south," to distinguish it from another town called Ap, situated in Lower Egypt. The name Ap, or Apt, has survived in the Coptic ⲁⲡⲉ or ⲧⲁⲡⲉ. The famous temple of Amen-Rā was situated here, and was considered specially sacred. The part of Thebes on the west bank of the river was called *em χeft Ȧptet* "Contra Apt." The town of Thebes generally was called or *Uast*, and was the capital of the fourth nome of Upper Egypt. See Brugsch, *Dict. Géog.* I. p. 20; Mariette, *Karnak*, (Texte), p. 2; Chabas, *Recherches sur le nom Egyptien de Thèbes*, p. 6; and Brugsch, *Geographische Inschriften*, I. p. 178.

[i] Nefer-hetep, or more fully, *Chensu nefer ḥetep*, is one of the names of the god Chensu, under which he was worshipped with great honour at Thebes. He is represented under the form of a man, having on his head a crescent and disk; on the right side of his head is a lock of hair, and in his hand he holds either a palm-notched branch or a sceptre, with the symbols of life, stability, rule, and dominion. The statue of this god was sent to Bechten in the 26th year of Rameses XIII. to drive out the evil spirit which had taken possession of the daughter of the prince of this land.

Nefer-hetep the little; prophet of Osiris, Horus, Isis and Nephthys of the temple of Het; prophet of Hathor, lady of Het-sechem, prophet of Mehit,[a] prophet of[b] Amsu, and Atmu, lord of Het-sechem,[c] vicar of Nefer-hetep[d] of the four orders; first prophet of Nefer-hetep, and prophet of the gods."

From this it is clear that Nesi-Amsu held several official appointments in the temples of Amen-Rā and the other gods at Thebes, and also in those of Diospolis parva, or Het.

The lines which form the second part of the colophon contain a prayer, a curse upon any one who shall dare to remove the papyrus from its resting-place, and a blessing upon the man who shall take the trouble to "establish the name and the *Ka*" of the deceased Nesi-Amsu. They read: "May their names (words?) be established and increased and never be destroyed before Osiris, Horus, Isis, Nephthys and the gods and goddesses whose names are written upon this book, in the presence of the gods and goddesses, whosoever they are, who are in the nether world and within the mighty and secret pylons which are there! May these names be made to come forth in the mighty nether world! Mayest thou (*i.e.*, the deceased Nesi-Amsu) be proclaimed by them (*i.e.*, the gods and goddesses) in the boat of Rā; mayest thou have given to thee by them sepulchral meals upon the table of the great god in the course of every day; mayest thou have given to thee by them fresh water and incense such as is given to the mighty kings of the north and south who are in the nether world; may there be given to thee by them coming forth and progress among the favoured ones of Osiris at the head of those in the nether world; and may they grant to thee that the rays of the disk may fall upon thy body daily."

"If any person from any foreign land, whether he be Negro, Ethiopian, or

[a] This god is, perhaps, the north wind personified. See Lanzone, *Dizionario di Mitologia Egizia*, p. 325.

[b] This line is omitted in my transcript. The text is 
 *Ḥet-ḥert nebt Ḥet-seχem neter ḥen en Meḥit neter ḥen en.*

[c] Het-sechem is the sacred name of the metropolis of the seventh nome of Upper Egypt, or *Diospolis parva*, which was dedicated to the worship of Hathor and Nephthys; the name is also written 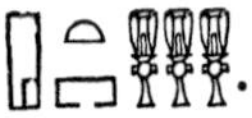.

[d] Nefer-hetep, called also 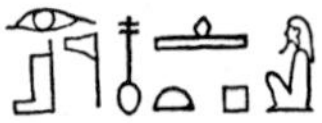 *Ȧusar Nefer-ḥetep*, and  *Nefer-χā-ḥetep*, was the name of Osiris under the form of a *bennu* bird  he was the husband of Hathor or Nephthys of Het-sechem and was venerated there.

Syrian, shall remove this book, or any thief (?) shall carry it off, may his body never draw near to [the presence of the god]; may he never be placed in the cool; may he never breathe the breezes of the north wind; may neither son nor daughter arise to him from his seed; may his name never be remembered on earth through his children; and may he never see the beams of the disk! But if any person shall look upon this book and shall so act that my name and my *ka* be established among the favoured ones of Osiris, may there be done likewise for him after his death in retribution for what he has done for me."

The papyrus of Nesi-Amsu is inscribed with three distinct compositions, which are entitled respectively: 1. The Festival Songs of Isis and Nephthys; 2. The Litanies of Seker; and 3. The Book of the Overthrowing of Apepi. Thanks to the liberality of the Society of Antiquaries, it has been possible to print the full text of each of these works with interlinear transliteration and literal translation. The order of the columns has been kept strictly, and the words written in red ink in the papyrus have been indicated in the hieroglyphic transcript by having a thick black line printed over them. The transcription has been made as uniform as possible, but the scribe was not always consistent in writing the same word; wherever the transcription of a character is doubtful it is represented by (?). In a few cases, where the signs are new ones, special types representing them have been cut. In transliterating I have followed the old system used by Lepsius, Brugsch, Birch, Renouf, and others; the other systems now in use in France and Germany may possess superior advantages, but they do not appear to outweigh their difficulties and disadvantages. The interlinear translation has been made as literal as possible, but a free rendering of each work is given in this introduction. Some passages are easy to translate and easy to understand; some are easy to translate but hard to understand; and some are both difficult to translate and to understand. In making my first transcript and translation I had the benefit of Mr. Renouf's supervision, and I gratefully acknowledge his kind assistance.

I. THE FESTIVAL SONGS OF ISIS AND NEPHTHYS.

This work fills seventeen columns of writing, and contains 463 lines. It is entitled "The Verses[a] of the Festival of the two 'Terti," and the rubric tells us that the whole of it was to be sung in the temple of Osiris on the occasion of the festival which was celebrated in the fourth month of the sowing season[b] (= November 27—December 29) from the twenty-second to the twenty-sixth day. 'Terti is the term applied to Isis and Nephthys in their character of protectors of the deceased; Isis is called *'terti urt*, "the great *'terti*," and Nephthys *'terti ne'teset*, "the little *'terti*." The rubric goes on to state that these verses were to be recited by two women who were virgins[c] and who were ceremonially pure; the hair of their limbs was to be removed, they were to wear ram's wool garlands upon their heads, and to hold tambourines in their hands; on the arm of one of them was to be a fillet inscribed, "To Isis," and on an arm of the other was to be a fillet inscribed, "To Nephthys." Thus arrayed they were to recite or sing the verses of the festival of the 'Terti. The rubric of a similar composition, which has been called the "Lamentations of Isis and Nephthys,[d] gives rather different directions; it reads,

[a] The word rendered "verses" is and means literally "houses." Dy. Pleyte translated the word by *traité*, *livre*, *chapitre*, and there is conclusive evidence that has, at times, the meaning of *chapitre*, as for example in the enumeration of the chapters of a composition. Here, however, the word is best rendered by "verses." Compare Arab. بَيْتٌ plur. ابيات Syr. ܒܝܬܐ plur. ܒ̈ܬܐ, Gr. *οἶκος*, Italian *stanza*. In Syriac we have the expression ܒ̈ܬܐ ܕܡܬܐܡܪܝܢ ܟܕ ܥܐܠܝܢ ܠܩܘܪܒܢܐ "verses which are to be said when they go in for the offering," and ܒ̈ܬܐ ܕܡܬܐܡܪܝܢ ܟܕ ܢܣܒܝܢ ܐܪ̈ܙܐ "verses which are to be said when they receive the Mysteries" (*i.e.*, the Lord's Supper). See Payne Smith, *Thesaurus*, col. 479, and Wright, *Arabic Grammar*, 2nd ed. vol. ii. pp. 378, 192.

[b] *I.e.* ⲬⲞⲒⲀⲔ. The days of the celebration of the festival correspond roughly with our December 25—29th.

[c] *ȧpt* appears to be used here in the sense of "defiled" (Comp. Heb. מְחֻלָּל Ezekiel, xxxvi. 23); *ȧn ȧpt*=undefiled, pure, unpolluted.

[d] A facsimile of the hieratic text from a manuscript at Berlin is published by J. de Horrack in his *Les Lamentations d'Isis et de Nephthys*, Paris, 1866. A hieroglyphic transcript is published in my *Egyptian Reading Book*, London, 1888, pp. 46-51, and an English translation by de Horrack in *Records of the Past*, 1st ed. vol. ii. pp. 117-126.

ȧn[a] *χertu set sen nefer em ḥāu — sen ertāt sene'tem-*
To be said by women two, beautiful in bodies their. Shall sit

sen er ta em āā ḥetepi en usuχut nāu ḥer
they upon the ground at the door chief of the hall, shall be inscribed upon

ermen er ren en Ȧuset Nebt-ḥet ertā nemmes ent θehen
their arms the names of Isis and Nephthys. Shall be placed vessels of glass

meḥ em māu em āāui- sen ȧment pau ȧri em Aneb-ḥ'tet
filled with water in two hands their left, and cakes made in Memphis

em āāui -sen ȧbt
in two hands their right.

The composition to which this rubric referred was to be recited or sung at the third and eighth hours of the day, and it is especially enjoined that the recital of it shall not be omitted during the period of the festival.

The Festival Songs of Isis and Nephthys were led off by an address to Osiris on the part of the *χer ḥeb*, or precentor, and they were continued by Isis and Nephthys, who sometimes sang together and sometimes singly; they appear to have accompanied their singing by the beating of tambourines. Throughout the composition there is no rhyme, but there is a very persistent rhythm; this is slightly monotonous, but is quite in keeping with what is known of oriental songs, and the way in which they were sung. The following lines will serve as an example of this rhythm.

a literally means "to bring." It must, however, be translated here by some such word as *said*, *recited*, *repeated*. M. de Horrack (*op. cit.* p. 15) translates *ȧn χertu set sen* by "étant amenées deux femmes."

Col. iv. l. 7	ut·f	χesef	Sebau
	māa	ti en	χennu-k
	χesef	mehi χent	het·n
	māa	ti en	χennu-k
	an tut	erek θas	em uāi
	neb-en	em hetep	auset-f

Certain phrases, like "come to thy temple," "come, thy relatives wait," and "come in peace," form refrains, and are repeated at frequent intervals. The structure of the composition has something in common with the non-devotional Hebrew psalms; there is the same parallelism in the members of the verses, the same manner of saying the same thing in different words, and there are many examples of address to the sun-god which begin in the second person and end in the third. The grammatical construction of many of the sentences is interesting and, when sufficiently examined and explained, will increase our knowledge of the grammar of the Egyptian language during the later period of its existence. The Egyptian vocabulary will be increased by this text, for there are words in it which do not exist in the great dictionary of Dr. Brugsch.

About the age of this work it is impossible to make any definite statement. Here and there in it the words *ki 'tet*, "otherwise said," occur; which show that other copies of the work existed, and that it was sufficiently ancient for variant readings to have crept in. There seems to be little doubt that services were held, and hymns sung in honour of Osiris at Karnak from very ancient times, and it is probable that these verses are either copies of ancient works, or redactions based upon them. Certain passages appear to be corrupt, but it is impossible to correct them without the help of other manuscripts. Judging from internal evidence, it will probably be right to assume that the work in its present form is not older than the twenty-sixth dynasty. Of the name of the author we are quite ignorant.

The subject of the verses throughout is the destruction of Osiris by Set, and the reconstruction of his body by Isis and Nephthys, his wife and sister respectively. As the references to this subject are so many and so frequent, the principal points of the story as given by Plutarch are here repeated. Osiris and Isis, having been united before their birth, were born on the first and fourth of the five days which formed the epact respectively; Osiris was the son of Rhea and the Sun, and Isis was the daughter of Rhea and Mercury. Rhea also bore to Saturn Typhon and Nephthys, the former on the third and the latter on the fifth day of the epact. Osiris became king of Egypt, and applied himself to the civilisation and improvement of his country. When the Egyptians had learned how to worship the gods, he set out to visit the other parts of the world, in order that all mankind might benefit by his teaching and assistance. Typhon, the half-brother of Osiris, was unable to work mischief in the land of Egypt during his absence, but on his return he joined himself to a queen of Ethiopia, called Aso, and seventy-two other persons, and entered into a conspiracy with them. Having secretly taken the measure of the body of Osiris, he caused a chest to be made exactly of the same size as it, and brought it into his banqueting room; when all those who were present had admired it, he promised to give it to the person whose body it would fit. One guest after another tried to get into it, but without success; last of all Osiris laid himself down in it, and it was found to fit him exactly. Before, however, he had time to get out of it again Typhon threw the cover over him, and, having nailed it down firmly, poured molten lead over it. The box was then carried away to the bank of the river, whence it was brought to the Tanaïtic mouth of the Nile; this happened either in the twenty-eighth year of the reign of Osiris, or in the twenty-eighth year of his age. When Isis heard of this she cut off one of the locks of her hair, and put on mourning apparel, and wandered about in sore distress seeking for the chest; finally some children who had watched Typhon told her by what mouth of the Nile it had been conveyed to the sea. About this time she also learned that Osiris had been united with her sister Nephthys, who, fearing the anger of Typhon her husband, had exposed the fruit of her unlawful commerce as soon as it was born. With great difficulty and by the help of dogs she finally discovered where the offspring was, and going to the place she bred it up, and it was afterwards named Anubis. Soon after she heard that the chest had been carried by the waves of the sea to Byblos,[a] and there gently lodged in the branches of a tamarisk tree, which in a short time had shot up into a large and beautiful tree, growing round the chest and enclosing it on every side, so that it was not to be seen. Isis came to Byblos and succeeded in obtaining the chest, which she carried away with her to Egypt, but intending to visit her son Horus, she deposited it in a remote and unfrequented place, where, however, it was found by Typhon one night hunting by the light of the moon. Having recognised the body of Osiris inside it, he tore it into fourteen parts which he scattered about

[a] Not Byblos in Phoenicia, but the papyrus swamps in the north-east of the Delta.

the country. Once more Isis set out in search of the scattered fragments of her husband's body, and whenever she found one she buried it and built a sepulchre over it. The phallus of Osiris was never recovered, for it was swallowed by the Lepidotus, Phagrus, and Oxyrhynchus fishes when it was thrown into the Nile immediately after its separation from the body. To make some amends for the loss, Isis consecrated a phallus made in imitation of it, and instituted a solemn festival to its memory. After these things Osiris returned from the nether world, and appearing to his son Horus, encouraged him to do battle with Typhon, and instructed him in the exercise of arms. In the battle with Typhon Horus was victorious, and Osiris his father was avenged.

The Egyptian inscriptions show us that Osiris, Isis, Nephthys, Anubis, Set or Typhon, and Horus, are all children of Nut, the Sky, and Seb, the Earth, and Mr. Renouf has proved that these gods are nothing more nor less than powers of nature. The greatest and most important of these was naturally Osiris, the sun, and the Festival Songs of Isis and Nephthys were composed in praise of this god. The two virgins who sang them assumed the characters of Isis and Nephthys, and as, in the myth, these two goddesses put together the fragments of the dead body of their husband and called upon him with pathetic and loving words to return to them, so in these the two virgins address the dead god with every endearing epithet possible. The prayers of Isis and Nephthys that Osiris should return again to them were answered, for that god lived again in the person of his son Horus, by whom he was avenged; and the Festival Songs refer to the resurrection and renewed birth of Osiris, the type of man after his death, who in this capacity is identified with the sun, the daily rising of which constantly recalled the idea of a birth eternally renewed.

TRANSLATION.

Column I.

1. The beginning of the verses of the festival of the two Terti, which shall be sung in the temple of Osiris, at the head of those who are in the nether-world, the great god, the lord of Abydos, in
2. the fourth month of the sowing season, from the twenty-second to the twenty-sixth days of the same. They are written expressly for the temple, and are to be sung by women whose
3. limbs are pure. They shall be virgins, the hair of their flesh shall be removed, their heads shall be bound round with ram's wool, and
4. they shall hold tambourines in their hands. Their names, Isis and Nephthys, shall be inscribed on their arms;
5. they shall sing the verses of this book in the presence of this god,
6. and shall say, " O lord Osiris, O lord Osiris, O lord Osiris, O lord Osiris."
7. The precentor, standing in the front of this temple, shall then say,
8. " O mighty one (?), chief of the earth," four times.
9. Then shall the women with ruffled flowing hair say,

10, 11. " O beautiful boy, come at once to thy temple, for we see thee not.

12, 13. " O beautiful boy, come to thy temple, draw near after thy departure from us.

14, 15. " Hail, beautiful boy, who leadest along the hour, who increasest except at his season.

16, 17. " Thou exalted image of his father Tenen,[a] hidden essence coming forth from Atmu.[b]

18, 19. " The lord, the lord, how very much greater is he than his father! eldest son of his mother's womb.

20. " O come back again to us with that which belongeth to thee, and we will

21, 22. " embrace thee; depart not from us, O thou beautiful and greatly-loved face,

23. " image of Tenen, virile one, lord of love!

[a] The god Tenen is a personification of the earth, and is also assimilated to the night sun. He is represented sitting on a throne, having on his head horns, disk, and feathers  and holding in his hands 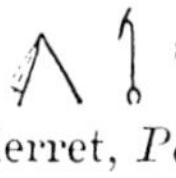 and  See Lanzone, *Dizionario di Mitologia Egizia*, pp. 246, 1257 (plate cccci), and Pierret, *Panthéon Egypt.* pp. 54, 55. He appears to have been the local god of the land on the borders of Lake Moeris, and in an inscription there he is represented as sitting on the hieroglyhic for an island  See Brugsch, *Dictionnaire Géographique*, p. 59.

[b] The night sun as opposed to Rā, the day sun.

24, 25. "The child (?) whose limbs are feeble by reason of his emotion in opening the womb,
26. "Come thou in peace, let us see thee, our lord.
27. "The two sisters will join thy limbs together, thou shalt feel no pain; they will put an end to thy calamity as if it never had befallen thee.

Column II.

1. "Our heads are turned back upon our faces.
2, 3. "O mighty and great one among the gods, the path which thou traversest cannot
4, 5. "be described; O babe, child at the two seasons, thou, together with that which belongeth to thee, goest round heaven and earth.
6. "Thou art the bull of the two sisters.
7, 8. "Come thou, O babe, who in setting renewest thyself, let us see thee, our lord.
9, 10. "Let thy phallus be with us like the phallus of Tebha at his block!
11, 12. "Come thou in peace, babe, mighty one of his father, be thou established in thy temple without fear, for
13-15. "thy son Horus avenges thee. May Nekau[a] (the devil) be carried away, may he be
16. "placed in his fiery cavern daily, may his name perish among the gods.
17. "May Tebha[b] die finally!
18, 19. "Thou shalt dwell in thy temple and shalt not be afraid of any evil thing that Sut[c] may do unto thee,
20. "for what Nut sent forth[d] has pierced him.
21-23. "Let him embrace us with joy travelling on earth with us. . . . .

[a] Compare 
 *maat-f pu seχer-s Sebâu ṯā-s māb-s em seχap Nut ṯā-s seshebsheb Nāk ām nef.* "His eye overthrows the Sebau, it makes its lance pierce Nut, and makes Nak to vomit what it has eaten." Grébaut, *Hymne à Ammon-Rā*, p. 10.

[b] Another name for Sut, or Apepi, the chief adversary of Rā.

[c] Sut, or Set, the Typhon of the Greeks, was one of the five sons of Seb and Nut, brother of Osiris, and husband of Nephthys. The worship of this god is as old as the Vth dynasty, and some of the greatest of the Egyptian kings delighted to call themselves "beloved of Sut," and attributed to him all the good qualities possible. About B.C. 1000-600, however, a violent reaction against this god set in; his statues were broken, he was expelled from the company of the gods, and from being considered the god of all good, he became the god of all evil, and his very name was a synonym of wickedness. "Nel mito di Hesiri, Set fu riguardato non solamente come il nemico implacabile di suo fratello ed il di lui uccisore, e quegli che ne usurpò il trono, ma pur anche, quale principio cattivo nel sistema de' due opposti principi; cosicchè in quella guisa che ogni bene essere attribuivasi ad Osiride, ogni danno ed ogni male assegnavasi a Set." Lanzone, *Dizionario di Mitologia*, p. 1130.

[d] *i.e.* Rā, the son of Nut.

Column III.

1. "Apostates (?).
2, 3. "Our two eyes are looking upon thy face blazing with radiance.
4-6. "Hail, lord, we cry to thee from the left, O beautiful face, lord of love, bull fecundating the cows.[a]
7, 8. "Come, boy with the saffron face, the ONE who increases and who is beautiful in his two eyes.
9-13. "O lord among women, male of the cows, O child, chief of beauties, once more let us see thee as well as what belongs to thee, for I love to see thee.
14-16. "I am thy sister Isis, the darling of thy heart, by reason of my love for thee when thou departest I water this earth with my tears this day.
17, 18. "Thou travellest along, thou art hymned by us, and life springs up for us out of thy nothingness.
19-22. "Come, lord, in peace, let us see thee! O prince, come in peace, and drive away the flame which is in our temple. May thy phallus be with us like the phallus of Tebha."
23. Then the women with ruffled flowing hair shall continue to say:
24, 25. "Hail, Osiris, bull of those in the underworld, the established ONE; how very
26. "much greater is he than the gods! O Baby, virile one,

Column IV.

1-3. "mighty heir of Seb, who art born god of the gods, come to the two widows.[b]
4, 5. "The entire cycle of the gods goes round thee [when] they meet thee.
6, 7. "Cursed be the name of Sut when he comes, behind the shrine, into the presence of thy father Rā, who darts out and repulses the fiend.
8-10. "Come, thy relatives wait, drive away sorrow from our temple, come, thy relatives wait for thee.
11-14. "There is none like unto thee, O thou that dwellest in solitude; the resting-place of our lord is in peace. Victorious one, his long-suffering is greater than himself when the
15. "Lock[c] hovers over his enemies. He fashions the earth according to his designs.

[a] *i.e.* Isis and Nephthys.

[b] *i.e.* Isis and Nephthys.

[c] The Lock was a name given by the Egyptians to that class of cloud which resembled a ringlet, curl, or tuft of hair, and which was supposed to be an enemy of the sun-god. He was a mythological personage, and is distinctly spoken of as a demon. In an inscription of the XVIIIth dynasty, he is called "the son of Nut," a fact which seems to imply an identification with Set. Renouf, *Trans. Soc. Bib. Arch.* viii. p. 212.

16-18. "O thou who comest forth mightily, O great one among the gods, inasmuch as thou art greater than the gods, the cycle of the gods is bowed

19. "down on their knees before thee. I stoop on the ground [before thee] O thou mighty one of the womb!

20, 21. "The uraeus crown is upon his head, he is born before his heart; how great

22-25. "is he in his coming! Divine body, lord of love, how exceedingly art thou loved! O soul, thou livest a second time, for the two sisters join thy limbs together drawing near [to thee] having waited for thee a long time.

26, 27. "Inasmuch as thou art greater[a] than the gods thou art proclaimed mighty in thy circuit.

Column V.

1, 2. "Come, thy relatives wait. Thy father Rā butts against the Lock.

3. "The cycle of the gods goes round thee as thou makest thy circuit, and they repulse the fiends for thee.

4, 5. "Remove thou the great grief (?) of thy images.[b] Thy temple is in festival, the evil one

6. "is at his block, the fiend is in evil case through what he has done. He drowns the earth with his empty schemes.

7-9. "Nut drives him off from the earth (?) turning back and bringing the fiend to the block in the storehouse (?).

10, 11. "Thy father Rā is for avenging thy constraint, thy son Horus will return an answer for thee.

12, 13. "Thou traversest the earth as thou revolvest, thou stridest over the four quarters

14, 15. "of Nut. Thou hoverest over the divine dwellings on earth, the two *rehti*[c] are

16, 17. "going round thee. Thou art exalted, thou art exalted! Verily Sut is in the dwelling, may that enemy of thine never rise up!

18. "Come thou to thy temple, Osiris, thy dwelling seeks to see thee.

19. "Thou hearest the report of Horus at the hands of his mother Isis.

20. "Placed in all lands, thou drivest off whatever comes against thy body, thou receivest what is in the house of thy books.

21. "O great god, thou art hidden in thy attributes.

22. "Go not away from thy temple, Osiris, come thou in peace to thy every dwelling,

23, 24. "victorious one, beautiful in his becoming, mighty bull, lord of love.

25. "Thy sister Isis is thy darling, she removes from thee that which causes thee

26, 27. "uneasiness, and embraceth thee; depart not from us, O Lord.

[a] The broken text in this line is probably to be restored by the insertion of  *tennu-k*. Compare line 17.

[b] *i.e.* Isis and Nephthys.

[c] *i.e.* Isis and Nephthys.

Column VI.

1. "Thou didst give life from the beginning . . . .
2. "Hail, protected art thou from that which floweth from the nome of Aphroditopolis,[a] from the
3. "evil as if it never existed.
4. "Thy sister comes to thee and cleanses thy limbs. The great and living god, the
5, 6. "greatly beloved one is dandled in the presence of the South and North.
7, 8. "Thou art decorated, O lord of decorations, mighty male, prince of beauties.
9. "Thy mother Nut comes to thee, and as she comes to thee she spreads herself out over thee.
10, 11. "She protects thy limbs against all evil, she advances . . . . within her, she, the
12. "solitary guardian of thee, has driven away all the disease which was in thy limbs
13, 14. "as if it never existed, she clothes the baby, the lord which cometh forth from her.
15-18. "The lord, the baby which comes forth from her womb, the mighty heir of the gods; the opener of Amenti at his season, makes this earth to be as in times
19-22. "of old. Behold, the blind baby advances, thy father Rā is avenging thee, and thy son Horus protects thee against Sut and all the evil which he has done. Come thou then to thy temple and be not afraid."
23-26. The women with ruffled flowing hair shall also say, "Hail, beautiful boy, come to thy temple; thou twice exalted Being, let thy side be turned to thy temple and towards the gods upon their thrones.
27. "I am the woman who defends her brother, I am thy wife, Osiris, thy mother's sister.

Column VII.

1. "Come thou to me running.
2. "O firm of heart, let thy face be seen because I see not thy face.
3. "Make clear thou for us the way before my face to Rā in heaven.
4 "Heaven unites with earth and darkness is thus made upon the earth daily.
5, 6. "My heart burns at thy escape from the evil one, my heart burns, turn thou thy
7. "side to me and remove it not from me for ever.
8, 9. "O thou that makest firm the two domains and turnest back the ways, I am seeking to see thee for my love's sake.
10. "I am in the town the walls of which are mighty.
11, 12. "I am overcome by reason of thy love for me, come by thyself, and depart not.
13. "Verily thy son [Horus] repulses Tebha at his block.
14. "I have concealed myself among the bushes to hide thy son that he might return
15. "an answer for thee, and that the moment of great distress might depart from thee.

[a] See Brugsch, *Dict. Géog.* p. 1357.

16. "Does not she (*i.e.*, Nephthys) collect thy limbs?

17. "I advance by myself and I go round among the bushes.

18-20. "There is a huge crocodile following after thy son, a female whose face is against the male; but Anubis and I know it.

21. "I go round the ways, and I turn back after my brother, who leaps away from the evil one.

22-27. "The hearts of myriads of people burn, O mighty splendour among the gods, may we see thee the lord! May there be no lack of thy love upon our faces, O phallus, lord of love, king, lord of eternity.

Column VIII.

1-3. "Thou who fliest as he lives, ruler of everlasting, destroyer of An-reχ,[a] king of the north and south, the lord going forth from Tasertet. May there never be to thee a time of misfortune with which my heart may be filled!

4-6. "O brother, lord, going forth from the nome of Akertet,[b] come thou to me with that which belongs to thee, come in peace, come in peace.

7, 8. "O king, prince, come in peace, let us see thy face again as before, for I love to see the

9-12. "My two hands are lifted up to protect thee, I love, I love the circuits of the two regions, the people of the north are in thy recollection (?) thou receivest a head of hair from them, the breezes which accompany them are of *ānti.*

13, 14. "O husband, my brother, lord of love, come thou in peace to thy seat; O beautiful boy, come to thy house at once, at once, come thou.

15, 16. "The things which concern thee as bull of those who are in the underworld are hidden, a place of secrecy is thy flesh in Pa-Hennu.[c]

17. "Hail to thee in thy name, 'Prince of eternity!'

18, 19. "Horus comes to thee with strength, he delivers thy limbs, he collects for thee the

20. "emanations which come forth from thee. The great god approaches thy body, O thou who art closed up in that which belongs to thee.

21-23. "Come thou in peace, lord, thou that becomest young a second time. Thy son Horus avenges thee, come to thy temple and inundate it with thy love.

24-27. "Sovereign, chief, distinguished in the egg, only one, strong one, mighty one, veritable son, opener of the womb,[d] divine germ of Seb[e] through his mother,

[a] A name of Apepi. (?)

[b] A general name for any Necropolis.

[c] , or  *Pa-hennu*, "the house of Hennu," is the name of the 10th nome of Lower Egypt (the Athribis of the Greeks), where the "divine heart"  of Osiris was deposited. Brugsch, *Dict. Géog.* p. 498.

[d] *i.e.* "firstborn." Comp. Heb. פֶּטֶר רֶחֶם Exodus xiii. 2; xxxiv. 19; Numb. iii. 12, etc.

[e] The god of the earth, father of Osiris.

Column IX.

1, 2. "decorated one, greatly beloved, working for those in the underworld, he overthrows

3-5. "disaster. Lord of the underworld, and bull of those who are in it, image of Rā Harmachis, baby beautiful in appearance, come thou to us in peace, in peace.

6, 7. "Thou repellest thy disasters, thou drivest away evil hap. Lord, come thou to us in peace, in peace.

8-10. "Hail thou that becomest young again, come in peace! hail, brother, come let

11, 12. "me see thee, the king and prince of eternity. Stay not, rest not, lord, come to thy temple, be not afraid."

13. . . . . Then shall the precentor say,

14, 15. "O beautiful boy, come to thy temple, the cycle of the gods seeks to see thee.

16-18. "Child, lord, opener of the womb, baby, who art beloved on account of thy face, perfect heir opening the womb, perfect son coming forth from the god of seeing and hearing,

19. "O Temple, Isis grieves for thee, go not away from thy dwelling.

20, 21. "May the heads [of Isis and Nephthys] be delivered by thy love, for they lament for thee and tie up the curls of their head.

22-25. "Un-nefer, lord of food, chief, mighty by reason of his terror, god, president of the gods, when thou inundatest [the land], things are engendered. Thou art gentler

26-28. "than the gods. The liquid which comes from the emanations of thy body makes the dead and living to live, O lord of food, prince of green things, mighty lord, the staff of life, the giver of offerings to the gods, and

Column X.

1, 2. "sepulchral meals to the beatified dead. Sesheta,[a] Lord of the sepulchral bier,

3-9. "Lord of the two eyes hidden in the horizon, who shinest in his season, who risest at his hour. Thou art splendour, dowered with splendour, thou shinest at the left-hand of Atmu, thou lookest forth from the habitation of Rā, thou collectest his splendours in thy noble form.

10-15. "Thy soul flies after Rā, thou shinest at dawn, thou settest at twilight, thou risest every day; thou wilt rise on the left hand of Atmu for ever and for ever. When thou risest the Lock is accursed, and is put an end to before his doom and before his failure.

16, 17. "Rā turns back the fiend, that attacking devil that comes against him; Amsehti is his heir.

18, 19. "All the gods worship him. The cycle of the gods rejoices when they meet thee,

[a]  The correct reading of this god's name was first shown by Mr. Renouf, in *Proceedings Soc. Bib. Arch.* Nov. 1884. See also Lanzone, *Dizionario*, p. 1112.

20-22. "Thy occupation is with Rā every day, thou lookest steadfastly from the left, thou lookest steadfastly at the living.

23-26. "Thou art Splendour, the deputy of Rā, the whole cycle of the gods comes to thee invoking thy face; its flame reaches unto thy enemies.

27. "We rejoice when thou hast gathered together thy bones, when thou hast summed up thy body daily.

Column XI.

1, 2. "Thou enterest like Atmu at his hour, without turning, thy bones are made

3. "strong for thee. Apuat[a] presents thee with a mountain of stone and hews out a

4, 5. "burial place for thee. The lord of Taser[b] comes to thee and the two sisters come

6-8. "to thee. They have obtained splendid things for thee, and they gather together thy limbs for thee from the mutilated pieces seeking to put thy body together.

9, 10. "The impurities which are upon them wipe upon our hair, and come thou to us without thy unpleasant recollections.

11, 12. "Come thou in thy attribute as prince of the earth, lay aside thy impetuosity, and

13, 14. "rest upon us, lord. Thou shalt be proclaimed heir of the world, the ONLY god, the fulfiller of the plans of the gods.

15, 16. "All the gods invoke thee, come to thy temple, be not afraid.

17, 18. "O Rā, thou art beloved, beloved art thou of thy two Images;[c] rest thou in thy habitation for ever."

19. The women with flowing hair shall also say:—

20, 21. "O beautiful boy, come to thy temple, turn, exalted one, turn thy side to thy temple; the gods are seated on their thrones.

22-24. "Hail, come in peace, king, come in peace, thy son Horus avenges thee.

25, 26. "Lay all thy great pain upon thy two images, who weep for thee at thy sepulchres.

27, 28. "O baby, how lovely will it be to see thee! Come, come to us, mighty one, strengthen thou for us our love.

Column XII.

1. "Come thou to thy temple and be not afraid.

2-4. "O ye gods in heaven, O ye gods on earth, O ye gods in the underworld,

5-7. "O ye gods in the watery deep, O ye gods who are among the followers of the deep, we follow after the lord, the lord of love.

a "The opener of the ways," a name given to Anubis.

b A name of the nether world.

c *i.e.* Isis and Nephthys.

8-10. "Brother, phallus, lord of love, hail! Come to me, unite heaven with earth, and
11. "let there be shadow on the earth daily.
12-14. "Messenger from heaven to earth, hail! may we come to thee! Thou makest fruitful the women in the town who seek our lord.
15. "I march over the earth towards my lord; come to me, O messenger from
16. "heaven to earth.
17-19. "May it be granted that the god shall come to his seat, may there be breathing of air to thy nose, may there be breath with the lord in his palace!
20, 21. "Hail, Rā is avenged, there are no disasters to him causing him trouble.
22, 23. "The limit of the desire of my heart is to see thee, heir, king, beautiful babe.
24-26. "Hail, lord of love, come to me, lord, that I may see thee daily, come, brother, that we may see thee.
27, 28. "My two hands are mighty to avenge thee, my two hands are raised up, raised up to protect thee.

Column XIII.

1. "Male, lord, babe, child, to avenge our lord.
2, 3. "I am the daughter of Seb, depart not from me, O thou who increasest except at his time.
4, 5. "I traverse the roads that thy love may come to me. I fly over the earth, I rest not from seeking thee.
6, 8. "I have in me a flame of love for thee, hail! come let me see thee; I weep for thy lonely condition.
9, 10. "Come thou to me quickly, for the extent of my desire is to see thee; come to me because of my desire to see thy face.
11, 12. "Hail, god invoked at the door of thy temple, thou art protected, protected
13-15. "in peace. Hail, hail, our lord cometh to his temple, the two arms of Isis and Nephthys protect his temple, their lord cometh to his habitation in peace.
16. "Be thou established in thy temple, be not afraid.
17. "Hail, twice exalted one, our lord; lament not in coming to us, O great god, come thou in perfect peace.
20-22. "Thou comest forth to Rā, O victorious one among the gods. O gracious one, come in peace, let me see thee: O child, come in thy attribute of Baby, Hai [a] is
23-25. "overthrown. Horus is like a prince, the mighty one is with thee, there is no work for thee.
26. "Thou art exalted as thou circlest, ... the two sisters.
27-30. "O beloved of his father, lord of rejoicings, thou delightest the hearts of the cycle of the gods, and thou illuminatest thy house with thy beauties, the cycle of the gods fear thy power,

[a] A name of Apepi. (?)

Column XIV.

1. "the earth trembles through fear of thee.

2-4. "I am thy wife who makes thy . . . . , the sister who protects her brother; come, let me see thee, the lord of my love.

5, 6. "O twice exalted one, mighty of attributes, come, let me see thee; O baby who advancest, child, come, let me see thee.

7-9. "Countries and regions weep for thee, the zones weep for thee as if thou wert Sesheta, heaven and earth weep for thee, inasmuch as thou art greater

10. "than the gods, may there be no cessation of the glorifying of thy *Ka*.

11-13. "Come to thy temple, be not afraid, thy son Horus embraces the circuit of heaven.

14, 15. "O thou sovereign, who makest afraid, be not afraid. Thy son Horus avenges thee and overthrows for thee the Semi [a] and the Lock.

16, 17. "Hail, lord, follow after me with radiance, let me see thee daily; the smell of thy flesh is like that of Punt.[b]

18, 19. "Thou art adored by the venerable women, in peace; the entire cycle of the gods rejoice.

20, 21. "Come thou to thy wife in peace, her heart flutters through her love for thee,

22. "she will embrace thee and not let thee depart from her; her heart is oppressed

23, 24. "because of her anxiety to see thee and thy beauties. She has made an end of prepara-

25. "tions for thee in the secret house, she has destroyed the pain which is in thy

26, 27. "limbs and the sickness as if it never existed. Life is given to thee by the most excellent wife.

28, 29. "Hail, thou protectest the inundation in the fields of Tepahet [c] this day.

Column XV.

1-3. "The cow [d] weeps aloud for thee with her voice, thy love is the limit of her desire. Her heart flutters because thou art shut up from her.

4, 5. "She would embrace thy body with both arms and would come to thee quickly, otherwise said, in peace.

[a] *i.e.* Fiends.

[b] The spice land of Arabia.

[c]  Tep-ahet, the metropolis of the 22nd nome of Upper Egypt (Aphroditopolis), Coptic ⲧⲡⲓⲉϩ, the modern اطفيح *Atfih*. See Brugsch, *Dict. Géog.*, p. 933; and Juynboll (مراصد الاطّلاع) t. i. p. ٧٥ "اطفيح بلد بالصعيد الادنى من ارض مصر على شاطى النيل فى شرقيّه"

[d] *i.e.* Isis.

6-9. "She avenges thee on account of what was done to thee, she makes sound for thee thy flesh on thy bones, she attaches thy nose to thy face for thee, she gathers together for thee all thy bones.

10-13. "Thy mother Nut comes to thee with peace offerings, she builds thee up with the life of her body. Thou art endowed with a soul, thou art endowed with a soul, thou art established, thou art established, thou hast a soul, O thou lord of women thou makest women fruitful.

14. "When thou comest from the Divine Land [a] there is odorous unguent on thy hair, there is unguent upon thy hair of *ānti* which flows of its own accord.

15-18. "O thou that comest forth, come in peace, come in peace: O king, prince, come in peace. O lord of Sais, the two hands of Nut are stretched out to thee; the heart of Shenthit,[b] turns to thee.

19, 20. "Thou art like a god, and comest forth like a god . . . .

21, 22. " . . . . . his baby. The hair upon thy body is like emerald when thou comest from the

23. "emerald fields. Thy hair is of the blue colour which appertains to lapis-lazuli, and

24, 25. "behold, thou thyself art more blue than thy hair. Thy skin and thy flesh are made

26. "for thee of the steel of the south, thy bones are moulded out of silver just as I am

27, 28. "from a babe. The teeth which thou hast are of emerald, *otherwise said*, the unguent of thy hair is of *ānti* which floweth of its own accord.

Column XVI.

1. "The crown of thy head is of lapis lazuli.

2, 3. "The god Seb is laden with peace offerings for thee, and he conveys them to the god who cometh forth from his nose.

4-9. "O heir, mighty one, coming forth from Rā, eldest one, prince, beautiful of face, living soul of Astennu,[c] babe, coming forth from the god of hearing and seeing, eldest one, prince of the two regions, heir of Seb, who gives to thee a circuit, O lord of the disk!

10, 11. "Come to thy temple, Osiris, messenger of the gods. Thy two eyes are opened that thou

[a]  *Neter ta*, "divine land," is the name given by the Egyptians to the lands to the east of the Nile on the shore of the Red Sea which extend from the mountains on the south nearly to Suez on the north. See Brugsch, *Dict. Géog.* p. 382.

[b] 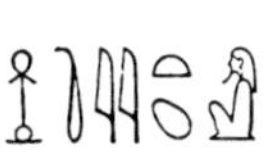 or 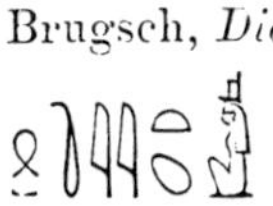 "Shenthit," is the name of a funereal form of the goddess Isis to whom sanctuaries in Abydos, Busiris, Denderah, etc., were consecrated. See Lanzone, *Dizionario*, p. 1178. The name of the sanctuary was 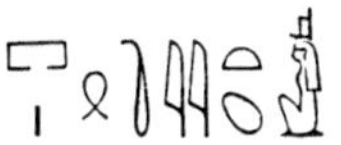 Pa-Shenthit. See Brugsch, *Dict. Géog.* p. 89.

[c] A name of the god Thoth.

12, 13. "mayest see with them. Thou drivest off rain storms, thou grantest that the earth may be lightened by the radiance of night.
14. "Come to thy temple, Osiris, at the head of those in the underworld, come to thy
15. "temple, O thou that proceedest from the body of the uraeus which is upon thy head.
16. "Thy two eyes light up the lands of the north and the south, and the gods; thou art
17. "twice exalted, O prince, our lord.
18. "That enemy of thine is laid upon the block and shall never rise up again; thou
19. "art established, established in thy name of 'established one.'
20. "Thou hast thy limbs, O Unnefer,[a] life, strength, health! thou hast thy flesh,
21. "O still heart.
22, 23. "Beautiful is that which cometh forth from thee, knowledge is the utterance of thy mouth.
24, 25. "Thy father Ta-tenen supports the heaven that thou mayest walk over its
26, 27. "four quarters; thy soul flies on the left hand, thou risest in the image of Rā.
28, 29. "Those who are in the underworld receive thee with shouts of joy, and Seb
30, 31. "opens out for thee a passage through it. They come to thee in peace, and thou comest in peace to Tettu.

Column XVII.

1, 2. "Exalted art thou, therefore, Osiris, exalted art thou, exalted art thou in peace.
3-5. "Isis, lady of the horizon, comes to thee, inasmuch as she has conceived the
6. "ONE, who is the guide of the gods; she avenges thee, she avenges thee, she avenges Horus,
7. "she, the woman who acts as the begetter of her own father."

Here endeth the book.

[a] A name of Osiris. For an explanation of the name, see Renouf, *Proceedings Soc. Bib. Arch.*, April, 1886, p. 111 ff.

II. THE LITANIES OF SEKER.[a]

This composition contains one hundred lines, and fills Columns XVIII. to XXI. of the papyrus. It is written in the same neat, careful hand, and appears to be a short rhythmical supplementary work, which was intended to be sung after the festival verses of Isis and Nephthys. It consists of three parts: 1, A Litany to the Sun-god; 2, A Recitation by Isis; and 3, A Litany to the Hathors. The subject-matter generally is easier to understand, but there are a few passages in it which are difficult. According to the rubric, it was to be sung sixteen times to the accompaniment of tambourines. The various names given to the Sun-god will probably be of much interest to the student of comparative mythology.

TRANSLATION.

The Litanies of Seker (Socharis).

Column XVIII.

1. The Litanies which Seker introduced: to be said in addition to the mysteries already recited.
2. Hail, prince coming forth from the womb!
3. Hail, eldest son of primeval matter!
4. Hail, lord of multitudes of aspects and evolutions!
5. Hail, golden circle in the temples!
6. Hail, lord of time and bestower of years!
7. Hail, lord of life for all eternity!
8. Hail, lord of myriads and millions!
9. Hail, thou who shinest in rising and setting!
10. Hail, thou who makest beings joyful!

[a]  Seker is, like Ptah, Osiris, and Tenen, a form of the night sun, with which the deceased is identified. The day of the festival of Seker, or Socharis, was celebrated in the various sanctuaries of Egypt at dawn, "at the moment when the sun casts its golden rays upon the earth." The festival consisted in drawing the Hennu boat 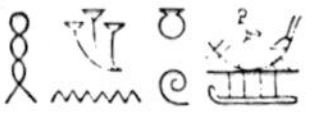 a symbol of the god Seker of Memphis, by a cord round the sanctuary. The god Seker is represented by a hawk-headed mummied figure as early as the time of Seti I. and in this form he is represented sitting on a throne, holding ,  and  in his hands; he appears on a coffin in the Imperial Museum at Vienna, in the form of a bearded man holding a knife  in each hand. A list of the shrines of this god is given by Lanzone, *Dizionario*, pp. 1117-1119.

11. Hail, thou lord of terror, thou fearful one!
12. Hail, lord of multitudes of aspects and divinities!
13. Hail, thou who art crowned with the white crown; thou master of the *urerer* crown!
14. Hail, thou sacred baby of Horus, praise!
15. Hail, son of Rā who sittest in the boat of millions of years!
16. Hail, restful leader, come to thy hidden places!
17. Hail, lord of terror, self-produced!
18. Hail, thou restful of heart, come to thy town!
19. Hail, thou that causest cries of joy, come to thy town!
20. Hail, thou darling of the gods and goddesses!
21. Hail, thou dipper in the sea, come to thy temple!
22. Hail, thou who art in the Nether-world, come to thy offerings!
23. Hail, thou that protectest them, come to thy temple!
24. Hail, Moon-god, growing from a crescent into an illuminated disk!
25. Hail, sacred flower of the mighty house!
26. Hail, thou that bringest the sacred cordage of the Sekti [a] boat!
27. Hail, thou lord of the Hennu [b] boat who becomest young again in the hidden place!
28. Hail, thou perfect soul in the Nether-world!
29. Hail, thou sacred visitor of the north and south!
30. Hail, thou hidden one, unknown to mankind!
31. Hail, thou illuminator of him that is in the Nether-world, that causest him to see the disk!

Column XIX.

1. Hail, lord of the *atef* crown, thou mighty one in Het-suten-henen! [c]
2. Hail, mighty one of terror!

[a] The *Sektet*  was the boat of the sun in the morning, just as the *Māti*  was the boat of the sun in the evening. A hymn to the sun-god says:

χā-k *em* *tuau* *em* *sekti*

Risest thou in the morning in the *sekti* boat;

ḥetep-k *em* *māti* *em* *māsher*

Settest thou in the *māti* boat in the evening.

[b] The *hennu* 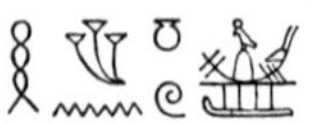 was the boat which was drawn around the sanctuaries of the temples at dawn. Drawings of it are given by Lanzone, *Dizionario*, plates CCLXV-CCCLXVII.

[c] Heracleopolis, the metropolis of the 20th nome of Upper Egypt.

3. Hail, thou that risest in Thebes, flourishing for ever!
4. Hail, Amen-Rā, king of the gods, who makest thy limbs to grow in rising and setting.
5. Hail, ... offerings and oblations in Ru-stau![a]
6. Hail, thou that placest the uraeus upon the head of its lord!
7. Hail, stablisher of the earth upon its foundations!
8. Hail, opener of the mouth of the four mighty gods who are in the Nether-world!
9. Hail, thou living soul of Osiris, who art diademed with the moon!
10. Hail, thou that hidest thy body in the great coffin at Heliopolis!
11. Hail, hidden one, mighty one, Osiris in the Nether-world!
12. Hail, thou that unitest his soul to heaven, thine enemy is fallen!
13. The goddess Isis cries unto thee, saying, "Hail, from the river,
14. "thou who separatest the pure *àbtu*[b] fish from the front
15. "of the boat of Rā! Hail, lord of the excretion which turns into the rejoicing gods!
16, 17. "Hail, egg which turns into Hen, cutting off the heads of the rebels in her name of 'Lady of Tep-ahet'![c]
18, 19. "Hail, lady of excretion, thou comest in front of the heads in name of 'Hathor, lady of emerald, lady of Thebes'![d]
20. "Thou comest in peace in thy name of 'Hathor, lady of Thebes.'
21. "Thou comest in peace, O Tait,[e] in thy name of 'lady of peace.'[f]
22, 23. "Thou comest forward to overthrow her enemy in thy name of 'Hathor, lady of Het-suten-henen.'[g]
24. "Thou golden one, thou comest in peace in thy name of 'Hathor,'
25. "'lady of Memphis. . . . .' Thou restest near Neb-er-ter[h] in the name of 'Hathor, lady of Shet-tesher.'[i]

[a] Literally "the door of the funeral passages," leading to the tomb.

[b] The *àbtu* and *ànt* were mythological fishes. See Lanzone, *Dizionario*, p. 16.

[c] Aphroditopolis, the metropolis of the 22nd nome of Upper Egypt.

[d] *i.e.* "lady of the peninsula of Sinai," where emerald mines were worked as early as the VIth dynasty.

[e] One of the names of the goddess Hathor mentioned in the eighty-second chapter of the Book of the Dead (Lepsius' ed. pl. xxxi.); it appears to be connected with *ta*, "fire."

[f] Neb-ḥetep or is one of the names of Hathor, the local divinity of *Pa-ḥeru*, near Tanis. See Brugsch, *Dict. Géog.* p. 333, and Lanzone, *Dizionario*, p. 370.

[g] Heracleopolis.

[h] *i.e.* "the lord of totality," a name of the god Osiris.

[i] The "town of the red pool," a district in the mountains east of Memphis.

26. "The golden one rises near her father in her name of 'Bast,' [a] advancing above
27. "the temples near the great double house in her name of 'Sati,' [b]
28. "verdifier of the north and south, leader of the gods in her name of 'Uatit.'
29. "Hathor gains the mastery of the enemies of her father in her name of 'Sechet.' [c]
30. "Uatit' [d] gains the mastery over the fire in her name of 'Lady of Ammu.' [e]
31. "There is perfume upon her hair and head in her name of 'Neith.' [f]

Column XX.

1. "Hail, O ye gods, on account of his virtues. [g]
2. "Hail, Hathor, lady of Thebes!
3. "Hail, Hathor, lady of Suten-henen! [h]
4. "Hail, Hathor, lady of Tep-ahet! [i]
5. "Hail, Hathor, lady of Nehau! [k]

[a] Bast was one of the four great Hathors and represented the life-giving heat of the sun. For the list of Basts and the towns protected by them, see Lanzone, *Dizionario*, p. 225.

[b] See Lanzone, *Dizionario*, pp. 1124, 1131.

[c] A form of Hathor, wife of Ptah, mother of Nefer-Aimu. She represented the blazing heat of the sun. See Lanzone, *Dizionario*, p. 1098.

[d] A form of the goddess Hathor, whose sanctuary *Pa-sat*, was situated in Sechem (Letopolis), the capital of the 2nd nome of Lower Egypt. See Brugsch, *Dict. Géog.* p. 659.

[e] Ammu, *i.e.* "the town of date trees," is the name of the sanctuary of the goddess Hathor, which was situated in "the town of Apis," , the metropolis of the 3d nome of Lower Egypt. is a variant of . There was a town also called Ammu in Upper Egpyt; it lay between Abydos and Panopolis. Brugsch, *Dict. Géog.* p. 327.

[f] There is a play here upon the words *ānti* and *Nit.*

[g] In the papyrus one-half of this line is written perpendicularly on the right-hand side of the list of the twelve Hathors, and the other half on the left.

[h] Suten-henen or Het-suten-henen, the metropolis of the 20th nome of Upper Egypt, called Heracleopolis by the Greeks, ϩⲛⲏⲥ by the Copts, and اهناس by the Arabs. See Brugsch, *Dict. Géog.* p. 601, and Juynboll, *op. cit.* t. i. p. ١٠٥

[i] Aphroditopolis, the metropolis of the 22nd nome of Upper Egypt; the local divinity was the goddess Hathor.

[k] *Neh*, or *Pa-neh*, a part of the town of Athribis *Het-ta-ḥer-ab*, the metropolis of the 10th nome of Upper Egypt, the modern Benha بنها which is famed for its honey, بنها اجود عسل مصر، see Juynboll, *op. cit.* t. i. p. ١٧٧ Brugsch, *Dict. Géog.* p. 349.

6. "Hail, Hathor, lady of Rehsau![a]
7. "Hail, Hathor, lady of Shet-Teshert![b]
8. "Hail, Hathor, lady of the Emerald Land![c]
9. "Hail, Hathor, lady of Aneb![d]
10. "Hail, Hathor, lady of Uaua![e]
11. "Hail, Hathor, lady of Ammu![f]
12. "Hail, Hathor, lady of Amem![g]
13. "Hail, Hathor, lady of the 'City of Sixteen.'[h]
14. "O ye nine *smeri*,[i] come ye bearing your father Osiris upon your two hands,
15. "come ye with divine adorations, come ye with divine adorations, come ye with divine adorations, come ye with divine adorations!
16. "Hail, crown of the festival! hail, crown of the festival! Sovereign!
17. "Hail, thou rejoicest the nurses who love thee!
18. "Hail, thou livest, thou livest, for ever!
19. "Hail, thou makest festival for ever!

[a] *Re-hesau*, a town famous for its temple of the goddess Sechet, was situated near Seχem (Letopolis), the metropolis of the 2nd nome of Lower Egypt. See Brugsch, *Dict. Géog.* pp. 71, 460.

[b] *Shet-tesher*, "the town of the red pool," was a district situated in the mountains to the east of Memphis, where are to-day the quarries of Ma'ṣara and Ṭurra. See Brugsch, *Dict. Géog.* p. 971.

[c] *Māfek*, *i.e.* the peninsula of Sinai, where the emerald mines were dedicated to this goddess as early as the Vth dynasty. Compare also the list of Hathors quoted by Brugsch, *Dict. Géog.* p. 971, and Mariette, *Dendérah*, t. i. pl. 27.

[d] A town situated to the east of Pelusium and north of Migdol. See Brugsch, *Dict. Géog.* pp. 50-52. In my interlinear translation for Memphis read Aneb.

[e] The country of *Uaua* was situated in Ethiopia, to the east of the modern town of Korosko. It is mentioned in the inscription of Una (line 16), where it is described as a Negro-land *Uauat neḥes*. In the list of ten Hathors printed by Brugsch, *Dict. Géog.* p. 1367, after "Hathor, lady of Aneb," we have "Hathor, lady of *χaχau*."

[f] See Note to column xix. line 30.

[g] *Āmemet* was the sacred name of *Pa-uátet*, Buto, the metropolis of the 19th nome of Lower Egypt. See Brugsch, *Dict. Géog.* p. 25.

[h] *I.e.* Lycopolis, the metropolis of the 13th nome of Upper Egypt. Compare [var] in Brugsch, *Dict. Géog.* pp. 1067, 1391.

[i] A title of a class of temple official.

20. " Hail, object of adoration, thou traverser of ways!
21. " Hail, thou who art established in the heavenly Tattu!
22. " Hail, god, who listenest to adoration, hail, thou listenest to adoration from the mouth of the divine nomes!
23. " Hail, thou who comest forth from thy two eyes, son of the prophet!
24. " Hail, thou who art protected by amulets when thou speakest!
25. " Hail, protect me, O king, to do thy pleasure!
26. " Hail, protect me, O king, to do thy will!
27. " Hail, Sitter, the restful of heart comes to thee!
28. " Hail, son of the prophet, the festal ritual is recited for him.
29. " Hail, thy name is established in the heavenly Tettu!
30. " Hail, thou sweetly smelling one in the heavenly Tettu.
31. " Hail, thou that comest to destroy the Sebau (fiends)!
32. " Hail, thou that comest to extol the Baby!

Column XXI.

1. " Hail, thou that settest thy terror in the evil-hearted!
2. " Hail, thou Worker, who followest after thy lord, there is not . . . . !
3. " Hail, ye evil-hearted, who hate the temple, strike death from his throat!
4. " Hail, the lord of the heavenly Tettu cometh, he has repulsed the evil-hearted!"
5. This book shall be recited sixteen times by players on tambourines.

Here endeth the book.

III.—THE BOOK OF THE OVERTHROWING OF APEPI.

This composition contains three hundred and seventy-seven lines and fills columns xxii. to xxxiii. of the papyrus; two columns are written on the back, and as the papyrus is in this place somewhat damaged, the reading of a few of the words is uncertain. The writing is neat and careful, but there are in it traces of more than one hand. The character of the subject-matter is quite different from that of the earlier works in the papyrus, and although rhythmical passages occur here and there, the work cannot be, like them, considered poetical. From the frequent repetition of certain passages parts of the work are monotonous; the varied and interesting nature of the other parts, however, amply atones for this, and makes it of considerable value, both to the Egyptologist, and to the student of comparative mythology.

The subject of the work is the daily battle which was waged by Rā, the Sun-god, against the demons and fiends of mist, clouds, rain, thunder, darkness, and night. The head of these veritable powers of darkness was named Apepi, and he seems to have been assisted in his dire work by fiends called Qettu, Sebau, Sheta, etc. Each night when Rā went to his home in the west he was assailed by squadrons of fiends under the leadership of Apepi; with these he waged war throughout the night, and chiefly by the might of sun-flame, he was enabled to show himself each morning to the expectant world. The fiercest and most violent attacks were made upon him during the night, but the fiends of darkness never lost an opportunity of sending clouds into the sky by day to obscure his light and to overcome his power. When they could send rain with their clouds they did so, and they rejoiced greatly when they succeeded in making a violent thunderstorm. Rain and cold were disliked by the ancient Egyptian as much as they are detested by his modern descendants. Everything then that he could do to cause the sun to shine, and to keep off the rain and cold he felt it to be his duty to do. Apart from his bodily comfort, he had a spiritual interest in the victory of the Sun-god over his foes. When the ancient Egyptian deposited his relative or friend in the grave, he identified the resurrection of his body with the daily renewed birth of the Sun-god. The dead man was identified with Osiris, the night sun, king of the dead, lord of the under-world, and a form of the Sun-god; if the god of the dead were overcome by the powers of darkness, what hope of renewed birth could remain for his subjects? The dangers which hovered over the path of the night-sun must necessarily stand in the way of the dead man; any deed or service which gave power to the Sun-god, or defeat to his enemies must also, necessarily, be of great benefit to the dead man. The name of the dead man is linked with that of Rā, the Sun-god, in the following manner: "Horus takes his steel lance and drives it into the heads of the enemies of Rā; Horus takes his steel lance and drives it into the heads of the enemies of P-āa[a] (the deceased). Therefore art thou exalted, O Rā, for thy enemies are smitten, Apepi is slaughtered, and the fiends of the Devil have been cast down.

[a] *P-āa, i.e.*, the "mighty one," written inside a cartouche, in this papyrus takes the place of the name "Osiris," by which in other papyri the deceased is usually designated.

Therefore art thou exalted, P-āa, for thy enemies are smitten, thy foes are slaughtered, and thy devilish opponents are cast down. Rā triumphs over Apepi, and P-āa triumphs over his enemies; Rā gains the mastery over thee Apepi, and P-āa gains the mastery over thee, Apepi." Hence provided that the dead man is justified before Osiris, whatever good is done for the god is also done for him; and a service recited by the priests in a temple to the honour and glory of the Sun-god became an act of worship in which each person would gladly join, as much for the sake of his beloved dead as for his own material comfort.

The "Book of the Overthrowing of Apepi," printed in the following pages was, as we learn from the title, recited in the temple of Amen-Rā in the Apts every day. It was divided into sections and chapters, each of which is clearly indicated in its proper place, and contained shorter compositions on the subject of the defeat of Apepi which were to be recited at suitable occasions. Of its author and date nothing is known. It contains variant readings, and it is evident from this that other copies of the work were extant, and also that it was sufficiently old for doubts to have arisen in the minds of scribes about the correct readings. The work is not entirely original, but appears to be a much amplified redaction of a number of chapters of the Book of the Dead which refer to the turning back of serpents in the under-world. A comparison of the seventh, thirty-first, thirty-third, and the thirty-fifth to the thirty-ninth chapters with the Book of the Overthrowing of Apepi will show that the redactor of this work was well acquainted with them, and that parts of them enter into it. Of these chapters the thirty-ninth is the most largely used, but it will be seen that there are many important variations between the two texts, due either to corruptions of the text, or to a change in religious views. The oldest hieroglyphic recension of this chapter has been given, with variants from three manuscripts, by M. Naville in *Das Aegyptische Todtenbuch* (Band 1, bl. liii. Bd. ii. ss. 107—109). In two manuscripts it is found with the sixty-fifth chapter, and in two others before or after the fortieth chapter. The text as given by Lepsius (*Das Todtenbuch der Aegypter*, bl. xviii.) is, in many places, quite different from that printed by M. Naville. Translations of it have been printed by Dr. Birch[a] and M. P. Pierret;[b] the following tentative version has been made from the text of M. Naville.

1. THE CHAPTER OF REPULSING HIS SERPENT IN THE NETHER-WORLD.

2. Get thee gone, depart, withdraw, thou baleful Serpent, retreat and be drowned at
3. the pool of the Sky, where thy father has commanded thy slaughter to be made. Depart thou to that birthplace of Rā, where exists that which makes thee afraid. I am Rā in his terror.
4. Get thee back, Sebau, by the darts of his beams Rā has overthrown thy words.
5. The gods have reversed thy face, the lynx has torn out thy heart, the scorpion has shot forth fetters upon thee, and Māāt has sent forth
6. destruction for thee. Those who are in the ways overthrow thee; fall down, depart, O Apepi, enemy of Rā! O pass away over the region in the east of the sky in the

[a] Bunsen, *Egypt's Place in Universal History*, vol. v. p. 193.

[b] *Le Livre des Morts des Anciens Egyptiens*, pp. 135—140.

7. voice of the roaring thunder cloud! Rā opens the gates of the horizon at once and comes forth; [Apepi] is ruined and cut to pieces.

I have performed thy will, I have performed thy will,

8. O Rā, I have done well, I have done well. I have worked in peace, making the ropes of thy boat to advance.

Apepi is overthrown! The gods of the south, north, west, and east tie and

9. fetter Apepi, they set fetters round about him; Rekes overthrows him, and Hertit fetters him. Rā sets, Rā sets, Rā strengthens himself in peace!

10. Apepi is overthrown, Apepi, the enemy of Rā, falls down.

The sting which thou art made to taste is stronger than the sting of

11. the scorpion; it has wrought death for thee and thy courses are over for ever. Thou shalt never experience sexual pleasure, there shall never be emissions of body to thee, O Apepi, enemy of Rā, who repulses thy face, O

12. hater of Rā, when he sees thee. Get thee back, thy head is crushed, thy face is slit, thy head is rolled along in the filth of the roads, thy head is broken in on his land, thy bones are broken, thy limbs are cut

13. in pieces, Nekker has condemned thee, O Apepi, enemy of Rā.

Thy sailors, thy green food, and thy necessaries, are

14. provided and offered to thee there. The advance to the house, the advance which thou makest to the house is a good advance. May there never come forth any evil disaster against me from thy mouth while thou workest for me.

15. I am Set, letting loose the storm clouds and the thunder clouds within the horizon of heaven, as his heart the Lock.

Says Atmu, "O ye soldiers of Rā, lift up your faces, for, by the

16. might of Powers, I have repulsed Nentā."

Says Seb, "O ye that are in your seats in the boat of Chepera, make

17. yourselves ready, find your roads, and hold ye your weapons in your hands."

Says Hathor, "O take ye your armour."

18. Says Nut, "Come, we will repulse that destroying one who follows after him that is in his shrine; he shall go forth [against] him . . . . . . Neb-er-ter is without repulse."

19. The gods who are in their cycles, going round the lakes of emerald, say, "Come, O mighty one, we adore and deliver the mighty one in [his] shrine, from whom proceedeth the substance of the gods.

20. Commemorations are made for him, shouts of acclamation are given for him, he is addressed by you and praised."

"Hail," says Nut, with reference to that Sweet One.

21. Those who are among the gods say, "He comes forth, he finds the way, he maketh captives among the gods, he drives away evil from Nut, Seb stands up."

Hail, victorious one!

The cycle of the gods marches along . . . . . . Hathor is trembling.

Rā triumphs over Apepi.

The Book of the overthrowing of Apepi is divided into the following chapters and divisions:—

I. The Chapter of Spitting upon Apepi.
II. The Chapter of defiling Apepi with the left foot.
III. The Chapter of taking a lance to smite Apepi.
IV. The Chapter of putting fetters upon Apepi.
V. The Chapter of taking a knife to smite Apepi.
VI. The Chapter of putting fire upon Apepi.
VII. The First Book of the Overthrowing of Apepi.
VIII. The Second Book of the Overthrowing of Apepi.
IX. The Book of Overthrowing the enemy of Rā.
X. The book of turning back Apepi. To be said at dawn.
XI. The Book of knowing the Evolutions of Rā and the overthrowing of Apepi.
XII. The Book of Overthrowing Apepi.
XIII. Another Book of Overthrowing Apepi.
XIV. The Accursed Names of Apepi.
XV. A Hymn of Praise to be recited after the foregoing Chapters.

The subject-matter of the first six chapters calls for little comment; they consist chiefly of adjurations against Apepi, and accounts of the various methods by which he was destroyed. The rubrics which follow these chapters order what acts were to be performed at the time of their recital. Apepi, the enemy of the Sun-god, was represented as a serpent of many folds, with a knife stuck in each. A wax figure of this fiend was made and taken by the priest into his hands. When he recited the words "An end to thee, an end to thee, Apepi, I have destroyed the enemy of Rā," he cast the wax figure of Apepi upon the ground and smote it four times with his left foot, saying "Thou art defiled, Apepi." A wax figure of Apepi, with his accursed name cut upon it, was also to be wrapped in a piece of new papyrus, upon which a figure of Apepi was drawn in green ink, and burnt in a dried grass [a] fire; what remained afterwards was to be mixed with excrement and burnt, and while it was burning it was to be spit upon by the priest several times. This was to be done morning, noon, and night, and at certain other times and seasons which are duly specified. If tempests were raging in the sky, or if heavy black-red clouds were stealing over the sky to obscure the sun's disk, or if heavy rain had set in, to make these pass away it was necessary to burn several such figures, and to recite these chapters over them while they were burning. The last part of the rubric which refers to this section of the papyrus states that it is a meritorious act for a man to perform these acts, that it is good for him upon this earth and good for him in the nether-world; they will enable him to attain to dignities which are above him, and he will be delivered from all evil things. Following this comes what appears to be a note by the scribe: "May I see these things happen to me."

The first book of the overthrowing of Apepi was to be recited by a person, ceremonially clean and pure, over a papyrus, upon which the name of Apepi was written in green colour, while it

[a] I am unable to find an exact meaning for the word *χessau* which is here translated by dried grass.

was burnt in the fire. The subject-matter is the injuries which are inflicted upon Apepi by Rā, Horus, and the deceased for whom the papyrus was written.

The second book of the overthrowing of Apepi was also to be recited by a person ceremonially clean and pure, and was devoted to the destruction, not only of Apepi, but also of Sebau, Qettu, Sheta, and the other rebels, fiends, and devils that accompanied him. The rubric is a little fuller than that of the first book, and orders that a wax figure of each demon and of his father, mother, and children shall be made, that they shall be wrapped up in pieces of new papyrus, upon which their names are written, and tied round with black hairs. These figures were to be spit upon, defiled with the left foot, and hacked with a stone knife, and then burnt in a blazing fire of dried grass. The rubric also orders that the book was to be recited, according to the original codex, when the *atep* boat of the sun went forth, at dawn, to overthrow the enemy of Rā, and every enemy of Horus. It was a meritorious act to recite it in the presence of the god at dawn every day without fail.

The short book of overthrowing Apepi which next follows is of small interest, and the "Book of turning back Apepi," which follows it, merely contains some interesting variants of the old theme, *i. e.*, the tortures which are inflicted upon Apepi by Rā, Horus, and the other gods.

Among this mass of half magical, half religious compositions, we meet with a very remarkable document entitled "the Book of Knowing the Evolutions of Rā," which relates to the origin of things and the genesis of gods and men. In Colums xxvi. and xxvii. one version of it is given, and in Columns xxviii. and xxix. is another; the first version is the shorter of the two, and is more easily understood. It is difficult to account for the presence of two versions of the same text in one papyrus; but it is fortunate that both occur, for the second helps to explain the first. Both are difficult to translate because it is nearly impossible to find exact equivalents for some of the Egyptian words, and it appears that, in places, the text is corrupt. The literal and the running translations of this document given below are not intended in any way to be final; they are only put forward to give an idea of the meaning of this, so far as can be ascertained, unique work.

The account of the creation is put into the mouth of the god Neb-er-ter, who is supposed to state how he came into existence, and what had happened since his birth. He begins by saying that there was no heaven and no earth, and that animals and reptiles did not exist; all animal life, according to his assertion, was made out of the watery mass of Nu, (the abyss or sky) which previous to his coming into being lay in an inert and chaotic state. There was not even a place upon which this god could stand; but his will was strong, and by an effort thereof he laid the foundation of everything which afterwards came into existence, and performed all that there was to be done. More than once the god points out that he was quite alone, and that there was none other who worked with him. As to his own origin he says that he developed himself out of the primeval matter which he himself had made, and that he evolved himself out of this matter by a series of evolutions which followed one after the other; from the same matter all other things were made by him. The word here translated "evolutions" is  *χeperu* which may be fairly accurately rendered by "rollings" or "turnings." The god  *χepera*, who performed these "turnings" or "rollings," was the form under which Neb-er-ter developed himself, and a common title of this god is 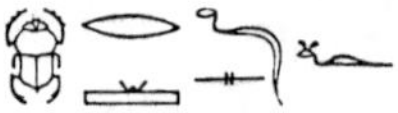 *χeper tesef, i. e.,* "becoming of himself" or "self-produced," like the Greek *αὐτογενής*. Without either insisting on the appropriateness of the word "evolutions" as a rendering of *χeperu*, or attempting to read into the text the modern technical ideas connected with it, it is nevertheless a remarkable coincidence that this word should so admirably suit, and make sense in many passages of a text written more than two thousand years ago to explain the various stages in the creation of the world, gods, men, and animals. The god Chepera not only created himself out of the matter which he himself had made, but he did so by uttering his own name from his mouth, thus using it as a word of magical power, and he straightway developed himself by evolutions or turnings. A little earlier the god tells us that his name is Ausares, which is the "matter (germ ?) of primeval matter"; Ausares, 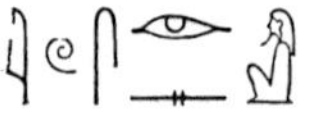 may possibly be a form of Ausar or Osiris. The conception of a god creating himself out of matter, which he had made, by the mere utterance of his own name is remarkable, and shows what an amount of power was attributed to the utterance of certain names. The word here translated "matter" is *paut,* and means literally the "cake" or "substance" from which all things were made.

Neb-er-ter, under the form of Chepera, having created matter and himself and animals, next brings the gods into existence. This he does by union with his own limbs, and as a result the gods Shu and Tefnut are produced. Thus, says the god, "from being one god, I became three gods, and they came out of myself into existence in this land." The origin of men and women were the tears which fell from the eye of the god. Thus far the meaning of the text appears to be perfectly clear, in spite of the repetitions of words and sentences which occur in it. A very difficult passage, however, follows here, and its meaning is not so easily perceived. It appears to have reference to the eclipse of the eye of Chepera or Neb-er-ter (*i. e.* Rā), and to a dispute which the god had with it. According to one version the god Nu complains that his eye is eclipsed, and Neb-er-ter says that it growled or raged at him because of some act of his. In the other version Neb-er-ter says that Shu and Tefnut brought his eye along with them, but that when it came, and saw that the god had collected his limbs and wept near them, and that men and women had sprung into existence from them, it growled at him. Both accounts agree in saying that Neb-er-ter restored it to its place in his face, that he filled it with radiance, that it put into order all things, and that it ruled the whole earth. Both accounts end by saying that Shu and Tefnut gave birth to Seb and Nut, and that Nut gave birth to Osiris, Horus, dwelling in invisibility, Sut, Isis, and Nephthys. This is the account of the creation as accepted by the Egyptians three hundred years before Christ at least. The text is, no doubt, corrupt, and from the frequent repetitions which occur, it is clear that a large number of variant readings, or glosses by scribes, have been incorporated into it. The number of glosses, or variant readings, shows that the work is of some antiquity, and hence it appears that the copy before us cannot be the first that was written. It is much to be hoped that future discoveries in Egypt will bring to light other copies of the text in a more correct form and of older date.

The formulæ for the destruction of Apepi are continued to a great length after the account of the creation, and the rubrics of the chapters are chiefly repetitions of those which are found early in the papyrus. Concerning one chapter it is said "It is a mystery, and is to be performed in the chamber; no eye shall see it. The Book of Words of Power is its name." At the end of it is a smaller chapter in which the gods Rā, Atmu, Chepera, Shu, Tefnut, Seb, Nut, Osiris, Horus, Isis, Nephthys, Hu, Sau, Osiris of Kochome and Hiku, the genius of Rā are taken to witness that the deceased P-āa has cast fire upon Apepi. This chapter is, in its turn, followed by "Another Book of overthrowing Apepi," and in it every dead person, every living person, and every person who is to be born is called upon to regard P-āa as a "great god, lord of heaven," for "Rā protects him, Rā protects his soul against every man, every woman, every dead person, and every unborn person. Rā will shut the mouth of every person who would speak evil against P-āa, and Rā will watch carefully to do harm to any person who would do any harm or evil thing to him." The rubric, which states at what time of the day this chapter is to be said, is mutilated; and with it the "Book of Neb-er-ter" comes to an end.

Next follow, written in red, twenty-nine of the abominable names of Apepi, many of which have been mentioned already in the chapters of the work. Owing to a break in the papyrus, one or two of them are incomplete; the meaning of most of them is evident.

In the last rubric of the work it is ordered that four wax figures of serpents are to be made, to represent the "children of inertness," *i.e.* Apepi, Sebau, Qettu, and Sheta. The first is to have the face of a . . . . . , the second the face of a cat, the third the face of a duck, and the fourth the face of a crocodile. The tail of each was to be thrust in his mouth, a knife was to be stuck in the back of each, each was to be tied round with fetters, and cast upon the ground while the priest uttered imprecations upon it. The names of the four wax figures were Hemhem (Roarer), Aaqaruaba, Hauna-aru-her-hra and Unti.

Following this rubric is the hymn of praise to Rā by the deceased, which ends the papyrus. In it P-āa addressed the god by his great titles of honour, and he claims to be his son in very truth. He says "O Rā, look with thy two eyes, and be graciously pleased with what I have done. I have destroyed Apepi for thee, I have overthrown him within his cavern. He is shut up in restraint, his body is destroyed and blotted out from the horizon of thy two heavens. Apepi has been cast down into the fire and the flame has carried him off; the heart of Amen-Rā, lord of the thrones of the earth, rejoices, for his enemy has fallen beneath him. Rā triumphs over his enemy, Amen-Rā triumphs over his enemy, Atmu triumphs over his enemy, and Thoth triumphs over his enemy."

The story of the daily battle waged by Rā, the sun-god, against Apepi has something in common with the Babylonian legend of the battle which took place between Marduk and Tiamat. Marduk, the Babylonian sun-god, corresponds to Rā or Horus, and Tiamat, the she-devil of blackness, mist, and night, with scaly body, claws, and tail, corresponds to Apepi. The Babylonian cycle of the gods sent forth their lord and master Marduk to do battle with Tiamat, and they provided him with a spear or club, of fabulous power, and bows and arrows wherewith he might overcome her. They commanded him to destroy her utterly, and to scatter her blood and person to the four winds; Marduk took with him a net wherewith to snare her, and also created a number of winds for his help. He drove across the sky in a chariot, and when he drew near to her he challenged her to combat. He first sent against her a mighty wind, which she tried to swallow, but she was unable to close her mouth by reason of its violence; this wind entered into her and smote her with great force so that she was overthrown. Marduk then seized his club and smashed in her head, he cast his net round her body, he cut out her entrails, he skinned her, and obtained the mastery over her. The fiends and devils, who accompanied her and formed her army, were scattered, her hosts were overthrown, and they fled away in great fear and trembling. They were, however, pursued by Marduk, who overtook them, and, having broken their limbs, cast his net round about them and fettered them. This brief summary is sufficient to show how great the resemblance between the two legends is; in matters of detail the resemblance is more striking. The Babylonian legend, unfortunately, gives us no rubrics, so that it is impossible to say if this composition was recited daily in the temples at Babylon, or if certain acts, such as the burning of wax figures, which accompanied the recitation of the Egyptian service for the slaughter of Apepi, were performed when it was read. In both the Egyptian and Babylonian legends the gods sing a hymn of praise to their victorious leader on the defeat of the great fiend that opposed him, and the sun shines and the heavens become bright.[a]

Of interest, too, for the subject of Egyptian magic, are the important details given in the rubrics to the Egyptian text of the service for the slaughter of Apepi. In these we learn that, in addition to the chapters and prayers which were to be recited in the temple of Amen-Rā at Thebes, it was necessary to perform certain acts of a magical nature. Apepi, the demon whose destruction was earnestly sought for, was supposed to exist under the form of a crocodile with a hideous face, and he was accompanied by hosts of demons in various forms and shapes. To annihilate his power it was necessary to make a figure of him in wax, and to write his name upon it in green ink. This figure was to be wrapped up in a papyrus case, upon which the figure of Apepi had been written in green ink, it was then to be tied up with black hair, and spit upon several times, and its back was to be gashed with a knife. The figure was then to be cast upon the ground, and trodden upon with the left foot several times, and then burnt in a fire made of a certain plant or grass. If this act was performed at morning, noon, and night, and at certain other stated times, and certain formulae or chapters were recited at the same time, the same injuries that were inflicted upon the figure of Apepi would be inflicted upon Apepi himself. When Apepi had been thus disposed of, wax figures of his principal demons were made and burnt in the same way. How old this piece of ritual is it is not possible to say definitely, but I believe it to be older than the xviiith dynasty. That the custom of performing acts of sorcery by means of wax figures is as old as the xixth dynasty is certain, for there is a case on record in which it appears that a certain superintendent of the cattle of the king was prosecuted in an Egyptian court of law for having made figures of men and women in wax, thereby causing paralysis of their limbs and other grievous bodily injuries.[b] He had by some means obtained a book of magic, which contained not only the formulae necessary for obtaining magical results, but also directions

[a] A summary of the contents of the Babylonian text was published by me in *Proc. Soc. Bib. Arch.*, November 1883, and the full text in *Proc. Soc. Bib. Arch.* December 1887, p. 86; an accurate German translation is published in Jensen, *Kosmologie*, p. 277 ff.

[b] See Chabas, *Le Papyrus Magique Harris*, p. 170.

how to proceed; he shut himself up in a secret chamber, and there proceeded to cast spells upon the people of his town.

A remarkable instance of the use of wax figures is recorded in the life of Alexander the Great by Pseudo-Callisthenes. Nectanebus II., the last native king of Egypt, was given to the study of magic, and, having become an expert, he used it in a remarkable way to preserve his country from invasion by enemies. Whenever they came to make war against him he used to go into his palace and overcome them from there by means of magical practices. If they came by sea he took a basin of water and set it in the middle of his room, and having made models of the soldiers of the enemy and of those of his own army he placed them in models of ships which he set upon the water opposite to each other. He then took a rod of wood in his hand, and uttered magical formulæ and the names of certain demons. Presently the ships would draw near to each other and the wax figures would begin to fight. If the figures which represented his own soldiers were victorious on the water in the basin his soldiers were victorious on the sea; but if they were beaten and the ships sunk, the same result whuld happen to his army if they attempted to fight. One day, by this means, Nectanebus discovered that the gods of Egypt had handed over the country to the invader, for his ships were scattered on the basin of water, and were driven hither and thither by those of the enemy; on seeing this he disguised himself and fled away.[a]

The above remarks will indicate the interesting nature of the texts which are transliterated and translated in the following pages. It is hoped that the attention of other students may be drawn to the consideration of them, and also that other copies may come to light to clear up the difficulties which now exist.

TRANSLATION.

The Book of the Overthrowing of Apepi.

Column XXII.

1. Here beginneth the book of the overthrowing of Apepi, the enemy of Rā, the enemy of Un-nefer, life, strength, health, triumphant! It shall be recited in the temple of Amen-Rā, lord of the thrones of the two lands, at the head of the Apts, in the course of every day.

The Chapter of spitting upon Apepi.

Then shall be said:—

2. "Be spit upon thou Apepi, be spit upon thou Apepi, be spit upon thou Apepi, be spit upon thou Apepi."

Rā rests with his *ka*, P-āa rests with his *ka*, Rā cometh mighty, Rā cometh victorious.

3. "Rā cometh exalted, Rā cometh dowered, Rā cometh with acclamation, Rā cometh in beauty, Rā cometh as king of the north, Rā cometh as king of the south, Rā cometh with divine

[a] For the Greek text see *Pseudo-Callisthenes* primum edidit C. Müller, Parisiis, 1877, lib. I. cap. 1., and see my *History of Alexander the Great*, p. xxxix.

4. "oblations, Rā cometh with triumph then, P-āa, life, strength, health! thou hast destroyed for him all his enemies as he has slain for thee Apepi. He slays Qettu for thee, he gives adoration to thy might,

5. "he adores thee at all thy risings in which thou risest for him, and he overthrows for thee all thy enemies in the course of every day."

The Chapter of defiling Apepi with the left foot.

To be recited:—

6. "Therefore art thou exalted, Rā, for thine enemies are destroyed.
"Shine, therefore, Rā, for thine enemies are fallen.
"Verily, Rā has destroyed for thee all thine enemies, O P-āa, life, strength, health! Verily, all thine enemies are destroyed for thee in life and death. Rā gains the mastery over thee, Apepi,

7. "his flame bristles against thee, it gains the mastery over thee, turning its flame against thee; its fire falls upon the enemies of Rā, its flame falls upon all the enemies of P-āa, life, strength, health!

8. "Rā gains the mastery; O Rā, thine enemy is trampled upon by thee in thy horizon. Those who are in the *sekti* boat adore thee, the *ahiti* go round thee and thy boat with acclamation, thou renewest festival in the valiant-hearted who are in the māāt boat.

9. "Adoration to thee, Rā Harmachis, adoration to thee, Rā Harmachis, adoration to thee, Rā Harmachis, adoration to thee, Rā Harmachis."

The Chapter of taking a lance to smite Apepi.

To be recited:—

10. "Horus takes his steel lance and thrusts it into the heads of the enemies of Rā; Horus takes his steel lance and thrusts it into the heads of the enemies of P-āa, life, strength, health! Of a truth Horus takes his steel lance and smites the heads of the fiends in front
11. of his boat.
"Therefore shalt thou be exalted, Rā, for thy fiendish enemies are hooked, Apepi is slaughtered, and the fiends of the Devil have been cast down. Therefore shalt thou also
12. be exalted, P-āa, for thy fiends are hooked, thy foes are slaughtered, and thy devilish opponents are cast down. Come then, Rā, in thy splendours, those who are in their
13. shrines adore thee in thy beauties in that thou risest and shinest unopposed by foes; thy words of power protect thy body. P-āa adores Rā, he thrusts his lance against Apepi, he
14. takes the flame of fire and casts it upon him, he sticks hooks into the bodies of his enemies. Be there fire upon you, be there flame upon you, be there burning to you, O ye enemies of P-āa, life, strength, health! may it consume you. Therefore shalt thou be exalted, Rā, for hooks are stuck into thy fiendish foes, fire is cast upon Apepi, and it gnaws
15. into the joints of his backbone. Hail, there is fire thrown on Apepi.

"Rā is in the midst of the breezes of the north winds, and the valiant-hearted ones who
16. navigate his boat in the horizon exult at the sight of him. He overthrows the fiend, his fire prevails over Apepi, and the Fiend roars, may he never be at peace, may he never be at peace!

"O Rā Harmachis, show thy beautiful face to P-āa, life, health, and strength! destroy
17. thou for him all his enemies, for he adores thee in very truth. Rā triumphs over Apepi, and P-āa triumphs over his enemies; Rā triumphs over Apepi, and P-āa triumphs over his enemies; Rā triumphs over Apepi, and P-āa triumphs over his enemies; Rā triumphs over Apepi, and P-āa triumphs over his enemies."

The Chapter of putting fetters upon Apepi.

To be recited:—

18. "O ye fetterers, fetter, fetter ye Apepi that enemy of Rā! Thou canst not know, O Apepi, what will be done unto thee, for justice meets thee.

19. "O thou that goest back at thy moment, thou destroyest thyself; by opening thy throat, thou holdest fast the fetter. Horus cries, 'Be thou fettered;' Rā cries, 'Be thou tied up, mayest thou never experience the delights of the pleasures of love,

20. "'mayest thou never escape from his fingers'; Rā cries, 'Mayest thou be damned;' and Horus dwelling in invisibility cries, 'Be thou tied up.'"

The Chapter of taking a knife to smite Apepi.

To be recited:—

"O slaughterer, mayest thou have the mastery, mayest thou have the mastery and over-
21. "throw the enemy of Rā with thy knife! O slaughterer, mayest thou have the mastery, mayest thou have the mastery and overthrow with thy knife those heads of yours, Sebau
22. and Apepi, slaughtering and slaying them with thy knife!

"O goddess Septet, who providest flame, O goddess Asbit who presidest over the spark, overthrow ye the Fiend with your knives, slaughter ye the Demon with your swords, slay
23. ye them because of the injury done to you, hack them in pieces because of what has been done to you, let there be justice done to them by you because of the evil which has been wrought upon you. Rā triumphs over you, ye fiends, Horus hacks you in pieces."

The Chapter of putting fire upon Apepi.

24. To be recited:—

"Fire upon thee, O Apepi, that enemy of Rā! The eye of Horus prevails over the accursed soul and shade of Apepi, the flame of the eye of Horus gnaws into

Column XXIII.

1. "that enemy of Rā, the flame of the eye of Horus eats into all the enemies of P-āa, life, strength, health! in death, in life."

When Apepi is put in the fire speak ye with words of power, and say, "Taste thou, death to thee Apepi! Get thee back, retreat thou enemy of Rā, fall down, wriggle away, depart, retreat. I have driven thee back, I have hacked thee in pieces. Rā triumphs over thee, Apepi; Rā triumphs over thee, Apepi; Rā triumphs over thee, Apepi; Rā triumphs over thee, Apepi. Taste thou, Apepi, taste thou, Apepi, taste thou, Apepi, taste thou, Apepi!

3. "Back, thou fiend, an end to thee! Therefore have I cast fire at thee, therefore have I caused thee to be destroyed, therefore have I judged and condemned thee to an evil doom. An
4. end to thee, an end to thee; taste thou, an end to thee, mayest thou never rise up again! An end, an end to thee, an end to thee, taste thou, and come to an end. I have destroyed the enemy of Rā.

"Rā triumphs over thee, Apepi, and P-āa triumphs over his enemies; Rā triumphs over thee, Apepi, and P-āa triumphs over his enemies; Rā triumphs over thee, Apepi, and P-āa triumphs over his enemies; Rā triumphs over thee, Apepi, and P-āa triumphs over his enemies."

5. Afterwards thou shalt smite Apepi with thy left foot four times, and shalt say, "Defiled art thou, Apepi."

After Rā has risen, standing facing him, with both thy arms bent shalt thou say, "Rā has triumphed over thee, Apepi; Rā has triumphed over thee, Apepi; Rā has triumphed
6. over thee, Apepi; Rā has triumphed over thee, Apepi; in very truth has Rā been made to triumph over thee, Apepi; destroyed is Apepi."

This chapter must be recited over [the name of] Apepi written in green ink upon a piece of new papyrus, and over a wax figure of Apepi on which his name is inscribed in
7. green ink; this figure shall be then put in the fire that it may devour the enemy of Rā. One must place such a figure in the fire at dawn, at daybreak, at eventide, when Rā sets
8. in the land of life, at midnight, at the eighth hour of the day, at the coming on of the evening, and even at every hour of the day and night; also, on the day of the festival, by
9. day, by month, by the sixth day festival, by the fifteenth day festival, and likewise every day. Then will Apepi, the enemy of Rā, be overthrown in the shower, for Rā will shine, and Apepi will be overthrown in very truth.

10. This figure of Apepi is to be burnt in a fire of dried grass, and when burnt, its remains (ashes) are to be mixed with excrement and thrown into a fire. The like of this must be done by thee at the sixth hour of the night, and at daybreak of the festival of the fifteenth
11. day. When the figure of Apepi is thrown into the fire, one must spit upon him very many times at the beginning of each hour of the day until the shadow comes round.

12. Afterwards, when thou hast thrown Apepi into the fire at daybreak of the festival of the sixth
day, spit upon him and defile him with thy left foot; thus will be repulsed the roarings of
the "Backward of face." Thou shalt do the like of this at daybreak on the festival of the
13. fifteenth day, for by it will Apepi be repulsed and slain before the *sekti* boat. Thou shalt
do the like of this when tempests rage in the eastern parts of the sky when Rā sets in the
14. land of life, to prevent the arrival of red threatening clouds in the eastern quarter of the
sky. Thou shalt do the like of this very many times to prevent the arrival of a shower
15. or a rain storm or thunder cloud in the sky. If thou doest the like of this many times as a
preventive against the shower, the sun's disk will shine, and Apepi will be overthrown in
very truth.

It is good for a man to do this, good for him upon earth, and good for him in the nether-
16. world; to this man is given power to attain to dignities which are above him, and he is,
in very truth, delivered from all evil things. May I see these things happen to me! [a]

17. THE FIRST BOOK OF THE OVERTHROWING OF APEPI THE ENEMY OF RA.

To be recited:—

"Down upon thy face, Apepi, thou enemy of Rā! get thee back, retreat, fiend! Sebau
18. is deprived of his arms and legs, thy snout shall be split; such are the things that shall
happen unto thee. Thou art cast down and overthrown. Rā Harmachis overthrows thee,
he destroys thee, he damns thee, he sticks hooks into thy body. Thou art thrown down
19. into the fire, the flames proceeding from it come forth, they blaze up at thee at their
opportunity."

20. "Isis says with vehement utterance, 'Thy soul is cut in pieces, thy vertebrae are hacked
asunder, Horus showers blows upon thee, and the children of Horus deliver crushing blows
on thee; thou art destroyed at their season.'

"Get thee back, retreat, retreat, thou art overthrown in going back and retreating,
21. Apepi. The great cycle of the gods who are in Heliopolis turn thee back. Horus drives
back thy crocodile, Sut destroys thy opportunity. Isis repulses thee, Nephthys cuts thee
in pieces, and the cycle of the great gods who are in front of the boat of Rā drive thee
22. back. The chain of Sut is upon thy neck, the children of Horus drive their spears into
thee, those gods who guard the secret portals repulse thee, and the flame from their fire
23. comes forth against thee.

"O thou that goest back and retreatest before the flames of fire which come forth from
their mouth, O thou fallen one, O wriggler, O Apepi, O thou who goest back

Column XXIV.

1. "and retreatest, thou enemy of Rā, thou art fallen at this moment of ill luck of thine!

"Those who are in the divine boat have overthrown thee, get thee back and begone.

[a] This sentence appears to be the remark of the scribe.

2. " Cursed art thou, destroyed art thou, repulsed art thou at thy moment of ill luck. O mayest
thou be tripped up! Thy accursed soul and body are turned back, thou thyself art turned
back, thy flesh is stripped off thee, thy blows are inflicted, the hacking in pieces and
3. " slaughter of thee is performed, and thy crocodile is destroyed. Thou art deprived of thine
ears, the flesh is smitten from thy limbs, thy soul is turned back from thy shade, thy name
is destroyed, thy enchantments have come to naught, destroyed art thou, overthrown art
4. " thou, thou shalt never come forth from that cavern of thine for ever and ever. Blows are
5. " inflicted upon thee a second time, thou art fettered and beaten by the cruel beaters, thine
opportunity is destroyed, thy crocodile is driven back, Rā seizes thee by the ear and makes
6. " thee go back upon that seat of thine, thou art tripped up and driven backward, thou art condemned for thy crime, Rā beats thee and thy opportunity of escape comes not. Thy
7. " accursed soul and shade are damned, the eye of Horus has condemned thee, it prevails over
thee and eats into thee to the fulness of its face. O, an end to thee, Apepi, it (*i. e.*, the
eye of Horus) darts at thee, it turns thee back, it destroys thee and makes an end of thee."
8. Then shalt be said firmly with the mouth:—
" Down upon thy face, Apepi, enemy of Rā! The flame coming forth from the eye of
9. " Horus comes against thee, a mighty flame which comes forth from the eye of Horus comes
against thee. Thou art thrust down into the flame of fire which rushes out against thee,
and which is fatal to thy soul, thy intelligence, thy words of power, thy body, and thy
10. " shade. The mistress of fire prevails over thee, it sticks hooks into thy soul, it makes an
end of whatever thou hast, and sends darts into thy form. Thou hast fallen by the eye of
11. " Horus which is powerful against its enemy, which devours thee and leads on the mighty
12. " flame against thee; the eye of Rā prevails over thee, the flame devours thee, and nothing
of thee remains.
13. " Get thee back, thou art hacked in pieces, thy soul is parched, thy name is buried in
oblivion, silence covers it, it is overthrown; thou art put an end to and buried under
threefold oblivion. Get thee back, retreat thou, thou art cut in pieces and
14. " removed from him that is in his shrine. O Apepi, thou doubly crushed one, an end to
thee, an end to thee! Mayest thou never rise up, may thy soul never
16. " rise up again! The eye of Horus prevails over thee, and devours thee daily, according to
what Rā decreed should be done unto thee. Thou art thrown down into
17. " the flame of fire which feeds upon thee; thou art condemned to the fire of the eye of
Horus which devours thee, thy soul, thy intelligence, thy body, and thy shade; mayest
thou never have the enjoyment of sexual pleasure, mayest thou never
18. " have issue of thy body for ever!"
Then shall be said four times, " Rā triumphs over thee, Apepi."
Then shall be said four times, " Horus triumphs over his enemies."
Then shall be said four times, " P-āa triumphs over his enemies."
" Get thee back, retreat before these words of power which come forth from my
19. " mouth on behalf of P-āa for ever, these (?) shall destroy thee; never shalt thou escape thy
fate, Apepi, enemy of Rā."

20. To be said four times, "Taste thou fiend, Sebau."
These words are to be said by a person ceremonially purified and clean. Behold, too, thou shalt paint the accursed name of Apepi upon new papyrus, and put it
21. in the fire when Rā shows himself in the morning, when Rā is in culmination and when Rā sets in the land of life. This shall be done on the eighth day, by day, and at every hour of every day, by month, on the festival of the sixth
22. day, on the festival of the fifteenth day, and likewise on every day for the overthrowing of the enemies of Rā Harmachis.

THE SECOND BOOK OF THE OVERTHROWING OF APEPI, THE ENEMY OF RA.

23. "Fall down upon your faces, O ye enemies of Rā, ye hostile fiends, ye children of inertness, ye rebels and enemies! Nameless sinners are they whose caverns of fire are prepared for them according to the commands of Rā. The rebels, fiends,
24. "and demons are fettered and tied fast; how many are the enemies who have rebelled! Fall down then upon your faces at the moment of Rā, and come to an end. He overthrows you,

Column XXV.

1. he casts down your head upon your faces, yea, he destroys you, he performs your slaughter. O an end, an end to you! Be ye destroyed, annihilated, brought to naught! May ye never exist, may ye never rise up, may your heads be broken,
2. "Your throats cut, your vertebrae severed, your blows inflicted and your slaughter performed! The eye of Horus endowed with flame falls against you and obtains
3. "the mastery over you. The eye of Horus rises against you and his power smites you. His eye gains the mastery over you, it consumes and devours you in its name of Devourer, and it gains the mastery over you in its name of Sechet; fall ye therefore
4. "by its deadly flame and by the burning which cometh forth from its fire. O it destroys, destroys, destroys you! the blaze cometh forth against you, ye enemies of Rā and fiendish foes of Horus, it comes against your bodies, and against
5. "your shades. The fire comes forth and roasts you, it frizzles, frizzles you, scorches, scorches you, and tries you; Apt-s-ur (*i.e.*, "the fire tries,") judges you, devours you, consumes
6. "you, destroys your souls, and her flames send burning darts into your shades. O, an end to you, an end to you! Ye are destroyed, destroyed, cut asunder, and hacked in pieces, and your slaughter is performed; ye are judged by the fire and the
7. "flame, the lord of blazing heat, the fire of which eats into your souls and drives darts into your accursed bodies, and fetters you with its fire. The fierce fire cuts at you with
8. "its cutting flames, it stabs you with its daggers, it consumes you with its heat, it burns you up with its burning, it sets you on fire with its conflagration, it burns you to ashes with its blazes; it eats you up with its flame, and bites

9. "into you in its name of Set ("fire"), it tries you in its name of Apt-s-ur ("the fire tries"). The fire, provided with huge flames, throws you down into itself and eats into your souls.

10. "O fall ye down, fall ye down, fall ye down therefore, for ye are overthrown; Rā has overthrown you, fall ye down therefore through the impact of his moment. He makes an end to you, an end to you, he destroys you, he overthrows you,

11. "he cuts you asunder, he damns you, he destroys you, he makes an end of your name, he hacks in pieces your soul, he roasts you, he annihilates you, he fetters you, he casts hooks into you, he overthrows you, fall ye down then

12. "through the flame of fire which destroys you; may there never be to thee again a rising up.

"O, come to an end, come to an end, come to an end! Come to an end then, come to an end. May your souls come to an end, may your bodies come to an end, may your shades come to an end, may you come to an end! May you never rise up, may your souls

13. "never rise up, may your body never rise up; may you never rise up, may your shades never rise up, may you never rise up, may your lives never rise up, may you never rise up, may a defender never rise up for you, may your heads

14. "never be fastened again on to your bodies. Retreat therefore ye before Rā, retreat therefore Sebau, may ye never rise up again at the words of power of Thoth. The great God is victorious over you, he casts hooks into you, he causes to be done unto you what your souls hate, fire comes forth from his mouth against

15. "you, be ye therefore consumed, O fiends, may ye never rise up again at the words of power of Thoth. He overthrows you, he hacks you to pieces, he destroys you, the fire coming forth from the eye of Horus judges you, it

16. "devours you to the fulness of its face, it destroys you with the intensity of its flame, and is not repulsed at the moment for which its heart wishes in its name of Mert. Come to an end therefore before it, retreat before it, go back before it,

17. "get thee gone before it, O every enemy of Rā, and every enemy of Horus. It shoots its arrows into you, it makes thee go back, it destroys you, it puts an end to you, it destroys you; may you never have the enjoyment of sexual

18. "pleasures, may ye never have issue from your bodies for ever!

So then Law makes Rā to triumph over you, Apepi, children of inertness, mighty ones of inertness.

Then shall be said four times, 'Rā triumphs over his enemies.'

Then shall be said four times, 'Horus triumphs over his enemies.'

19. "Then shall be said four times, 'Osiris, at the head of those in the nether-world, triumphs over his enemies.'

Then shall be said four times, 'P-āa, life, strength, health, triumphs over his enemies.'

"I have overthrown Apepi, Sebau, Sheta, and Qettu, children of inertness,

20. "in every place in which they are. I have overthrown all the enemies of Rā in every place in which they are. I have overthrown all the enemies of Horus in every place in which they are. I have overthrown all the enemies of

21. "Amen-Rā, lord of the universe, at the head of the Apts, in every place in which they are. I have overthrown all the enemies of Ptah of Memphis, lord of the universe, in every
22. "place in which they are, likewise every enemy of Atmu; likewise every enemy of Thoth,[a] lord of Chemennu;[b] likewise every enemy of Iusāset,[c] lady of Annu (Heliopolis), Hathor, lady of Hetep-hemt,[d] the shade of Atmu; likewise
23. "every enemy of Horus-Chent-Chattha,[e] lord of Kakam;[f] every enemy of Chuaut[g] Neter (?) Shes (?); every enemy of Bast, the mighty lady, lady of Bubastis; every enemy of Osiris, lord of Tattu[h]; every enemy of the 'Ram, lord of Tattu (Mendes),' the great god, the life of
24. "Rā. I have overthrown every enemy of Anher-Shu,[i] the son of Horus the Concealed, every enemy of Amen-Rā Sam-Behutet,[k] every enemy of Anubis, lord of Siut,[l] every

[a] The divine intelligence, the inventor of arts and sciences and the god of astronomy, numbers, geometry, weights and measures, architecture, sculpture, painting, and music.

[b] 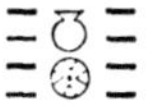 *χemennu*, Coptic ϣⲙⲟⲩⲛ, was the sacred name of  *Pa-Teḥuti*, "the town of Thoth," *i.e.*, Hermopolis Magna, the metropolis of the fifteenth nome of Upper Egypt.

[c] A goddess whose shrine 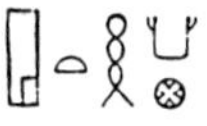 *Het-heka*, was situated at  *Annu*, Heliopolis; she was a form of Hathor of Lower Egypt.

[d]  or  *Hetep-hemt*, the name of a district belonging to the Heliopolitan nome, which, at the time of Ptolemies, formed a kind of supplementary nome with the metropolis  *i.e.*, Bilbeis. See Brugsch, *Dict. Géog.* p. 546.

[e] See Lanzone, *Dizionario di Mitologia Egizia*, p. 621.

[f] A name of the great necropolis of Memphis, near the Serapeum, in the desert of Sakkârah; the *κωχώμη* of Manetho.

[g] *I.e.*, "the protectress," the feminine counterpart of Horus-Chent-Chattha.

[h] Mendes and Busiris both bore the name of Tattu; here Busiris, the metropolis of the ninth nome of Lower Egypt, is referred to.

[i] Anher was the son of Rā, and a form of the god Shu; his name means the "guide of heaven." He is called "the god of lofty plumes residing in Thinis," and is represented wearing  See Lanzone, *Dizionario di Mit. Egizia*, p. 75.

[k] Another name for 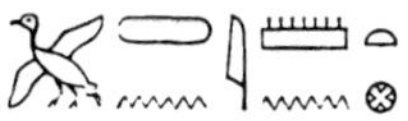 *Pa ḥen-en-Àmen*, the metropolis of the seventeenth nome (Diospolis) of Lower Egypt. See Brugsch, *Dict. Géog.* p. 705. The reading Sam-behutet was first proved by Mr. Renouf.

[l] Lycopolis, the modern Asyûṭ اسيوط. For a list of the Anubis gods see Lanzone, *Dizionario Mit. Eg* p. 67.

enemy of Horus, lord of those in the east (?), every enemy of Horus of the two eyes[a], lord of Shetenna[b], every enemy of Horus in . . . . . .[c]

Column XXVI.

1. "every enemy of Horus-sam-taiu,[d] lord of Chatet,[e] every enemy of Horus in Pe, Uátit in Tep,[f] every enemy of Horus the aged,[g] lord of the south[h] in every place in
2. which they are; I have overthrown every enemy of Seb in every place in which they are."
Then shall be said by a person washed and ceremonially pure:
"Now are ye done for, O every enemy of Rā, and every enemy of P-āa, life, strength, health! in life and in death together with all the schemes which are in your hearts."
3. Then shalt thou write the name of their fathers, mothers, and children, with every . . . . . with green paint upon new papyrus, and shalt also inscribe their names upon wax figures of them which shall be tied round with dark hair; these
4. figures shalt thou spit upon and defile with thy left foot, and pierce with a stone knife. Put these into the flaming fire of the burners, in addition to the [figure with the] name of Apepi, and turn it with the *χessau* plant when Rā rises, when Rā is
5. in culmination, when Rā sets in the land of life, on the first hour of the day, on the . . . . . hour of the night, on the second hour of the night and until the third hour of the night, at daybreak, and likewise at every hour of the day, and every hour of the night. Let a figure be burnt on the festival of the new moon, on the
6. festival of the sixth day, on the festival of the fifteenth day, and likewise [by day] and by month. Then will be overthrown the enemy of Rā, then Apepi will be overthrown in very truth, then will be overthrown the enemy of Rā.

This book shall be performed after the manner of that which is laid down in writing when the atep boat of the sun goes forth to overthrow the enemy

a *I.e.*, lord of the two *utats* He is thought to be a form of *Àmsu ááh*. Amsu, the moon god of Panopolis, is represented with the head of a hawk and wears and ; in each hand he holds See Lanzone, *Dizionario*, p. 617.

b The metropolis of a supplementary nome in Lower Egypt; for the identification of this place see Brugsch, *Dict. Géog.* p. 805.

c I am unable to transcribe this name.

d *I.e.*, Horus, uniter of the North and South.

e A name of one of the sacred quarters of Denderah, the metropolis of the sixth nome of Upper Egypt; this name appears to have some reference to the victory of Horus-behutet over Set. See Brugsch, *Dict. Géog.* p. 370.

f Pe and Tep were the names of two districts, which together formed the town of *Pa-Uatet*, the metropolis of the nineteenth nome of Lower Egypt, where the goddess Uatet was worshipped.

g He was the son of Hathor of Apollinopolis Parva, and brother of Osiris.

h See Brugsch, *Dict. Géog.* pp. 355, 847.

7. of Rā, and every enemy of Horus of the two eyes in Aaat-Peka.[a] It is good for a person if this book is recited before the venerable god regularly and always.

THE BOOK OF OVERTHROWING THE ENEMY OF RA IN THE COURSE OF EVERY DAY.

To be recited:—

8. "Fall down upon thy face Apepi, enemy of Rā; be drowned, be drowned! O thou that comest forth from unknown places, get thee back, get thee back, quickly, quickly; hasten thou to go back as quickly as thou didst come forth. Let there be
9. "overthrow to thee at the pool of heaven, for Rā has commanded thee to be slaughtered. Mighty flame rises up against thee, provided and coming forth from Ap-Hekau,[b] whose two eyes are open observing the two earths. The mighty spell comes forth from the chamber, which is in the shrine, against thee; the hawk
10. "comes forth against thee; the two uraei rear themselves up; and the flame from out of the mouth of the guardians of the secret pylons comes forth against thee. Come to an end, enemy, fiend; be fettered, Apepi. Rā reposes upon his station
11. "within his shrine. Hail to thee Rā, in thy serpent goddess, Mehenet!"

Then shall be said four times:

"Thy voice is triumphant over Apepi, thy voice is Law against thy enemies, and the voice of P-āa, life, strength, health! is triumphant against his enemies.

"Be thou vomited upon, Apepi.

12. The Book of turning back Apepi Char, (the thunder?), which is to be performed at dawn.

To be recited:—

"Be thou vomited upon, Apepi, enemy of Rā [To be said] four times.

"O thou that must turn back from him that is in his coffin, come to an end,

13. "thou fiend, and fall down upon thy face, vomit over it! Get thee back to the place whence thou camest, may thy roads be blocked up, may thy paths be obstructed, mayest thou be confined in the place where thou wast yesterday; may thy body be powerless, thy heart feeble and thy limbs torpid.
14. "Thou shalt be annihilated, thou shalt never come forth, thou art decreed for those who preside over the block, the slaughterers who are provided with knives. May they cut off thy head, may they cut in pieces thy neck, may they do for thee a second time, may they throw thee into the flame, and goad thee and terrify thee more
15. "than the flame at its moment. The flame gains the mastery over thee, it devours thy limbs, it gnaws into thy bones, it drives hooks into thy flesh, Chnemu[c] carries off thy

[a] The necropolis of the nome Pharbaethites, the capital of which was Shetennu. See Brugsch, *Dict. Géog.* p. 227.

[b] See Brugsch, *Wörterbuch*, p. 929.

[c] Chnemu is usually styled the creator and maker of men.

children to his block, thy limbs are transferred to the flame, and thy soul is fettered; may it never traverse the earth, may

16. "thy two hands nevermore exist on this earth, O Apepi, enemy of Rā! Horus the Aged, son of Isis, destroys thee. Thou shalt never have heir or child, thy soul shall never attain to the heaven which Shu supports, thou shalt never

17. "see nor look out of thine eyes, thou art destroyed, and thy shade, O Apepi, enemy of Rā, shall never more exist, vomit thou fiend! Thy name shall come to nought and thou shalt never more be remembered, and thy mastery is completed; be sick over thyself each time thou art mentioned. Rā inflicts thy blows upon thee, thou art

18. "tied up by Isis and fettered by Nephthys, and the virtues of Thoth destroy thee. Thy accursed soul shall never rise up among other souls, thy accursed body shall not be with other bodies; may the fire bite into thee and the flame devour thee, burning thee

19. "up as soon as it rests upon thee, Apepi, enemy of Rā. Rā rejoices, Atmu is full of delight, and the heart of Horus the Aged is glad because Apepi is transferred to the flame, Nekau is transferred to the fire; may he never again exist, and may

20. "the shade of Apepi, the enemy of Rā, never again exist in heaven or earth."

Then shall be said four times, "Be thou spit upon and come to an end, Apepi!"

The above is to be said over a figure of Apepi made of wax, and likewise written on new papyrus. Throw them into the fire in the presence of Rā every day, likewise on the first day of the month, and on every day, and on the festivals of the sixth and

21. fifteenth days; then will Apepi be overthrown on water, on land, and with the stars.

THE BOOK OF KNOWING THE EVOLUTIONS OF RA, AND THE OVERTHROWING OF APEPI.

Column XXVI.

The words of Neb-er-ter who speaks after (or concerning) his coming into existence.

22. "I am he who evolved himself under the form of the god Chepera. I, the evolver of evolutions, evolved myself, the evolver of all evolutions, after many evolutions and developments which came forth from my mouth. There was no heaven, there was no earth, ground—animals and reptiles were not then in existence. I constructed their forms out of the inert mass of watery matter,

23. "I found no place there upon which I could stand. By the strength which was in my will I laid the foundation [of

Column XXVIII.

20. The words of Neb-er-ter who says:—

"I have evolved the evolving of evolutions. I evolved myself under the form of the evolutions of the god Chepera, which were evolved at the beginning of all time. I evolved the evolutions

21. "of the god Chepera, I evolved by the evolution of evolutions, that is to say, I developed myself from the primeval matter which I made, I developed myself out of the primeval matter. My name is Ausares (Osiris?), the germ of primeval matter. I have

22. "wrought my will to its full extent in this earth, I have spread abroad and filled it,

things] in the form of the god Shu, and I made for them every attribute that they have. I was quite alone, for I had not evacuated the god Shu, and I had not spit forth the god Tefnut; there

24. "existed none other who worked with me. I laid the foundation of all things out of my own heart, and the evolutions of things, the evolutions out of the evolutions of their births which took place through the evolutions of their children, became multiplied.

My hand acted for me as a husband, and I copulated with my shadow (or hand);

COLUMN XXVII.

1. "I poured seed into my own mouth, I evacuated the god Shu, and I spat out from my mouth the god Tefnut. My father Nu (the sky) says, 'They eclipse my eye behind them since for long periods of time they depart from me, after that I from being one god became

2. "three gods, from myself, evolved in this land.' Shu and Tefnut rejoiced in the watery mass in which they existed, and they brought to me my eye along with them. After this, then, I collected my limbs, and I wept

3. "over them, and men and women sprang into existence from the tears which fall from my Eye. When it came and found what I had done in its place, it growled at me; with the splendour (*or* might) which I wrought, I restored it and made it take up its place in my face, and afterwards it ruled the

4. "whole of this earth. Their moment fell upon their plants (?), and I restored to it what had been carried off from it. I made plants to spring up, I created all

I lifted up my hand (?) I was quite alone, nothing existed, for I had not evacuated Shu, and I had not yet spit forth Tefnut. I uttered my name, as a word of power, from my own mouth, and I straightway developed

23. "myself by evolutions. I evolved myself under the form of the evolutions of the god Chepera, and I developed myself out of the primeval matter which has evolved multitudes of evolutions from the beginning of time. Nothing existed on this earth [before me], I made all things. There was none

24. "other who worked with me at that time. I made all evolutions there by means of that soul which I raised up there from inertness out of the watery matter. I found no place there upon which I could stand, I was strong in my resolution, and I laid the foundation [of things] out of my own

25. "self, and I performed all that was done. I was quite alone. I laid the foundation [of things] by my own will, I created also the multitudes of things by the evolutions of the god Chepera; and their offspring came into existence from the evolutions of their

26. "births (*or* children). I evacuated and Shu arose, I spat and Tefnut arose; thus from being one god, I became three, out from myself, coming into existence in this land. Shu and Tefnut, then, rejoiced in the watery mass in which they were.

27. "Through my eye I brought them along after long periods of time, and they advanced towards me. I gathered together the limbs of my own person from which they had come forth

reptiles, and everything that existed from them (*i.e.*, Shu and Tefnut ?)

5. "Shu and Tefnut give birth to Nut, Seb, Nut giving birth to Osiris, Horus, dwelling in invisibility, Sut, Isis, Nephthys at one birth, one after the other, and their children multiply upon this earth."

after I had begotten them with my hand, and my heart came to me out of my shadow (hand ?). I poured seed into my own mouth, I evacuated

Column XXIX.

1. "Shu, and I spat out Tefnut; thus from being one god I became three gods, out of myself, who came into existence in this earth. Therefore Shu and Tefnut rejoiced in the watery mass from which they had arisen. Through my eye I brought them along after long
2. "periods of time. I gathered together the limbs of my own person from which they had come forth after I had begotten them with my hand, and my heart came to me out of my shadow, I poured seed into my own mouth, I evacuated Shu and I spat out Tefnut.
3. "My father Nu (the sky) says, They eclipse my eye behind them, for numbers upon numbers of centuries. Plants and reptiles [came into existence] from the god Rem, [*i.e.*] from the tears which I let fall. My eye cried out and men and women sprang into existence.
4. "I filled [my eye] with flame, it growled against me, and afterwards came another growth in [its] place. Its force fell upon the masses (?) and masses (?) which I
5. "had placed before (*or* in) it, it put order into them and drew near to its place in my face, and ruled the whole earth. Shu and Tefnut bring forth Nut, Osiris, Horus dwelling in invisibility, Sut, Isis and Nephthys, [who] by their children make multitudes
6. "of evolutions upon this earth from the evolutions of the births from the evolu-

tions of their children. They invoke my name and they overthrow their enemies; they create words of power for overthrowing Apepi."

Column XXVII.

6\. "The mighty words of power, which are the genius of enchantments, are to be recited, for they are fated to destroy the enemies of Rā by the might of their utterance. May it be fated for me to hear what has become of my limbs. That evil enemy is overthrown, Apepi has fallen into the flame, a knife is stuck

7\. "into his head . . . . his name no longer exists on this earth. It is fated for me to inflict blows upon him, I drive darts into his bones, I destroy his soul in the course of every day, I sever his vertebræ from

8\. "his neck, cutting into his flesh with a knife and stabbing through his hide. He is given over to the fire which obtains the mastery over him in its name of "Sechet;" it has power over him in its name of "Chut-ubti-cheft" (Eye

9\. "burning the enemy); darts are driven into his soul, his bones are burnt, and his limbs are transferred to the fire. Horus, mighty of strength, has decreed that he shall come in front of the boat of Rā; his fetter of steel ties him up and makes his limbs so that they cannot move; Horus repulses his opportunity during

10\. "his eclipse, and he makes him to vomit that which is inside him. Horus fetters, binds, ties up, and Aker takes away his strength that I may separate his flesh

11\. "from his bones; that I may fetter his feet, and cut off his two hands and arms; that I may shut up his mouth and lips, and break in his teeth; that I may cut out his tongue from his throat, and carry away his words; that I may block

12\. "up his two eyes, and carry off his ears; that I may tear out his heart from its seat and throne, that is to say, from its station; and that I may make him so that he exists not. May his name never exist, and may what is born to him never exist; may he never exist, and may his kinsfolk never exist; may he never exist, and may his relatives never exist; may he never exist,

13\. "and may his heir never exist; may his offspring never grow to maturity; may his seed never be established; moreover, may his soul, body, intelligence, shade, words of power and his bones and his skin never more exist! May he fall down and be overthrown and never rise up again! Let the flame

14\. "of the eye of Horus grip him. The Striker and the Executioners have their knives and hack at him, they drive their knives into him, and he falls to the ground through the infliction of those evil blows which I have decreed to be

15\. "inflicted in the course of every day upon his damnable form. The eye of Horus falls upon him cutting and hacking his head from his neck; the goddess Sechet tears out his intestines and kicks them on the fire

16. "with her left leg; she places them on the fire and burns into him in her name of "Set-usert-āa" (Fire, victorious mighty one); she burns into him, and drives out his soul from his body; she obtains the mastery over him in her name of "Sechet;" and she overpowers him in her name of "Chut-nebat."

17. "She consumes his interior and blazes in it with the flame of her mouth; Uatit devours [him] and casts herself down against his cavern so that he may never come forth from it again for ever and ever. She constrains those who

18. "have fetters, and they cut in pieces his soul, his body, his shade, his intelligence, and his words of power; they tear out his heart from its place and they destroy his name. He has fallen down, and shall never rise up again, for I have

19. "decreed his annihilation, and the annihilation of his soul. Uatit has seized the bones of Shu (?) at the storehouse of the eater of green things, and she causes his tongue to be split; the goddess Sati also provides destruction for him at the moment of her strength. Sechet places his heart in the flame of the utterance of her

20. "mouth; he falls by her slaughter, and his eye is stopped up. Darts are driven into Apepi and he is overthrown by Rā himself; Rā triumphs over Apepi in the presence of the cycle of the great gods, and a dagger is driven into

21. "his head in the presence of Rā every day. The gods of the south overthrow him, the gods of the north overthrow him, the gods of the west overthrow him,

22. "and the gods of the east overthrow him. The starry deities of Orion of the southern skies fetter him, the Great Bear in the northern heavens turns him back, and those who are in the decans involve him in chains. The fire devours him, the flame consumes him, it drives fiery darts into his bones

23. "and hair, it burns up his members, it shrivels up his skin, and he is utterly overthrown by the hands of the gods. May his name nevermore exist in the mouth of men, and may he nevermore be remembered in the heart of the gods! May he be spit upon each time that his name is mentioned. Rā

24. "has inflicted disasters upon him, he is twice annihilated, he is doubly stabbed by darts of fire, the flame has gripped him, Henbu has fastened upon him; he shall never more breathe, he shall never more breathe, he shall never more smell the breezes, he shall never more smell the breezes. He is

25. "cast into the fire and it burns into his two eyes, its flame slays and devours his face. The gods who are in the divine boat of Rā desire to attack him. O tears that come forth from my eye inflict your blows

26. "upon him, and upon that damnable form of his! Behold, O ye gods, and grant, O ye gods, that his dwelling place and tomb may never exist; grant, O ye gods, that his name may never exist; grant, O ye gods, that his soul, intelligence, shade, bones, and hair may never exist; and grant not unto him, O ye gods, the space of his two hands and arms!

Column XXVIII.

1. "That his children and his accursed heirs may never exist, grant, O ye gods; that his seed may never grow nor lift up its ears, grant, O ye gods; that his words of power may be of none effect, grant, O ye gods; that he may never rise up in heaven or upon earth, grant, O ye gods; that he may never rise up among
2 "the dwellers in the south, north, west and east, grant, O ye gods; and that he may never exist among mortals, grant, O ye gods! May he be in the flame of that eye of Horus, may it obtain the mastery over him in the course of every day,
3. "may it burn in him and never be extinguished for ever and ever. May it seize him at his moment, may it repulse his crocodile, may it burn him and may he come to an end. If Apepi rises up may it grip him, may the flame overthrow him, may Rā himself overthrow him. Rā triumphs over thee. Verily I have
4. "slain thee, verily I have blotted out thy name, and thou art therefore committed to the flame every day, according to what Rā commanded should be done to thee. Behold then, Rā, hear then, Rā, verily I have destroyed thy enemy, I have defiled and trampled upon him with my feet, and I have spit upon him. Rā is made to triumph over thee, and over all his enemies, they have fallen
5. "down and shall never rise up again. The name of Apepi is consumed, inasmuch as I have destroyed his place of habitation, his throne, and his tomb; I have destroyed his soul, his intelligence, his body, his shade, his words of power, his seed, his egg, his bones, and his hair, and he shall be given to the fire
6. "every day according to what Rā has commanded to be done to him. There shall be therefore destruction and seizure and burning for all the enemies of P-āa, life, strength, health! in death and in life. May their members be hacked in pieces, may they be torn out of their skins, may the lords of Heliopolis make
7. "them their possession and destroy them before thee, O Rā, every day, and may the fire which is in them consume them. May their souls, intelligences, bodies, shades, words of power, bones, hair, strength, utterances and words of power
8. "never more exist; may their graves, homes, habitations and tombs never exist; may their fields, trees and plants never exist; and may they never have water,
9. "bread, fire or warmth; may their children and kinsfolk and heirs and families never exist; may their heads, arms, legs, ears and seed never exist; may their place of habitation upon their own lands never exist; may water never
10. "be poured out for them in this land among the living, and may water never be poured out for them in the Nether-world among the blessed dead.
Thou hast decreed them to the block of Sechet in Aat-nebt-Asher, thou hast overthrown them at the victorious moment of the Mighty Baby, thou hast
11. "adjudged them to the power of the fetterers among those who dwell in the Nether-world. May their souls never be permitted to come forth from the Nether-world, may they never be among the living upon earth, may they never see Rā

12. "daily, may they be chained in fetters in the depths of the nethermost hell, and may their souls never be permitted to come forth thence for ever and ever. These things are decreed to happen to them because of their cursing Rā in his shrine. The gods in the shrine mete out justice to them, they lay hold upon

13. "the two hands of Apepi, the eye of Horus obtains the mastery over them, and they consume and burn away upon the altars of Sechet, upon the brazier which devours limbs. They are seized in thy presence, Rā, daily, according to what the great god (Rā) decreed should be done to them for ever and for ever.

14. "Thou, O Rā, art seated in thy shrine, thou advancest in the *sekti* boat, thou restest in the *ati* boat, thou traversest thy two heavens in peace, thou obtainest the mastery, thou livest, thou art strong, thou increasest, thou art mighty, thou destroyest by thy decree all thy enemies who do wrong to P-āa, life, strength,

15. "health! with all evil spears (?), every man, every woman, every damned person, every beatified person whatsoever, all the easterns of all foreign lands, and all the enemies of P-āa in death and in life. I have destroyed and made of none effect what thou hast vomited, and thou art fallen, O Apepi. Rā triumphs over thee, Apepi. Four Times. P-āa, life, strength, health! triumphs over

16. "his enemies. Four Times."

This chapter is to be said over a figure of Apepi, inscribed upon new papyrus with green ink, and placed inside a covering upon which his name is written. It must be tied around tightly and put into the fire every day; thou must

17. stamp upon and defile it with thy left foot, and thou shalt spit upon it four times during the course of each day, and when thou placest it in the fire thou shalt say four times, 'Rā triumphs over thee, Apepi, Horus triumphs over his enemies, and P-āa, life, strength and health! triumphs over his enemies.' Next thou shalt

18. write down the names of all the male and female devils of which thy heart is afraid, the names of all the enemies of P-āa, life, strength, health! in death and in life, and the names of their father, mother, and children inside the covering, together with a wax figure of Apepi. These shall then be placed

19. in the fire in the name of Apepi and shall be burnt when Rā rises in the morning; this shalt thou repeat at noon and at evening when Rā sets in the land of life, while there is light at the foot of the mountain. Over each figure of Apepi shalt thou recite the above chapter, in very truth, for the doing of this is of great effect upon earth and in the Nether-world.[a]

Column XXIX.

7. "Rā fetters the two hands and arms and feet of Aker that they may not exist, and he is fastened to one place while Rā inflicts upon him the blows which are

8. "decreed for him. He is thrown over upon his accursed back, his face is gashed because of the

[a] For lines 20—27, col. xxviii., and lines 1—6, col. xxix., see above, col. xxvi., lines 22—24, and col. xxvii., lines 1—5.

evil which he has done, and that accursed form of his remains prostrate. The children of Horus are overthrowing him, they drive away his soul from his body and his shade, and the sages who are in the boat, and the tears of my eye

9. "desire to proceed among them. The disasters of Apepi are decreed, may he never make his courses in this land according to his will! He is annihilated, and his soul is annihilated; those who are in the south overthrow it, those who are in the

10. "north overthrow it, those who are in the west overthrow it, those who are in the east overthrow it. The sages who are in this land, and the cycle of the gods who sprang into existence from the body [of Rā] are watching to overthrow Apepi.

11. "His soul is accursed, his name is destroyed, he is overthrown by your two arms, and his name is caused to be dissipated. May children never exist for him, and may his place of habitation, his soul, his body and his intelligence never more exist. He is given over to the eye of Rā, and it obtains the mastery over him and consumes him. I am decreed to rise up to destroy him, to overthrow his

12. "name, and to make his words of power of none effect. I have decreed them to the flame, I have decreed them to the fire, I have given them over to the eye of Ra, the eye that will consume and devour his soul, his

13. "intelligence, his body, his shade, and his words of power; may he never have sexual pleasure or emission from his body for ever."

This is to be said over a wax figure of Apepi upon which his name has been written with green ink, and over a figure of Apepi inscribed

14. upon new papyrus. Thou shalt also make in wax figures of every enemy of P-āa, in death and in life, and thou shalt write their names upon them in green ink; then shalt thou tie them up inside wrappers, spit upon them, trample upon and defile them with thy left foot, make gashes in them with a knife and throw them into a fire

15. of *χessau* grass, and quench it with the urine of a crocodile. Also, thou shalt paint the names of Apepi and of every enemy of P-āa, in life and in death, upon a slab (?) on the ground and thou shalt trample upon it and defile it

16. with thy left foot, as if it were in very truth an actual person. This figure will know (?) Rā and his evolutions, and will make him to triumph over his enemies.

This book is a mystery [to be said] in the chamber, let no eye see it. The "Secret book of overthrowing Apepi" and the "Book of words of power" are its names.

17. "Apepi is destroyed, his fiends are cut off, Rā triumphs over his enemies, and the divine boats are made to advance in peace. Apepi is made to retreat to the fire, he is made to advance to the divine block of execution, that filth (*i.e.*, Apepi)

18. "is beaten into nothing in very truth, repulsed and made to turn back are his soul, his body, his intelligence, his shade, his children, his kinsfolk, his family, his relatives, his heirs, his hair, his belongings, his evolutions, his body, his

19. "egg, his name, his substance, his arms, his legs, his speech, his words of power, his strength, his seat, his cavern, his tomb, and his two accursed hands; he is overthrown, and his ear is taken off from him. O Rā, thy *sekti* boat

20. advances, and the knife which is in it is made to gain the mastery over him in the presence of Rā every day. When Rā hears this book recited his heart is fortified, his boat is made to advance in peace, and Apepi in his every name is destroyed. "Adoration to the god who causes his strength

21. "to come into existence, the writing is tied up, Nekau and Kettu are cut in pieces, and the god rejoices in coming into existence," says Isis.
Rā, who makes the Fiend to retreat, who blinds his two eyes from covering up the height of heaven, in very truth, who drives darts into his soul as well

22. as into his body, who turns back his bones and places them in the fire, who makes him drive his teeth into his own body, says, "He is given over into the hand of the executioners of Rā, he is made to retreat."
To be recited:—
"Back thou Apepi, thou thing upon which Rā treads! Back thou claw of strife,

23. "thou enemy, thou legless and armless Fiend, whose children are destroyed in coming forth within thy cavern, thou thing upon which Rā treads and which he has turned back. I know the evil which thou hast wrought. Thy head

24. "shall be cut off, thy slaughter shall be consummated, thou shalt not lift up thy face against the great god, let there be fire upon thy face, let there be flame upon thy soul, may the mighty block of execution destroy thy flesh, mayest thou smell the slaughter of the great god! The goddess Serqet curses thee and turns

25. "thee back. O thou that didst twice attempt to come in, twice wast thou overthrown by this word of power which came forth from my mouth. Thou art given over to the flame and it destroys thee; thou art cast down into the fire by the eye of Horus upon thy face. Thou art fallen upon thy face and thy soul is overthrown. The eye of Rā obtains

26. "the mastery over thee. Thou art fallen, thou art fallen, thou art driven back, thou art driven back; O legless and armless serpent, fall down upon thy face. Duration of life shall not be to thee, for thou shall go into the fiery brazier, and the Great God, the self-produced, shall

27. "overthrow thee; those who are in his boat shall destroy thee with the might of their utterance and with the words of power which come forth from their bellies. Thou art thrown upon thy back and thy throat is cut open. The executioners of Sechet are for slaying thee,

Column XXX.

1. "their mouths are buried in thy flesh, they stab thee, letting thy blood fall on the fire, they cut open thy head with a knife, and the mighty god removes thy ears. Retreat, retreat, go back, go back, thou art overthrown, thou

2. "art destroyed, thy footsteps are removed, for the great god carries away thy legs. Rā comes forth and Horus the mighty rises up; they curse thee and Rā triumphs over thee. Thou art spit upon, O thou enemy, Rā slays thee,

3. "vomit thou over thyself. Thou art fallen, thou art come to an end and thy two eyes are

blocked up (?); Rā utters words of power to fetter thee. That which cometh into existence from thee has come to an end, thy belongings are destroyed, they body and shade are made an end of, and thy words of power are made of none effect.

4. "Rā takes away thy life from thee, and the moisture of thy mouth and thy breath shall never more exist. Thou art thrown down, thou art made an end of, the god lays hold of thee with fettering irons, thou art decreed for a mighty slaughter, thy fiends are destroyed, thou art without hands and feet, and thou hast no strength of heart in

5. "its place. Thou art cut in pieces and hacked asunder. Retreat, retreat, go back, for the dagger of Horus comes forth against thee. The chain of Sut is thrown over thy head, Rā himself destroys thee, thy voice is broken and thy cries

6. "cannot be heard. O, thou art destroyed, and made an end of; may that which cometh into existence from thee never rise up. Thou art given over to the eye of Horus and it obtains mastery over thee in the course of every day. O Apepi, enemy of Rā, Rā and Atmu destroy thee, they turn thee back

7. "by the might of their utterances. Thou hearest my words of power, and thou diest according to what Rā commanded should be done unto thee. O enemy of Rā, I know what thou doest. Come, get thee back in thy accursed turn, thou art fallen at thy evil moment. Rā blocks thy way and curses

8. "thee, and the great cycle of the gods judges Apepi, the enemy of Rā. Thou art cast down and overthrown, and thou art seized by irons at that moment. Thou art given over to the knife, and together with those knives which are in the boat of Rā, it obtains the mastery over thee. Thou art given over to

9. "the fire, and it obtains the mastery over thee in the course of every day. Thou art given over to the block, and Isis overthrows thee with her words of power. Thou art given over to the eye of Horus, and Usert Ubti [a] consumes thy soul. Thou art given over to Horus, into the two hands

10. "of the mighty god, and he comes against thee having his dagger in his hand. Thou art given over to Sut, the son of Nut, and he severs thy vertebrae and cuts into thy neck, and he fetters thee with that victorious chain of his which is in his hands. Thou art given over to the eye of Rā, and the burning fiery eye

11. "of Horus bites into thy carcase. Thou art given over to the rowers and sailors of Rā, and they set thy head down on the ground. Thou art given over to Horus, dwelling in invisibility, which is in Sechem, and art cut to pieces by his knife.

12. "Thou art given over to the keepers of the secret pylons, their flames come forth against thee and devour thee, and mighty dread rests upon thy body, O enemy of Rā; thou shalt never advance nor pass on, thou shalt never [again] come

13. "into existence, and there shall never rise up and come forth to thee a soul from among those who are in the Nether-world. Thou art given over to the flame of the utterance [of Rā], and the hawk of Horus comes forth against thee from among those who are in the East. Thou art given over

[a] *I.e.*, "mighty flame."

14. " to the words of power which are in him, those who are in their shrines accomplish their purposes against thee, and they slay thee again and again. Thou art given over to the fire of the God which is on the altar of the eater of limbs (?) in the cavern of the rowers of Rā

15. " at the block of Thoth. Each god receives his weapon(?), and their hearts are satisfied in performing thy slaughter. O Apepi, enemy of Rā, get thee back, retreat, down with thy head, even to the dust! Thy ears are destroyed, thy eyes are blinded, and there is an end to thee. Mayest thou and thy form and

16. " thy attribute never more exist, mayest thou never come to Rā in his two heavens. Rā is in heaven and he triumphs over thee. May thy tail be placed in thine own mouth, mayest thou bite into thine own skin, and

17. " mayest thou be hacked in pieces upon the altar of the gods of the great cycle in Heliopolis! thou art cast down and overthrown, and they make thee to fall. Disasters and flames come forth against thee out of the fire, out of the midst of the fire they cry out to thee, they set their faces against thee

18. " from out of their flames, they hack at thee with knives of flint, they burn thee in thy windings, they destroy thee with the knives which are in their hands, the children of Horus destroy thee, their words of power enter into thee,

19. " their powers turn against thee, thou art accursed upon the water (?), and thou art accursed in all the deeds which thou didst perform in that evil hour. Make no attempt upon the *sekti* boat of the gods, get thee back,

20. " Fiend, thy soul is destroyed, thou art cut asunder, thou art driven back from the divine bark, thou art accursed, thou art driven back, the eye of Rā devours thee. Get thee back, Fiend, an end to thee; Horus has

21. ". . . . . . . in thee. O broken Apepi, Rā has obtained the mastery over his enemy. The eye of Rā devours thee in its name of " Devourer," it gnaws into thee and consumes thee by the magical words of the utterances

22. " [of Horus and Rā], the flames smite thee and thou diest through them, they cast thee down, they repulse thee and they obtain the mastery over thee! Thou vomitest, there is an end to thee, thou art turned back, and the great cycle of the gods in Heliopolis cuts thee in pieces; the mighty ones who multiply

23. " the deadly spark of the flame fetter thee with hooks. Thou art given over to the flames of those who are in its name [of . . . .], it (*i. e.* the spark) makes an end of thee, and meets thee in thy accursed exit. There is fire against thee, it bites into thy flesh, it makes an end to thee with

24. " flame which burns up thy soul, and it consumes thy bones and thy flesh. The eye of Horus and the eye of Rā work against thee, and Sut drives his lance into thee. The deadly lion, the soul of Bast, the

25. " lady of slaughter, is against thee, and he reposes on thy blood. Let there be fire upon all thy ways! The goddess Pechit, blazing with fire, the mighty lady of slaughter, the mistress of the spark, works evil against thee, she removes thy flesh, she does harm to thy soul, and she burns thee

26. "up with flame. O Apepi, enemy of Rā, the cycle of the great gods who are in their shrines in front of the boat of Rā consumes thee that thou mayest nevermore exist. Mayest thou never be avenged, mayest thou lie down prostrate and nevermore be roused up! Rā has overthrown thee for ever, thou shalt never be stationed in

Column XXXI.

1. "heaven, thou shalt never exist upon earth. Thou shalt be a victim to that great knife, and thou shalt be slaughtered again and again. Fall down, then, by the knife of the god, a net is thrown over thy head, the spear is in
2. "thy stomach, and the darts of Rā are driven into thy form. Thou art overthrown at thy evil moment, thou art burnt up at the moment of Horus. The god comes forth against the Fiend, Apepi is overthrown. Thy face, Apepi, is on the block
3. "at that place where Rā spits, thou art destroyed by it for ever. Mayest thou never have sexual pleasure or emission from thy body, may thy male offspring never exist, may thy egg never grow! The gods that come forth from the eye of
4. "Horus shall cut thee in pieces and thou shalt pass away. Thou art fallen and Rā-Harmachis overthrows thee, he comes against thee with the dagger in his hand, he makes a successful design against thee, and thou becomest non-existent. An end to thee, then, Apepi, enemy of Rā! Four times.

   Mayest thou never come into existence! May thy soul never exist, may thy *ka*
5. "never exist, may thy body never exist, mayest thou never exist! May thy limbs never exist, mayest thou never exist, may thy arms never exist, may thy limbs never exist, mayest thou never exist, may thy bones never exist, mayest thou never exist, may thy words of power never exist, mayest thou never exist, mayest
6. "thou never exist, mayest thou never exist, may thy form never exist. Mayest thou never exist, may thy attributes never exist; mayest thou never exist, may that which springs from thee never exist; mayest thou never exist, may thy hair never exist; mayest thou never exist, may thy possessions never exist; mayest
7. "thou never exist, may thy emission never exist; mayest thou never exist, may the material of thy body never exist; mayest thou never exist, may thy seat never exist; mayest thou never exist, may thy tomb never exist; mayest thou never exist, may thy cavern never exist; mayest thou never exist, may thy funeral chamber never exist;
8. "mayest thou never exist, may thy paths never exist; mayest thou never exist, may thy seasons never exist; mayest thou never exist, may thy words never exist; mayest thou never exist, may thy entrance never come to pass; mayest thou never exist, may thy journeyings never exist; mayest thou never exist,
9. "may thy advances never exist; mayest thou never exist, may thy coming never exist; mayest thou never exist, may thy sitting never exist; mayest thou never exist, may thy growing never exist; mayest thou never exist, may thy body never exist; mayest thou never exist, may thy prosperity never exist!
10. "Thou art smitten, Apepi, enemy of Rā, thou shalt die, thou shalt die. Thou shalt perish,

thy name shall perish, thy teeth shall become powerless, thy . . . . shall pass away, thou shalt be blind and shalt not see. Fall down

11. "upon thy face! Thou art overthrown, overthrown, destroyed, destroyed, made an end of, made an end of, hacked in pieces, hacked in pieces, slaughtered, slaughtered, cut to pieces, cut to pieces, chopped asunder, chopped asunder, butchered, butchered. Thy head is cut off by that knife in the presence of Rā daily. Aker thee to judgment dooms,

12. "and he turns back Apepi's bones. Retreat thou, for Rā Harmachis overthrows thee. Thou art given over to the god who brings destruction upon thee. He says,

"The daggers of Horus are driven into thy head, and they cut it off from thy neck; thy soul is overthrown, thy shade shall never exist, thou art destroyed

13. "at the divine block. Thy head is cut off and thou art thrown down upon thy back; get thee back, O fiend, enemy of Rā. Thou art cut to pieces at thy accursed exit. The eye of Horus eats thee and bites into thee, its heart is satisfied

14. "when its fire and its flame are directed against thee. Get thee back, Apepi, with that accursed foot of thine! The cycle of the gods lift up their faces against thee, and they spit their flame into thy eye. There is fire against thee, a deadly

15. "fire, which masters thee, and burns thee away, and consumes thee. Thou art given over to the flame which is in its mouth, it cuts thee in pieces; Rā turns back thy eyes, and Horus blinds thee from his boat; the flame obtains mastery over thy throat and it performs thy slaughter. There is a knife in thee, and it

16. "destroys thy limbs. Thou shalt never come to the boat of the great god, for Rā himself turns thee back. Thou art at the block and thy face is laid upon it. The gods who are in the shrine of Rā overthrow thee, and the shrine overthrows

17. "thee; thou art walled up, and thy two ears are removed."

Isis overthrows thee with her words of power, she smashes thy mouth, she removes thy ears, she will never give Rā over to thee, for ever, for ever

18. "and for ever. That spear of Rā turns back into thy limbs, be silent, be stabbed, die, live not! Isis and Nephthys overthrow thee, and together they turn back thy crocodile; get thee gone, retreat, be blind, perish, be destroyed thy

19. "soul, live not, for ever and ever. Thy opportunity departs, and the flame of fire which is in thy body takes away thy strength. There is fire upon thee, it grips thy body, and burns thy bones, when thou comest forth it burns thy

20. "soul and gnaws thy body. Thou art seized by the mighty fire which flames against thy limbs, and then returnest to thy block.

Rā makes Thoth to slay thee with his words of power. Thou shalt never come to the

21. "boat of Rā, for Rā himself turns thee back. He knows all the evil which thou hast done. "The flame of those who are in the south is against thee, and masters thee," says divine Sothis Anqet, decreeing what is to be done to thee. "The flame of those who are in the north is against thee and masters

22. "thee," says Uatit, lady of Pe and Tep, decreeing what is to be done to thee. "The flame of those who are in the west is against thee and masters thee," says Kesun, lord of those in

the west, decreeing what is to be done unto thee. "The flame of those who are in the east is against thee and masters thee," says Sept, lord of those

23. "who are in the east, decreeing what is to be done to thee. Mayest thou never exist in any place in which thou art. Behold thou, the flame masters thee. Thou art given over to the flame of the eye of Rā, it decrees its flame against thee in its name of

24. "Uatit, it eats into thee in its name of "Eater," it obtains the mastery over thee in its name of "Sechet," and it flames against thee in its name of "Flame." Die thou by the flame of fire, be there blindness to thee! The eye of Horus obtains the

25. "mastery over thee, it removes thy two hands, it carries away thy two feet, and decrees thy disasters. Rā says, "Let evil arise to thee." Horus says, "Let slaughter be made of thee, be thou spit upon, fettered, and overthrown!

26. "May thy soul be carried away from thy shade, may thy head be fettered, *otherwise said*, may thy head be cut off, may thy bones be smashed, may thy flesh be torn from thy limbs, may thy soul be turned back from thy shade, and thy body be brought to nought: and mayest thou nevermore exist! Thou art seized

27. "by the fire, tortured and turned back." The might of the uraei of Rā overthrows thee, the fire of their mouths chews thee up. Thou art given over to the fire, it blazes in thee, it sparkles in thee, it destroys

Column XXXII.

1. "thy soul at the divine block; the great cycle of the gods rages at thee by reason of that work which thy two hands have wrought. Amen in his Apts enfeebles

2. "thee, and drives his horn into thy neck. Isis says, "It is decreed that thy ways shall be stopped." Her son Horus shuts up thy name. Tefnut says, "The water is turned away from thee, and thou art seized when thou comest forth from it." Shu drives his spear into thee, saying, "Be thou drowned, and never come forth, O Apepi, enemy of Rā."

3. "Be thou spit upon, Apepi. Four times. Be spit upon O every enemy of P-āa, life, strength, health! in death in life."

THE BOOK OF OVERTHROWING APEPI.

To be recited:—

4. "O Rā, O Atmu, O Chepera, O Shu, O Tefnut, O Seb, O Nut, O Osiris, O Horus, O Isis, O Nephthys, O Shu, O Tefnut, O Hu, O Sau, O Osiris, lord of Kakam (Cochome), O Hiku, the genius of Rā, the deceased P-āa comes to you,

5. "he casts fire against Apepi, he carries off the . . . . of the Fiend, he gives joy to the boat of millions of years. The hearts of the rowers of Rā are in exultation within his shrine, the souls of the gods rest in his horizon,

6. "the gods who are in it give to him adorations. Rā is at the head of Het-Mesq, Horus comes forth upon his station.

"Rā triumphs over his enemies. Four times.

"P-āa triumphs over his enemies. Four times."

ANOTHER BOOK OF OVERTHROWING APEPI.

"O every man, woman, dead person, and unborn person whatsoever who would

7. "do harm to P-āa, O ye gods who would do violence to him, may he be in your sight like a great god, lord of heaven! May all his tongues cry out to Nebau when he travels over the two heavens and earth with fulness

8. "of breezes, when Rā destroys his enemies! May he be a messenger to Heliopolis to propitiate the heart of Atmu and his Powers, and to put Northern and Southern

9. "Heliopolis in delight! May he be in your sight like the golden *abtu* fish under the boat of Rā! He terrifies all the enemies of Rā, he gives power to the heart of Horus; he crushes the enemies of Rā, he gives joy in the heart of Horus; he

10. "sets the rudder in the boat of the great heart of Rā reposing in its shrine: he destroys all fiends. The *māāt* boat is in strength of heart, the *sektet* boat is in peace, *otherwise said*, in fair winds. The goddess Heset is united to her lord in exultation. Rā is protecting him, Rā is

11. "protecting the soul of P-āa, Rā protects him, protects him against every man, every woman, every dead person, and every unborn person whomsoever. Rā will shut every mouth which would speak any evil thing against P-āa. He will make thy face

12. "blind and he will watch carefully any person who would do any evil or wicked thing to him. Rā opens the mouth of P-āa life, strength, health! against every man, every woman, every dead person, and every unborn person whatsoever."

This chapter is to be said when Rā is . . . . in order to make him live long.

Here endeth the book of Neb-er-ter.

13. The Accursed Names of Apepi.

14. Apepi, Fiend, bristling with terror.
15. Apepi, Fiend, Doubly evil One.
16. Apepi, Fiend, with face turned behind.
17. Apepi, Fiend, Roarer.
18. Apepi, Fiend, Evil doer.
19. Apepi, Fiend, Qerner or Qelnel.
20. Apepi, Fiend, Iubani.
21. Apepi, Fiend, Devourer.
22. Apepi, Fiend, Adversary of the world.
23. Apepi, Fiend, Eclipser of the earth.
24. Apepi, Fiend, Chermuti.
25. Apepi, Fiend, Monkey (?).
26. Apepi, Fiend, Tortoise.
27. Apepi, Fiend, Destroyer of the world (?).
28. Apepi, Fiend, Strong-face.

29. Apepi, Fiend, Unti.
30. Apepi, Fiend, Karau-ememti.
31. Apepi, Fiend, Repulsive of face.
32. Apepi, Fiend, Devil of Devils.
33. Apepi, Fiend, Rebel.
34. Apepi, Fiend, Chan-re- . . . . -uāa, *otherwise said*, Cha . . . .
35. Apepi, Fiend, Nai.
36. Apepi, Fiend, Am.
37. Apepi, Fiend, Turre-pa (?).
38. Apepi, Fiend, Iuba.
39. Apepi, Fiend, Uai.
40. Apepi, Fiend, Fourfold Charebutu.
41. Apepi, Fiend, Sau.
42. Apepi, Fiend, Beteshu (Inert One).
43. The inscriptions which are to be written upon new papyrus for the coverings [of the wax
44. figures of Apepi and the other fiends] which are to be thrown upon the ground and put in the fire.

Make a figure of a serpent having his tail in his mouth, and a knife stuck in his back,
45. and cast it upon the ground, saying, "Apepi, Fiend, Betet."
46. Make another mystery of words, *i e.*, make four other figures of the
47. enemies [of Rā] having the faces of . . . . . . , fetter them and tie their hands
48. behind them [and call them] "Children of inertness."

Make another serpent with the face of a cat, having a knife stuck in it, [and cast it upon the ground] saying, "Roarer."
49. Make another with the face of a . . . . . . , having its knife [stuck in it, and cast it upon the ground] saying, "Aat-qar-Uaba.
50. Make another with the face of a crocodile, having its knife [stuck in it, and cast it upon the ground] saying, "Hauna-aru-her-hra."
51. Make another image of the Fiend with the face of a duck, having its knife [stuck in it, and cast it upon the ground] saying, "Unti."
52. Make another figure with the face of a white cat, tie it up and fetter it and [put] its knife [in it, and cast it upon the ground] saying, "Apepi, the Fiend."
53. Make four other images each having the face of a duck, tie their hands and their feet together, and stick knives in their backs; [let them represent the] "Children of inertness."

A Hymn of Praise to be recited after the foregoing.

1. "Hail father! lord of the gods, mighty one of the great cycle of the gods!
2. Hail thou primeval matter from which the gods were formed, hail creator of men, hail thou evolver of all evolved things which came into existence after thou thyself wast evolved!
3. I am thy son, thy heart in very truth, that strength of heart which comes forth from thy mysterious being, and commemorates their coming into existence from thee with words of power for

4. making thy beautiful virtues which come forth from my mouth to make protection for thee; I am perfect with plans.
5. Come, O Rā, look with thy two eyes, and be graciously pleased with what I have done. I have overthrown Apepi for thee
6. at his moment, I have destroyed him within his cavern. Horus the two-eyed has his weapon to cut off the head of thy enemy. Menhi (*i.e.*, the executioner)
7. has his mighty knife and he cuts off the head of thy fiend: the flame
8. devours him and shoots fire into his soul [as he lies] on his block.

   Thy soul is joyful, thy soul is joyful. Thou sailest along the sky with fair
9. winds. Come, O look thou with thine eye at what I have done with the limbs of Apepi . . . the enemy. He is shut up in restraint, his body
10. is destroyed and blotted out from the horizon of Aa-Peqa, and of thy two heavens; thy towns are saved and possess stability. Thou art
11. firm, thou art strong, thou growest, thou growest, thou risest, thou risest, thou shinest, thou shinest every day.
12. Thou risest in thy boat, thy heart is dilated with joy, thy children fill thy heart.
13. Rā cries out to the Enemy, the serpent whose face is turned behind him, "Away with thee," and utters horrible cries against him when
14. he is at his block; he then turns round and crushes him.

   Hail thou who comest forth from the horizon over all lands with strength of heart, thy heart, O Rā, rejoices every day.
15. Apepi the fire has cast down, and the flame has carried away Nekau; the heart of Amen-Rā, lord of the thrones of the earth, at the head of
16. the Apts, rejoices, for his enemy has fallen beneath him.

   Rā triumphs over Apepi, Rā triumphs over Apepi,

   Rā triumphs over Apepi, Rā triumphs over Apepi.
17. Amen-Rā, lord of the thrones of the earth, at the head of the Apts, triumphs over his enemy.

   Amen-Rā, lord of the thrones of the earth, at the head of the Apts, triumphs over his enemy.

   Amen-Rā, lord of the thrones of the earth, at the head of the Apts, triumphs over his enemy.

   Amen-Rā, lord of the thrones of the earth, at the head of the Apts, triumphs over his enemy.

   Atmu, lord of Setemet, triumphs over his enemy.

   Atmu, lord of Setemet, triumphs over his enemy.

   Atmu, lord of Setemet, triumphs over his enemy.

   Atmu, lord of Setemet, triumphs over his enemy.
18. Thoth, perfect in enchantments, lord of divine words, triumphs over his enemy.

   Thoth, perfect in enchantments, lord of divine words, triumphs over his enemy.

   Thoth, perfect in enchantments, lord of divine words, triumphs over his enemy.

   Thoth, perfect in enchantments, lord of divine words, triumphs over his enemy."

Here endeth the book.

THE FESTIVAL SONGS OF ISIS AND NEPHTHYS.

(British Museum Egyptian Papyrus 10188.)

Column I.

1. *Ḥā em ḥet nu*[a] *ḥeb t'erti ȧri em pa*
Beginning of the chapters of the festival of the two Terti, made in the temple of

Ȧusar χent Ȧmentiu neter āāi nebt Ȧbṭu em 2. *ȧbeṭ ftu*
Osiris, at the head of the Amentiu, god great, lord of Abydos, in month four

ša hru t'at-sen neferit er hru t'at-sas seri χertu
of the sowing, day twenty-two up to day twenty-six. Written with reference to

pa ȧu t'er - f ȧn χertu set āb 3. *ḥā*
temple to entirety its, brought with reference to women pure of limbs,

ȧn ȧpt - sen χersek šennu en ḥāu - sen meḥu
not polluted are they, removed (is) the hair of limbs their, crowned (are)

ṭep - sen em ser 4. *ser em āāui - sen*
heads their with ram's wool, [placed are] tambourines in two hands their,

[a] The words over which a black line is printed are, in the papyrus, written in red.

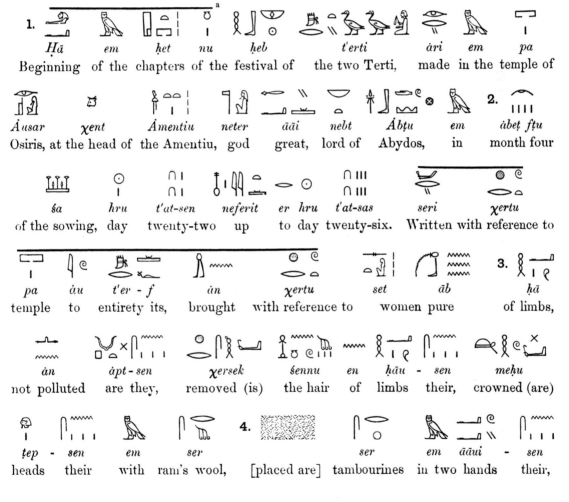

mātennu ren - sen ḥer ermen-sen er Ȧuset Nebt-ḥet
inscribed (are) names their upon two arms their 'To Isis and Nephthys.'

5. *ḥes-sen em ḥet nu śāt ten embaḥ neter pen* 6. *t'eṭ χer sen*
chant they in the chapters of book this before god this, is said by them.

ȧ neb Ȧusar sep ftu 7. *t'eṭtu ȧn χer - ḥeb ḥer nerȧu en*
'O lord Osiris,' times four. Says the precentor at the front of

pa pen 8. *āa ḥer (?) en ta sep ftu* 9. *t'eṭtu ȧn ḥenksti*
temple this, 'O..... chief of earth' times four. Say the women with flowing hair.

10. *ḥunnu*[a] *nefer māȧ er pa-k* 11. *t'erā ȧn maa-n-θ*
"Boy beautiful, come to house thy at once; not see we thee.

12. *ȧ ȧḥi nefer māȧ er pa-k* 13. *χenti emχet*
O boy beautiful, come to house thy, approaching after

teś-k er-n 14. [*ȧ*] *ḥunnu nefer śem - ta ennu*
departure thy from us. O boy beautiful, piloting the hour.

15. *renp ȧn ȧs er trȧ-f* 16. *senen seri ent ȧtf-f*
increasing except at season his. Image exalted of father his

[a] In this papyrus, after every title of the Sun-god, and the name of everything relating to him, the determinative of divinity, [hieroglyph], is placed.

17. 18.

Tanen mãi šeta per em Ȧtmu neb sep sen

Tanen, essence hidden coming forth from Atmu. The lord, twice,

19.

tennu su er ȧtf-f sems em χat en

how great (is) he more than father his! Eldest from the womb of

20. 21.

mut-f ḥa iu-k en n em ȧru-k ḥapt-n-tu

mother his. Back come thou to us in attribute thy. Embrace will we thee,

22. 23.

ȧn ḥeru-k er n nefer ḥrȧ ur mertu senen Tanen

not depart thou from us. beautiful of face, great of love. The image of Tanen,

24. 25.

t'a nebt net'emt'em em ȧp χat ḳenen

the male, lord of love. [child]? opening the womb. feeble (are)

26.

ḥāu-f em ennuḥ-f iu-k em ḥetep neb-n

limbs his in emotion his. Come thou in peace lord our

27.

maa-n-tu χnem senti ḥāu-k ȧn ȧm-k ȧuset-ā

see we thee. Unite the two sisters limbs thy. not (is there) in thee pain,

28. [1⅜ inch broken]

. . . . tu mȧ enti ȧn χeper-f

[they destroy] the evil as if never happened had it.

Column II.

1. 2.

ṭep-n ān ḥer ḥrȧ-n perti āat emma neteru

Head our (is) turned back upon face our. Mighty one great among the gods,

(1)*

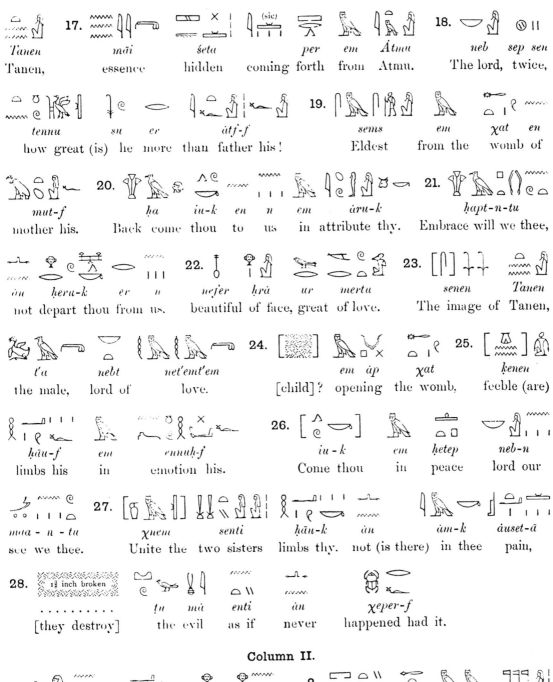

3. *àn neχebu-s mātennu àri - nek* 4. *pa χi ḥunnu*
not described (is) it the road (which) makest thou, the babe, child

àu tràui àn às (?) 5. *rer-k pet ta em*
at two seasons . . . . Goest round thou heaven and earth in

àru-k 6. *àu-k em ka ent senti* 7. *iu-k χi*
attribute thy. Art thou like a bull of the two sisters. Come, thou babe,

renp em ḥetep 8. *neb-n maa-n-tu* 9. *sam-k àm-n*
renewing in setting, lord our, let see us thee. Let phallus thy be among us

mà sam 10. *Tebha er nemmat-f* 11. *iu-k em ḥetep nu*
like the phallus of Tebha at (*or* against) block his. Come thou in peace, babe,

ur nu àtf-f 12. *men-tu em pa-k àn senṭ-k*
great one of father his. Established art thou in house thy, not fearest thou.

13. *se-k Ḥeru net' - ḥrà-k* 14. *nekàu māš-su* 15. *àu-f*
Son thy Horus avenges thee. The devil may carried off be he, may be he

em χebait-f ent χet hru neb 16. *šāṭ ren-f emmā*
in cavern his of flame day every, may be slain name his among

neteru nebu 17. *Tebha χep-s āṭi* 18. *àu-k àu pa-k*
the gods all, Tebha may die it finally. Art thou in house thy,

àn *sent-k* 19. *Sut* *em* *ṭu* *nebt* *àri* *nef* 20. *uṭ-nef*
not fearest thou Sut in evil all (that) does he. Has shot him (what)

sehab *Nut* 21. *ànq-f* *en* *n* *maatu* 22. *seḥ* *en* *ta*
sent forth Nut Embraces he us joyfully travelling on earth

àm-n 23. *à . . . s* *ḥer* *àpt* . . . .
among us, ... to open . . . .

Column III.

1. *stastau* 2. *maa-n* *em* *bàf* *ḥer* *ḥrà-k* 3. *ufiḥ*
apostates (?) Two eyes our (are) looking upon face thy blazing with

maatu 4. *àhai* *t'er* *àbṭ* *neb-n* *er-n* 5. *pa* *nefer*
radiance. Hail from the left lord our from us. The beautiful

ḥrà *nebt* *mertu* 6. *pa* *ka* *sati* *em* *kauit* 7. *māā*
face lord of love, the bull sowing seed in the cows. Come

àḥi *θeḥen* *ḥrà* 8. *pa* *uā* *renp* *ānnu* *em* *maa-f*
boy saffron face, the ONE increasing, beautiful in two eyes his.

9. *neb* *em* *ḥemt* 10. *t'a* *en* *kauit* 11. *pa* *χi* *ḥer* *neferu*
Lord among women, male of the cows. the child chief of beauties.

12. *ḥa* *maa-n-tu* *mà* *àru-k* 13. *mà* *mertu-à* *maa-k*
Once more let see us thee as well as what belongs to thee, as love I to see thee.

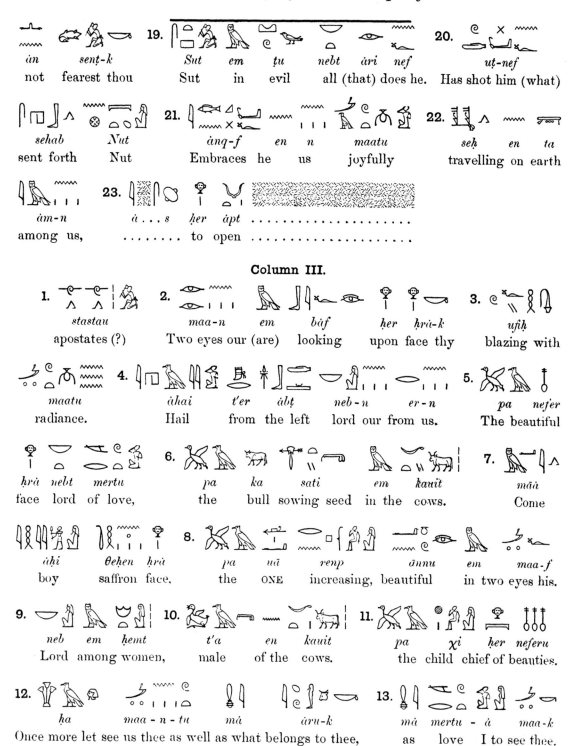

14. *nuk senàt-k Àuset mertu àb - k* 15. *ḥer - sa mertu-k*
I am sister thy Isis the darling of heart thy, because of love for thee

ḥer-tu 16. *meḥ - à ta pen em hru pen* 17. *seḥ-k ḥes - tu*
when departest thou. Inundate I earth this on day this. Travellest thou, hymned (art) thou

àm-n 18. *un-n ānχ em ḳa-k* 19. *iu-k em ḥetep*
by us, springs up to us life out of nothingness thy. Come thou in peace

neb-n maa-n-tu 20. *à ser māā em ḥetep* 21. *seḥeràut*
lord our, let see us thee. O prince coming in peace, drive away the

χet χent ḥet-n 22. *sam-k àm-n mà sam*
flame which is upon temple our, may phallus thy be among us like the phallus of (Tebha)."

23. *s-āšt t'eṭtu àn ḥenksti* 24. *à Àusar ka Àmentiu*
Repetition of words by the women with flowing hair. "O Osiris, bull of the Amentiu,

25. *uā men tennu [su] er neteru* 26. *χi benen*
ONE, established, how great is [he] more than the gods! Baby, virile,

Column IV.

1. *āuāā ur en Sebu* 2. *mestu neter em neteru*
heir mighty of Seb, born god of gods,

3. *iu-k en χart* 4. *rer-nek paut neteru tem-θ*
come thou to the two widows. Go round thee the cycle of the gods entire,

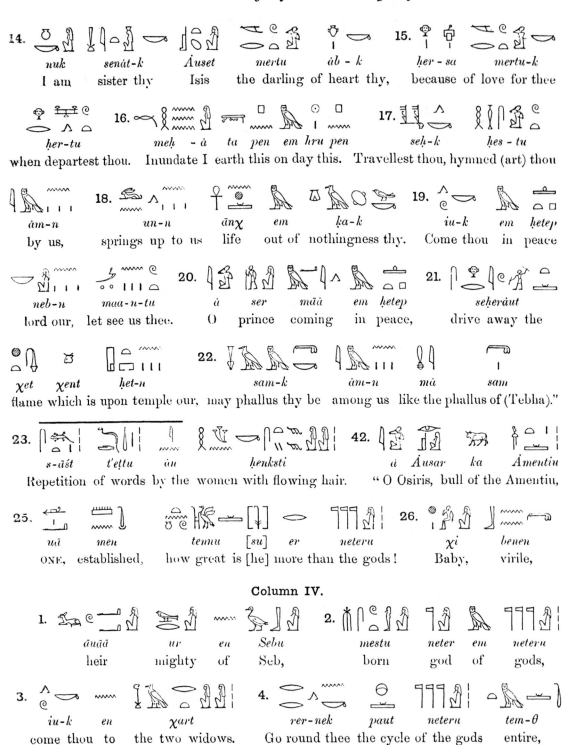

5. *χesef - sen nek Sut em ī-f*
meet they thee. Sut in coming his

6. *aha ren-f*
cursed (be) cursed name his

em ḥa kerȧut em baḥ ȧtf-k Rā
behind the shrine before father thy Rā.

7. *uṭ-f*
[who] darts out

χesef Sebȧu
repulsing the fiend.

8. *māȧ ṭi en χennu-k*
Come, wait relatives thy,

9. *χesef meḥi*
drive away sorrow

χent ḥet-n
from temple our,

10. *māȧ ṭi en χennu-k*
come, wait relatives thy.

11. *ȧn tut erek*
Not (is there) like unto thee

θȧs em uāi
sitting in solitude.

12. *neb-n em ḥetep ȧuset-f*
Lord our in peace (is) seat his.

13. *seqernu*
Victor,

ur eref sef ḥrȧ-f
greater than he [is] long-suffering his,

14. *t'er seχennu nebṭ ḥer*
when hovers the Lock upon

χerui-f
enemies his.

15. *ḥut-f ta em seχeru-f*
Moulds he the earth according to designs his.

16. *pertet*
Mighty comer forth,

āat emmā neteru
great one among the gods,

17. *paut neteru nek em ḥetep maȧuset*
the cycle of the gods (are) to thee upon shanks (their),

18. *mȧ tennu-k er neteru*
inasmuch as greater (art) thou than the gods.

19. *χenṭ - ȧ ta tennu*
Tread I the earth, O very

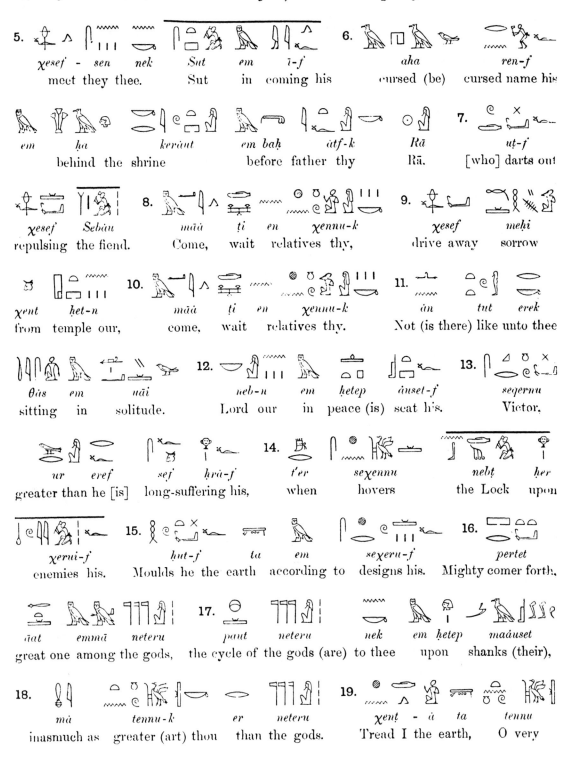

ur enti χat 20. *χut em tep-f* 21. *mes-su em baḥ àb-f*
great one of the womb! The crown (is) upon head his, born (is) he before heart his,

em ī tennu 22. *t'et neter nebt mertu tennu āšt*
in coming, how great! Body divine, lord of love, how exceedingly manifold

mertu 23. *pa ba ānχ-k em nem* 24. *χnem senti*
of love! O soul livest thou a second time, unite the two sisters

ḥāu-k 25. *speru ṭi erek t'er em-baḥ* 26. *neχtu - nek*
limbs thy, approaching waiting for thee long time. Proclaimed mighty art thou

em šen-[k] 27. *mà* [¾ inch broken] .... *neteru nebt*
in circuit thy, as .... the gods all.

Column V.

1. *māà ṭi χennu-k* 2. *àtf-k Rā kahabu*
Come wait relatives thy. Father thy Rā butts

àu nebt 3. *rer-nek paut neteru em šen-k χesef-sen*
against the Lock. Go round thee the cycle of the gods in circuit thy, repulse they

nek Ṭešu 4. *ṭer-k āu ur en erpetet-k*
for thee the fiends. Remove thou the unpleasantness great of images thy.

5. *pa-k em ḥeb ṭu àu nemmat-f Sebàu em ṭu em*
Temple thy (is) in festival, the evil one (is) at block his, the fiend (is) in evil case by what

àri-nef 6. *āuḥenu-f* *ta* *em* *seχeru-f* *qesn* 7. *habu-f*
done has he. Drowns he the earth with schemes his empty. Drives off him

Nut *er* *se-taiu* 8. *χetχet* *mās* *em* *hebt*
Nut from Setaiu, turning back bringing into the storehouse,

9. *mās* *er* *nemmat* *Sebàu* 10. *àtf-k* *Rā* *er* *net'* *ser-k*
bringing to the block Sebàu. Father thy Rā (is) for avenging constraint thy,

11. *se-k* *Ḥeru* *er* *uśebt* *ḥer-k* 12. *seḥ-k* *ta* *màtet*
son thy Horus (is) for answering for thee. Traversest thou earth as

χeper-k 13. *nemmetau-k* *Nut* *ḥer* *àfṭ-s* 14. *χen-k* *ta*
turnest thou, stridest thou Nut over four quarters its. Restest thou on earth

ḥer *neterui* *het-āt* 15. *reḥti* *ḥer* *rer* *nek* 16. *χi-tu*
upon the divine dwellings, the two *reḥti* are for going round thee. Exalted (art) thou,

sep sen *māk* *Sut* *em* *hebt* 17. *Sebàu-k* *àn* *un-nef*
twice, verily Sut is in the storehouse. Sebàu thy not may rise up he.

18. *iu-k* *er* *pa-k* *Àusar* *àuset-k* *heḥ* *maa-k* 19. *setem-k*
Come thou to house thy Osiris, seat thy (is) seeking to see thee. Hearest thou

semàu *ent* *Ḥeru* *ḥer* *āāiu* *mut-f* *Àuset* 20. *χesef-k*
the report of Horus at the two hands of mother his Isis. Keepest off thou

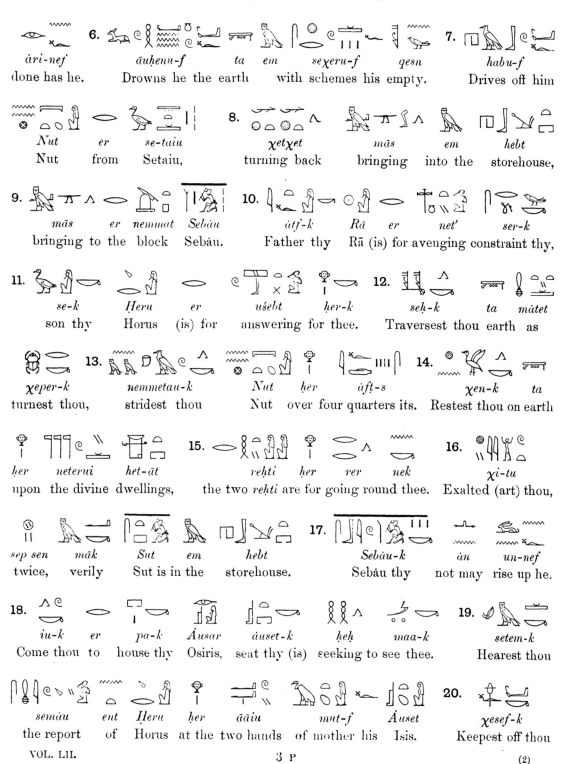

ertāt em taui neb āb t'et-k seśep-f àm pa
placed in lands all what comes against body thy, receives he what is in the house

śāt-k **21.** *neter āā ḥetem-tu em àru-k* **22.** *em ḥeru*
of books thy. O god, great, shut up art thou in attributes thy. not go away

er pa-k Àusar **23.** *iu-k em ḥetep er àuset-k nebt neràu*
from house thy Osiris. Come thou in peace to place thy every, victorious one

ānnu em χeperu-f **24.** *pa ka ur nebt nt'emt'em*
beautiful in becoming his, the bull, great, lord of love.

25. *apṭ-k senà-k Àuset* **26.** *χersek sati àri*
Duck thy (is) sister thy Isis removing the impurity which (is)

àm-k **27.** *ḥapt-s-tu àn ḥeru-k er-n neb-n*
in thee. Embraces she thee, not depart thou from us lord our.

Column VI.

1. *Ṭā-k ānχ em ḥāt em śeb* (?) **2.** *àhai χau-k*
Gavest thou life from the beginning .... Hail, protectest thou

meḥ em sept Tes **3.** *ṭu mà enti àn χeper-f*
(what) flows from the nome of Aphroditopolis, evil as if never became it.

4. *iu-nek senàt-k χersek-s ḥāu-k* **5.** *neter āā ānχ*
Comes to thee sister thy, cleanses she limbs thy. God, great, living one,

6. 7.

ur mertu rertu su er ḥer en ḥetep qemā meḥit χaker-tu

great of love, dandled (is) he in the presence of Qemā Mehit Decorated art thou

8. 9.

nebt χakeru t'a ur ḥer neferu iu-k en

the lord of decorated things. male, mighty one, chief of beauties. Comes to thee

10.

mut-k Nut peš-s ḥer-k em iu-k nes māket-s

mother thy Nut, spreads out she herself over thee in coming thy to her. Protects she

11. 12.

ḥāu-k er ṭu nebt šem-s ten (sic) *em χennu-s seḥerȧu-s*

limbs thy against evil all, advances she . . . . . . within her, drives away she

13.

ṭu nebt ȧri ḥāu-k ȧri uā mȧ enti ȧn χeper-f

evil all which is in limbs thy, the guardian solitary, as if never had happened it,

14. 15.

set χi neb per em Nut ȧri nef ta pen

clothing the baby, the lord, coming forth from Nut. Makes he land this

16. (?)

mȧ ḥetep-ā neb χi per em kaut ten āuur en

as in olden time, the lord, the baby, coming forth from womb this, heir, mighty one of

17. 18.

neteru ȧp Ȧmentet er trȧ-f ȧs šem χi ȧn

the gods, opener of Amenti at season his. Behold, advances the baby not

19. 20.

ennu ȧtf-k Rā er net' ḥrȧ-k se-k Ḥeru

seeing. Father thy Rā is for avenging thee, son thy Horus is

ḥer nubȧu - tuk 21. *sut em ṭu nebt ȧri nef* 22. *iu-k er*
for protecting thee (against) Sut in evil all (which) done has he. Come thou to

pa-k ȧn senṭ - k 23. *t'eṭtu ȧn ḥenksti* 24. *ȧ*
house thy without fear thou." Say the women with flowing hair: "O

ȧḥi nefer māā er pa-k 25. *qa sep sen sa-k er*
boy, beautiful, come to house thy. Exalted twice, let side thy be to

pa-k 26. *ȧu neteru ḥer ȧuset - sen* 27. *nuk set χut en*
house thy, towards the gods upon seat their. I am a person the defender of

senȧ-s 28. *ḥemt-k senȧ en mut-k*
brother her, wife thy, the sister of mother thy,

Column VII.

1. *iu-k nȧ em χeχ* 2. *t'er-ȧb maa ḥrȧ-k ȧu sa ȧn maa-ȧ*
come thou to me running. Firm of heart, let be seen face thy, because (?) not see I

ḥrȧ-k 3. *sam-tu uat en - n em ḥrȧ-ȧ ȧu Rā em pet*
face thy. Make clear thou the way for us before face my to Rā in heaven.

4. *sam pet ta ȧri χebit em ta mȧn* 5. *tau ȧb - ȧ*
Unites heaven (with) earth making shade on the earth daily. Burns heart my

er sefeχ-k em nefiȧ 6. *tau ȧb-ȧ erṭā - nek sa-k*
at escape thy from the evil one. Burns heart my, give thou side thy

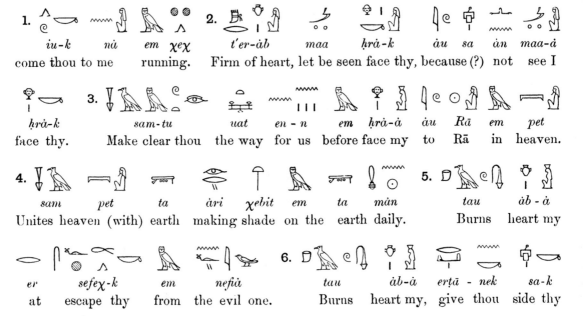

7. 8.

er-à *àu* *àn* *sep* *qem* *nek* *su* *er-à* *āṭi* *àat*

to me, for not ever remove thou it from me. Making firm the two domains

9. 10.

tenemem *uat* *àu-à* *ḥeḥ* *en* *mertu* *maa-k* *un-à*

turning back the roads, am I seeking of love to see thee. Am I

11.

em *nut* *āat* *nehat - s* *meḥt - à* *en* *mertu-k*

in the town mighty (are) fortifications its. Overcome am I by love thy

12. 13.

er-à *māā* *em* *uā* *em* *ḥeru* *māk* *se-k*

for me, come alone do not depart. Verily son thy (is)

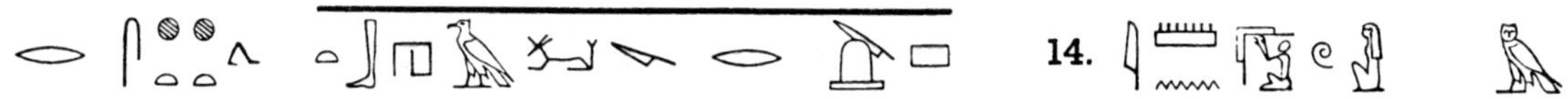

14.

er *seχetχet* *Tebha* *er* *nemmat* *àmen - uà* *em*

for repulsing Tebha at the block. Concealed have I myself in

15.

bàa *er* *seḥapu* *se-k* *er* *uśebt-k* *ḥer* *sep*

the bushes to hide son thy for answering thee, for the time

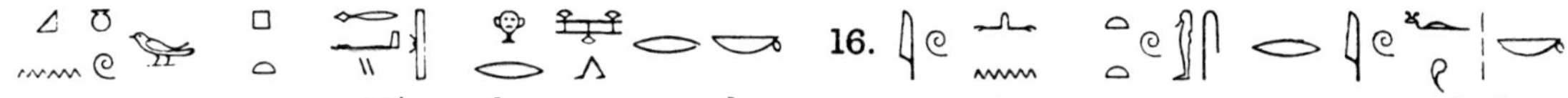

16.

qennu *pu* *āāi* *ḥer* *er-k* *àu* *àn* *tut-s* *er* *àuf - k*

of distress to wit great departing from thee. Is not gathering she for limbs thy?

17. 18.

śem-à *em* *uā* *rer-à* *em* *bàa* *àu* *tennu* *em*

Advance I alone, go round I among the bushes. Is a very great

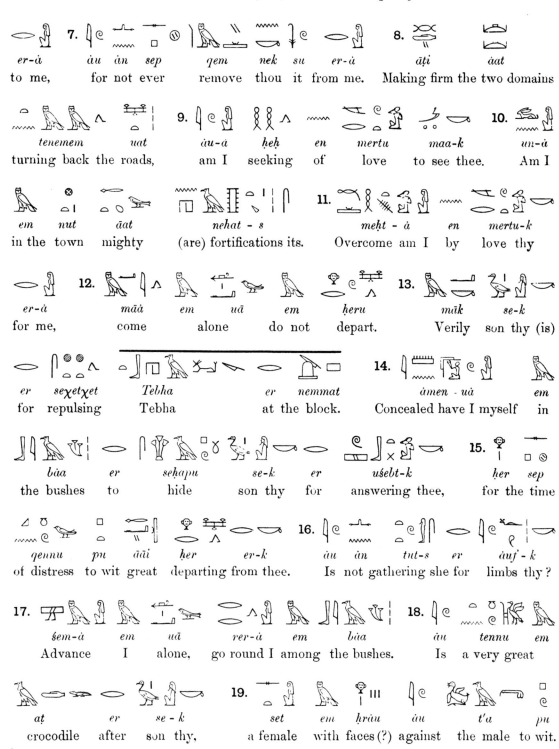

19.

aṭ *er* *se - k* *set* *em* *ḥràu* *àu* *t'a* *pu*

crocodile after son thy, a female with faces (?) against the male to wit.

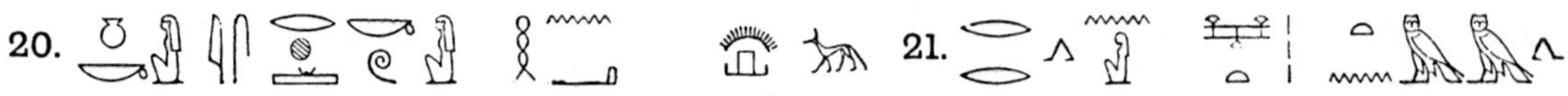

nuk às reχ-kuà ḥnā Ȧnpu rer-nà uat tenemem

I but know I in conjunction with Anubis. Go round I the ways, turn back

nà ḥer senà bati em nefi tau àbu en

I after brother [my] leaping from the evil one. Burning (are) the hearts of

ḥefnu ḥràu maut āāi em neteru bef - n neb

myriads of faces. Splendour great among the gods, may see (?) we the lord.

àn uśer en mertu-k ḥer ḥrà-n pa sam

Not may there be lack of love thy upon faces our, the phallus,

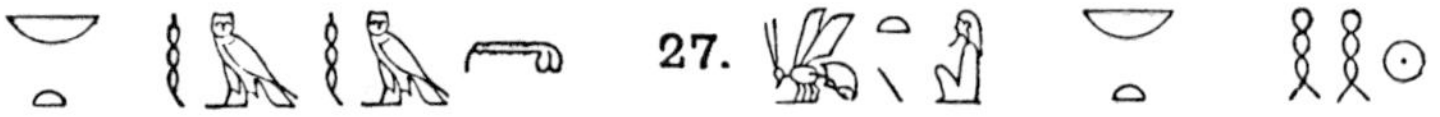

nebt net'emt'em net nebt ḥeḥ

lord of love, king, lord of eternity,

Column VIII.

āχ em ānχ ḥeq t'etta ḳau àn reχ

flying as he lives, ruler of everlasting, destroyer of Ȧn-reχ

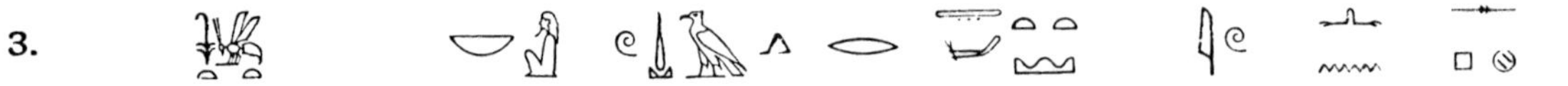

suten net neb ut'a er Tasertet àu àn sep-

king of north and south, the lord going forth from Tasertet. May there never be a time

k meḥ-nà àb-à àm-f senà neb ut'a er sept Ȧqertet

to thee fill I heart my with it. Brother, lord, going forth from the nome of Aqertet.

iu-k nà em àru - k māā em ḥetep sep sen net ser

Come thou to me in attribute thy, come in peace twice. King, great one,

8.
māā em ḥetep ḥa maa-n ḥrà-k mà χent mà mertu - nà
come in peace. Again may see we face thy as before according as love I

9.
maa-k āāui-à qa er χau - tuk mertu - nà
to see thee. Two hands my (are) exalted to protect thee, love I,

10. 11.
mertu - nà šenti àat meḥtiu ḥer maatu àu
love I the circuits of the two regions, the northern ones (are) in recollection. Is

12.
sešep - nek ṭep art àm sen χemu-k em ānti
received by thee a head of hair (?) from them, breezes thy (are) of incense.

13. 14.
hai senà nebt mertu iu-k em ḥetep er àuset-k à
Husband, brother, lord of love, come thou in peace to seat thy. O

àḥi nefer māā er pa-k t'er-ā sep sen àuk em àb
boy, beautiful, come to house thy at once, twice. Art thou coming.

15. 16.
šeta χet-k em ka Àmentiu àuset šeta àuf-k χent
Secret (are) things thy as bull of the Amentiu, place of secrecy (is) flesh thy in

17.
pa ḥennu hai em ren-k en ḥeq t'etta
the house of Ḥennu. Hail in name thy of prince of eternity.

18. 19.
iu - nek Ḥeru em neχt χersek-f ḥāu-k seqā - f
Comes to thee Horus with strength, delivers he limbs thy, collects he

nek *erṭuu* *per* *àm-k* 20. *āb* *t'et-k* *neter*
for thee emanations coming forth from thee. Approaches body thy the god

āāi *ḥetem - tu* *em* *àru-k* 21. *iu-k* *em* *ḥetep* *neb-n*
great, O closed up thou in attribute thy. Come thou in peace lord our

renp *em* *nem* 22. *se-k* *Ḥeru* *net' ḥra-k* 23. *māā*
rejuvenescent a second time. Son thy Horus avenges thee. Come

χent *pa-k* *bāḥu* *neter* *ḥet-k* *em* *mertu-k* 24. *àθi*
to house thy, inundate divine house thy with love thy. Sovereign,

χerp (?) *seṭ* *nes* *em* *suḥt* 25. *uā* *user* *peḥti*
chief, distinguished was it in the egg, only one, strong one, powerful one,

26. *se* *às* *pu* *àp* *χat* 27. *seχem* *seb* *ḥer* *mut-f*
son, in sooth, opener of the womb, divine power of Seb by mother his.

Column IX.

1. *χaker* *āāi* *mertu* 2. *àri* *er* *Àmentiu* *qennu-f* *aṭi*
Decorated one, great of love, working for the Amentiu, overthows he disaster.

3. *nebt* *ṭuaut* *ka* *Àmentiu* *mestu* *en* *Rā* *Ḥeru-χuti*
Lord of the underworld, bull of the Amentiu, image of Rā and Horus of the double horizon.

4. *χi* *ānnu* *en* *maa-f* 5. *iu-k* *en* *n* *em* *ḥetep* *sep sen* 6. *χersek-k*
Baby, beautiful in sight his, come thou to us in peace, twice. Repellest thou

nešeni-k *seḥer-k* *at* 7. *neb-n* *iu-k* *en* *n* *em* *ḥetep*
disasters thy, drivest away thou hap. Lord our, come thou to us in peace

sep sen 8. *hai* *renp* *māā* *em* *ḥetep* 9. *hai* *senà*
twice. Hail, rejuvenescent, come in peace. Hail brother,

10. *māà* *maa-tu-à* *net* *ḥeq* *t'etta* 11. *em* *urtu* *em* *urtu*
come, let see thee me, king, prince of eternity. Not let stop, not let stop

àb-k *neb-n* 12. *iu-k* *er* *pa-k* *àn* *sentti-k* 13. *pa*
heart thy lord our. Come thou to house thy not fear thou, O

s-āšt *āā* *àn maa* *àn setem* *t'eṭtu* *àn* *χer-ḥeb* 14. *à* *àḥi*
multiplying one, great, not seeing, not hearing. Says the precentor, "O boy,

neferi *māà* *er* *pa-k* 15. *paut* *neteru* *ḥer* *ḥeḥ* *er* *maa-k*
beautiful, come to house thy, the cycle of the gods (are) seeking to see thee.

χi *neb* *àp* *χat* 16. *set* *mertu - k* *ḥer* *ḥrà-k*
Child, lord, opener of the womb, baby, beloved (art) thou for face thy,

17. *āuāā* *menχet* *em* *àpt - s* 18. *se* *menχet* *per*
heir perfect, in opening it. Son perfect, coming forth

em *maa* *setem* 19. *ḥet* *meḥt* *en* *Àuset* *ḥer - k* *em*
from the god of hearing and seeing. O house, grieves Isis over thee, not

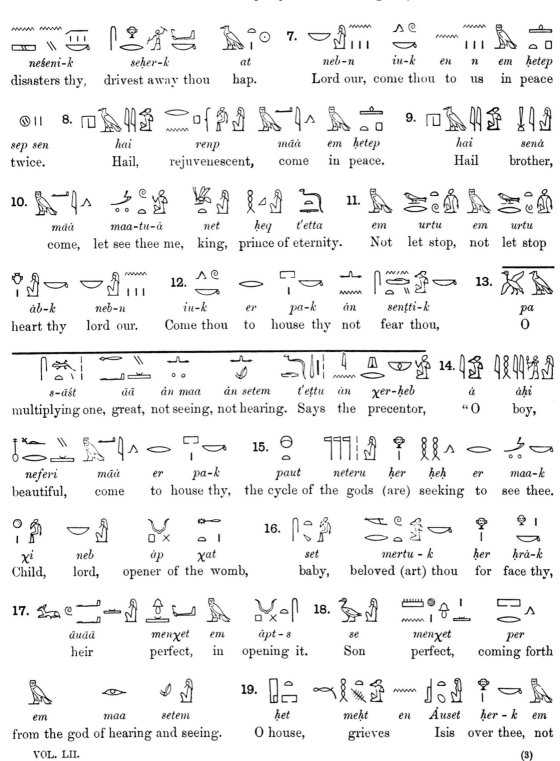

20.

ḥeru er àuset-k nehem tep-sen en mertu-k

go away from place thy. May be delivered head their by love thy,

21. 22.

àkebu - sen nek em àar mās tep Un-nefer

lament they for thee tying up the curls of the head. Un-nefer,

23.

nebt t'efau ser ur em šefi-f neter ḥer

lord of food, chief, mighty by terrors his, god, president

24. 25.

neteru meḥ-k utet su entek heru àu neteru

of the gods; inundatest thou, engendered are they. Art thou gentler than the gods.

26.
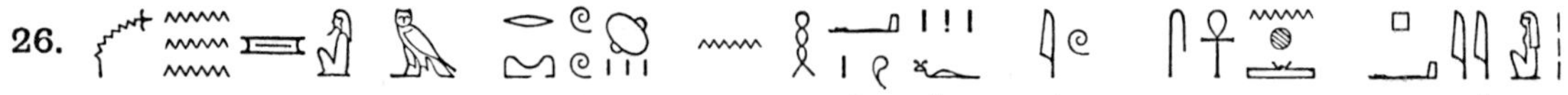

. . . . em erṭuu en ḥāu-f àu seānχ pāi

The liquid of the emanations of limbs his (is) for making live the dead

27. 28.
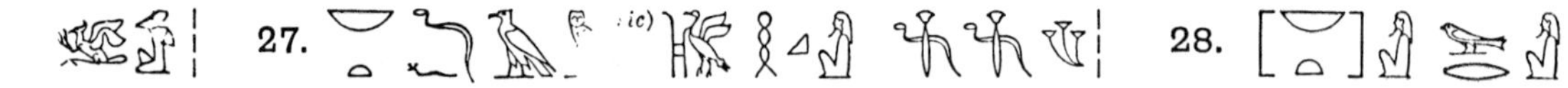

reχiu nebt t'efau ḥeq uat'uat' nebt ur

and the living. Lord of food, prince of vegetables, the lord, great,

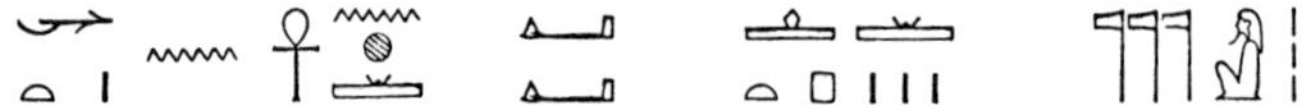

χet en ānχ ṭāṭā ḥetepu neteru

staff of life giving offerings (to) the gods and

Column X.

1. 2.

per χeru en χu Sešeta nebt nemmàt

sepulchral meals to the beatified dead. Sešeta lord of the couch,

3. 4.

nebt ut'au sešeta em χut sešep er trà-f

lord of the eyes hidden in the horizon, shining at time his,

5. *uben er ennu-f* — rising at period his. 6. *entek χu āper mau* — Thou art χu provided with splendour.

7. *sešep-k en àb en Àtmu* — Shinest thou at the left hand of Àtmu, 8. *maa-k em àuset Rā* — lookest thou from the seat of Rā

9. *sam maaui - tuf sāḥu - k* — collecting splendours his (in) form thy. 10. *āpi ba-k* — Flies soul thy

emχet Rā — after Rā, 11. *pesṭ-k em ṭūau ḥetep-k em māšer* — shinest thou at dawn, settest thou at twilight,

12. *hru neb pu un-nek* — day every to wit risest thou. 13. *un-nek em àb en Àtmu* — Risest(?) thou from the left hand of Àtmu

ḥeḥ t'etta χā-k — for ever and ever, risest thou. 14. *batu Nebṭ ḥetem embaḥ* — Accursed (is the) Lock, destroyed before

15. *àpi-tuf ḥer-baḥ qennu-f* — doom his, before failure his, 16. *un χer-f ān Sebàu* — is he turning back Sebau

neken tui ī er - f — attacker that coming against him. 17. *Àmseḥti āuāā -* — Àmseḥti heir

f erek — is he to thee. 18. *suaš - f neteru nebt* — Worship him gods all, 19. *ḥāā paut neteru* — rejoices the cycle of the gods

(3)*

em χesef-k 20. *urśu-k χer Rā hru neb* 21. *tut maa-k*
in meeting thee. Occupation thy (is) with Rā day every, steadily lookest thou

em àbt 22. *tut maa-k en ānχiu* 23. *entek χu*
from the left, steadily lookest thou at the living. Thou art χu,

àtennu en Rā 24. *iu nek* (*sic*) *paut neteru ṭemθ* 25. *ḥer*
the vicar of Rā, comes to thee the cycle of the gods all at

ṭep-k hen em ḥrà-k 26. *peḥ nesert-s er χeft-k*
head thy invoking at face thy. Reaches flame its (*sic*) unto enemies thy.

27. *ḥāā erek en n ànq-nek qesu-k* 28. *àpi-tu*
Rejoicing therefore (is) to us (when) collected hast thou bones thy, reckoned up (is)

t'et-k hru neb
body thy day every.

Column XI.

1. *āq-k mà Åtmu er ennu-f àn ḥepḥep*
Enterest thou like Åtmu at hour his, without turning,

2. *t'art-nek àaχeχ-k* 3. *àp uat āba-f*
strengthened (are) for thee bones thy. Åp-uat presents he

nek ṭu neka-f sam-ta 4. *iu-nek* (*sic*) *nebt*
to thee a mountain, hews out he a burial place. Comes to thee the lord of

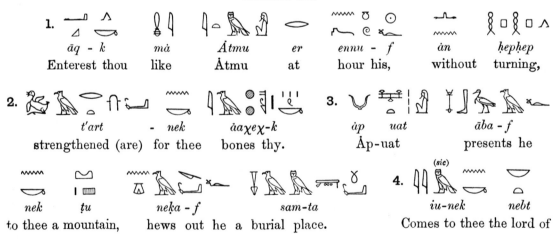

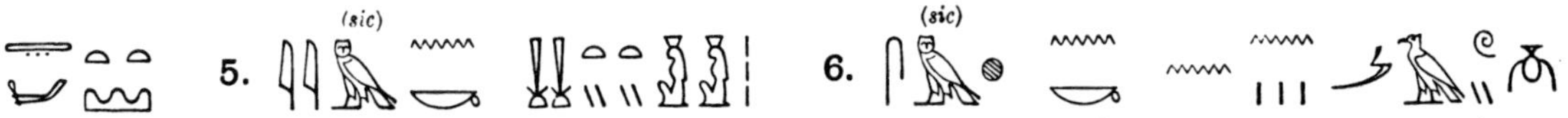

Tasertet 5. *iu-nek* *sentiti* 6. *seχem* *nek* *en-n* *maui*

Tasert, come to thee the two sisters. Obtained hast thou for us splendours,

7. *tut - sen* *ḥāu-k* *nek* *em* *kemtu* 8. *ḥeḥ* *er*

collect they limbs thy for thee from the mutilations, seeking to

ennu *χa - k* 9. *enen* *āu* *ḥer-sen* *seχent-k er* *šennu-n*

put together body thy. Those impurities (which are) upon them set thou upon hair our,

10. *iu-k* *en - n* *tem* *seχau - k* 11. *iu-k* *em*

come thou to us without unpleasant recollection thy. Come thou in

àru-k *ḥer* *ḥetep* *ta* 12. *ruàa* *tenten - k* *ḥetep-k* *en-n*

attribute thy as prince of the earth, lay aside impetuosity thy, rest thou upon us

nebt 13. *šeṭu* *āuāā* *taui* 14. *neter* *uā* *menχet*

O lord. Be proclaimed heir of the two earths, god, only one, completing

seχeru *en* *neteru* 15. *hen - nek* *neteru* *nebu* 16. *iu-k* *àu*

the designs of the gods. Invoke thee the gods all, come thou to

pa-k *àn* *senṭ-k* 17. *mertu - tu* *Rā* *mertu-tu* *erpati - k*

house thy, not fear thou. Beloved art thou Rā, beloved art thou of Likenesses thy.

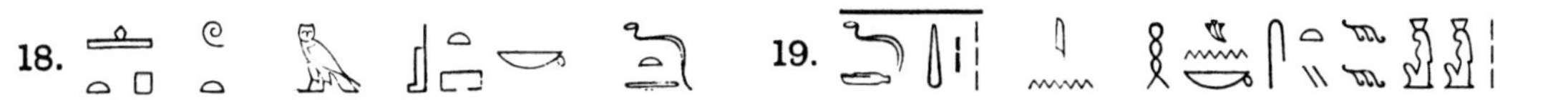

18. *ḥetep - tu* *em* *àuset-k* *t'etta* 19. *t'eṭtu* *àn* *ḥenksti*

Restest thou on seat thy for ever." Say the women with flowing hair,

20. *à àḥi nefer māā er pa-k* 21. *qa sep sen sa-k*
"O boy, beautiful, come to house thy, exalted, twice, back thy

er pa-k àu neteru ḥer àuset-sen 22. *hai māā em ḥetep*
(is) to house thy. Are the gods upon seat their. Hail, come in peace,

23. *net māā em ḥetep* 24. *se-k Ḥeru er net' ḥrà-k*
king, come in peace. Son thy Horus (is) for avenging thee.

25. *ṭā-k āu ur er erpati-k* 26. *ḥai-n*
Give thou unpleasantness great to two Likenesses thy. Weep we

ḥer-k em χentàu-k 27. *χi mà mertu maa-k* 28. *māā*
for thee at sepulchres thy. Baby how lovely to see thee! Come,

māā en-n ur χau-k mertu-n
come to us great one, protect thou love our.

Column XII.

1. *iu-k er pa-k àn sentti-k* 2. *à neteru àmu pet*
Come thou to house thy, not fear thou. O gods in heaven,

3. *à neteru àmu ta* 4. *à neteru àmu ṭuaut*
O gods on earth, O gods in the underworld,

5. *à neteru àmu . . . .* 6. *à neteru àmu*
O gods in the watery deep, O gods who are among

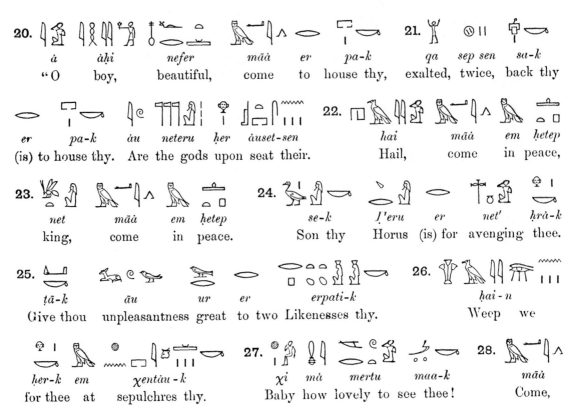

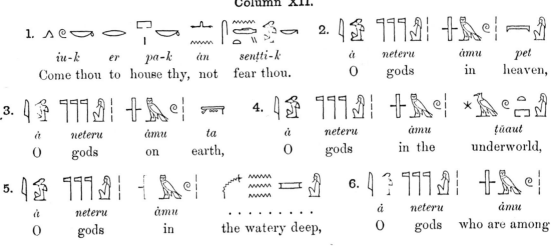

7. 8.

śesu . . . . śes-n χer nebt nebt mertu senȧ

the followers of the deep, follow we after the lord, the lord of love. O Brother,

9. 10. (*sic*)

[sam] neb net'emt'em ȧhai mȧȧ nȧ sam

phallus, lord of love, hail! come to me, uniting

11. 12.

pet er ta χeper χebit em ta mȧn hab pet

heaven to the earth, becoming shadow on the earth daily. Messenger of heaven

13. 14.

er taiu ȧhai mȧȧ - n ḥnā-t t'a

to earth, hail, come we with thee (?), the impregnator

15.

ḥemt em nut ḥeḥ neb-n śem-ȧ ta er hau

of the women in the town (who) seek lord our. Traverse I the earth towards

16. 17.

neb-n mȧȧ - nȧ hab pet er taiu erṭā iu

lord our. Come to me messenger of heaven to the earth. Is given to come

18. 19.

neter er ȧuset-f sensen em nefu er fent-k ȧu nef em

the god to seat his. Is breathing of winds to nose thy. Is the wind with the

20. 21.

nebt em ḥet - āt-f hai Rā net' su ȧn bu-k

lord in palace his. Hail, Rā avenged is he, (are) not disasters thy

22. 23.

erek ȧri ṭu t'er ȧb ȧb-ȧ maa-k āu net

to thee making evil. The limit of the desire of heart my is to see thee, heir, king,

24., 25.

χi ānnu hai neb mertu māȧ - nȧ neb

babe, beautiful! Hail, lord of love, come to me, O lord,

26., 27.

maa-ȧ-θ mȧn senȧ māȧ maa - en - n θ āāui-ȧ ur

may see I thee daily! Brother, come, may see we thee! Two hands my mighty

28.

ȧu net' ḥrȧ-k āāui-ȧ qa sep sen ȧu χau-k

(are) for avenging thee, two hands my exalted, twice, (are) for protecting thee,

Column XIII.

1., 2.

t'a nebt neχen χi ȧu net' neb-n nuk

male, lord, babe, child, to avenge lord our. I am

(sic) 3.

set en Seb ȧb-k er-ȧ renp ȧnȧs er

the daughter of Seb [not] depart thou from me, increasing except at

4.

trȧ-f šem-ȧ uat t'er iu mertu-k er-ȧ

time his. Traverse I the ways because comes love thy to me.

5., 6.

χennu-ȧ ta ȧn urṭu-ȧ em ḥeḥ-k ȧu nebȧt er-ȧ

Fly over I earth, not rest I from seeking thee. Is a flame to me

7., 8.

en mertu-k hai māȧ maa-ȧ-θ rem-ȧ en

of love thy. Hail, come let see me thee. Weep I at

9.

uā-k iu-k nȧ em χeχ t'er ȧb-ȧ en maa-k

loneliness thy. Come thou to me in haste for the limit of desire my is to see thee,

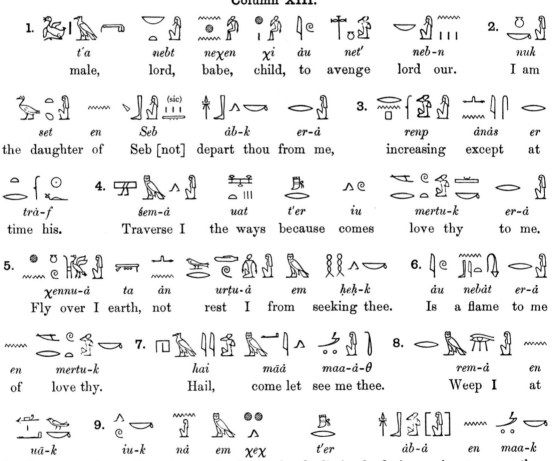

mȧ ur-k er neteru 10. *ȧn un šu em ṭuau*
inasmuch as greater art thou than the gods. Not is there cessation in glorifying

ka-k 11. *māā er pa-k ȧn senṭti-k* 12. *se-k Ḥeru*
ka thy. Come to house thy not fear thou. Son thy Horus

ȧḥi šen en pet 13. *seχet em sepeḥu ȧn senṭti-k*
embraces the circuit of heaven. Sovereign, repulsing not fear thou.

14. *se-k Ḥeru er net' ḥrȧ-k* 15. *seχer-f nek Semi*
Son thy Horus (is) for avenging thee. Overthrows he for thee the *Semi*

nebt 16. *hai nebt emχet-ȧ em ḥet'* 17. *maa-ȧ-θ mȧn*
and the Lock. Hail, lord after me illuminating, let see me thee daily.

ȧu seti en ḥāu-k en Puntet 18. *ṭūau-tu šeps-tu*
Is the smell of limbs thy of Punt. Adored art thou by the venerable women

em ḥetep 19. *ḥāā paut neteru temθ* 20. *iu-k en ḥemt-k*
in peace. Rejoices the cycle of the gods entire. Come thou to wife thy

em ḥetep 21. *apṭ ȧb-s en mertu-k* 22. *ḥept-s-tu ȧn*
in peace Flutters heart her at love thy, embraces she thee, not

ḥeru-k er-s 23. *χenteš ȧb-s er maa-k neferu-k*
depart thou from her. Straitened (is) heart her to see thee and beauties thy.

24. *ḥeru - nek - s em pa šeta* 25. *χersek-s ṭu ȧri*
Finished for thee has she in the house secret, destroyed has she the evil which is

ḥāu-k 26. *ȧuset-ā mȧ enti ȧn χeper-f* 27. *ṭā-k ānχ*
in limbs thy and the sickness as if never existed it. Art given thou life

em ḥetep ḥemt 28. *ȧhai χuau-k meḥi em*
by the best of a wife. Hail protectest thou the inundation in the

seχet Ṭep-ȧḥet em hru pen 29. *pert āat sep qesn ȧn mȧtet-f*
fields of Tepahet on day this, corn much disaster lacking without like its.

Column XV.

1. *rerem-nek aha em χeru-s* 2. *mertu-k t'er*
Weeps aloud for thee the cow with voice her, love thy (is) the limit of

ȧb-s 3. *apṭ ȧb-s χent-k eres* 4. *ḥapt-s ḥāu-k*
desire her. Flutters heart her, shut up art thou from her. Embraces she limbs thy

em āāiu-s 5. *iu - nek em χeχ ki t'eṭ em ḥetep* 6. *net' - nes -tu*
with two hands her, coming to thee in haste, otherwise said in peace. Avenges she thee

mā ȧri er - ek 7. *sut'a - s - nek ȧuf-k er qesu-k*
on account of what is done to thee. Makes healthy she for thee flesh thy upon bones thy.

8. *ṭes - s - nek fent-k er ḥāt-k* 9. *seqā - s nek qesu-k tem-tu*
Attaches she for thee nose thy to face thy. Collects she for thee bones thy all.

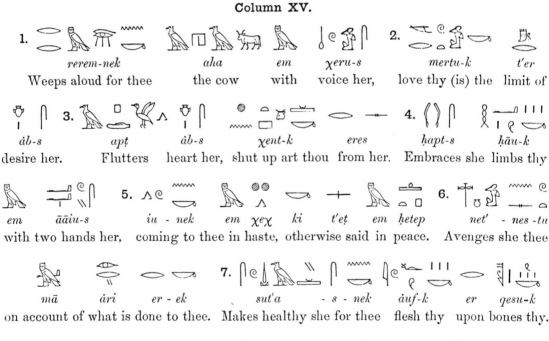

10. *ḥer - sa mertu-à maa ḥrà-k* 11. *àhai hen er*

in consequence of desire my to see face thy. Hail, invocation at the

12. 13. *re ḥet-k χuau - tu sep sen em ḥetep hai sep sen*

door of temple thy. Protected art thou, twice, in peace. Hail, twice,

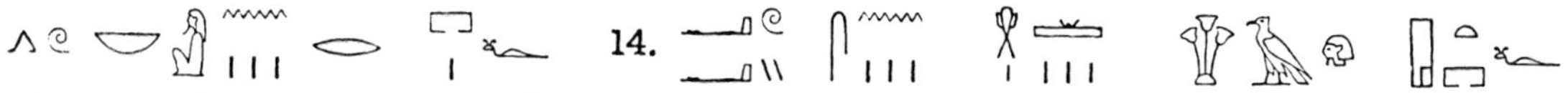

14. *iu neb-n er pa-f āāui sen sau ḥa ḥet-f*

comes lord our to house his. Two hands their (are) protectors behind temple his.

15. 16. *iu neb-n em ḥetep ḥer àuset-f men-tu em pa-k àn*

Comes lord our in peace upon seat his. Established (art) thou in house thy, not

17. 18. *sentti-k à qa-θ sep sen neb - n em ka*

fearest thou. O exalted (art) thou, twice, lord our. Do not cry,

19. 20. *ḥer neter āāi iu-k em ḥetep māāt per-k χer*

departing god great. Come thou in peace veritable. Comest forth thou to

21. 22. *Rā seχem em neteru heni māà em ḥetep maa-à-θ*

Rā victorious among the gods. O gracious one come in peace. May see I thee,

23. *χi iu-k em àru-k en χi hai χer*

child, come thou in attributes thy of Baby. Hai falls down.

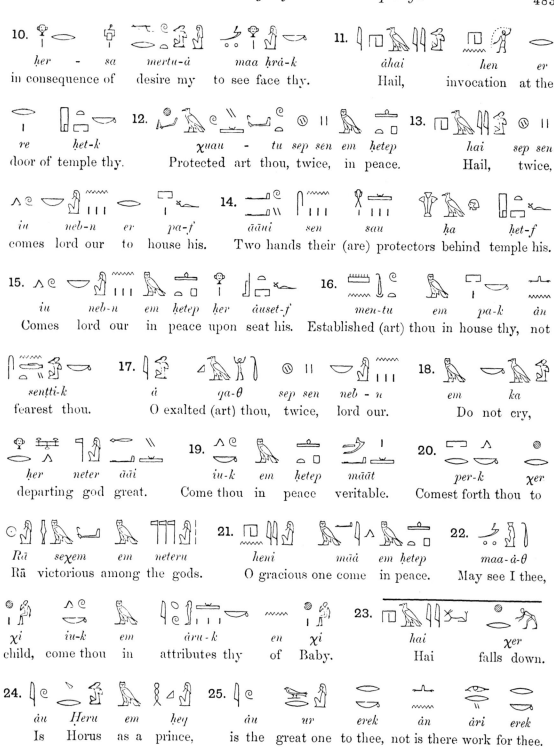

24. 25. *àu Ḥeru em ḥeq àu ur erek àn àri erek*

Is Horus as a prince, is the great one to thee, not is there work for thee.

26. *θes-tu em uben iu* (sic) *senȧti* 27. *pa mertu*
Exalted (art) thou in circling, come (?) the two sisters. The beloved of

ȧtf-f nebt θeθheḥtu 28. *ša - nek ȧbu paut neteru*
father his, lord of rejoicings. Delightest thou the hearts of the cycle of the gods;

29. *ȧpeš neter ḥet-k em neferu-k* 30. *nerȧu paut*
illuminating divine house thy with beauties thy. Fear the cycle of

neteru em šefi-k
the gods before might thy.

Column XIV.

1. *ta setet en ḥeri-k* 2. *nuk ḥemt-k ȧri iu-k* (sic)
The earth trembles at fear thy. I am wife thy making progress (?) thy,

3. *senȧt χut en senȧ-s* 4. *māȧ maa-ȧ-tu nebt*
the sister protector of brother her, come may see I thee lord

mertu-ȧ 5. *qa sep sen āā ȧru māȧ maa-ȧ-tu* 6. *nu*
of love my. Exalted twice great of attribute, come may see I thee. Baby

šem χi māȧ maa-ȧ-tu 7. *rerem-nek taiu taiu*
advancing, child, come, may see I thee. Weep for thee districts and lands,

8. *ḥeteb nek ȧat mȧ entuk Sešeta* 9. *rerem - nek pet ta*
lament for thee the zones inasmuch as thou art Sešeta Weep for thee heaven and earth

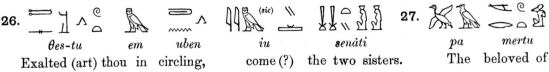

šen nebt en āten 10. *māā er pa-k Āusar āp*
circuiting, O lord of the disk. Come to house thy Osiris messenger of

neteru 11. *un - nek maa-k maa-k ām-sen*
the gods. Are opened for thee two eyes thy (that) mayest see thou with them.

12. *χersek-k ḥaθātu* 13. *ṭā-k ḥet't'au en ta em*
Drivest off thou rain storms, grantest thou to be lightened the earth by the

sati qerḥ 14. *māā er pa-k Āusar χent Āmentiu māā*
radiance of night. Come to house thy Osiris at the head of the Amentiu, come

er pa-k 15. *per em χat ārāt em ṭep-f* 16. *seḥet'*
to house thy, coming forth from the belly of the uræus upon head his. Light up

maa-f taiu neteru 17. *θes- tu sep sen seru neb-n*
two eyes his the two earths and the gods. Exalted art thou, twice, prince lord our.

---

18. *sebāu-k er nemmāt ān un-nef* 19. *ṭeṭṭeṭ sep sen em*
Sebau thy (is) upon the block, not may rise up he. Established twice in

ren-k Ṭeṭ 20. *ḥāu-k nek Un-nefer ānχ ut'a senb*
name thy Tat. Limbs thy (are) to thee Un-nefer, life, strength, health!

21. *āuf-k nek urṭu - āb* 22. *Āusar nefer tu per*
Flesh thy (is) to thee, O still heart. Osiris, beautiful is that coming forth

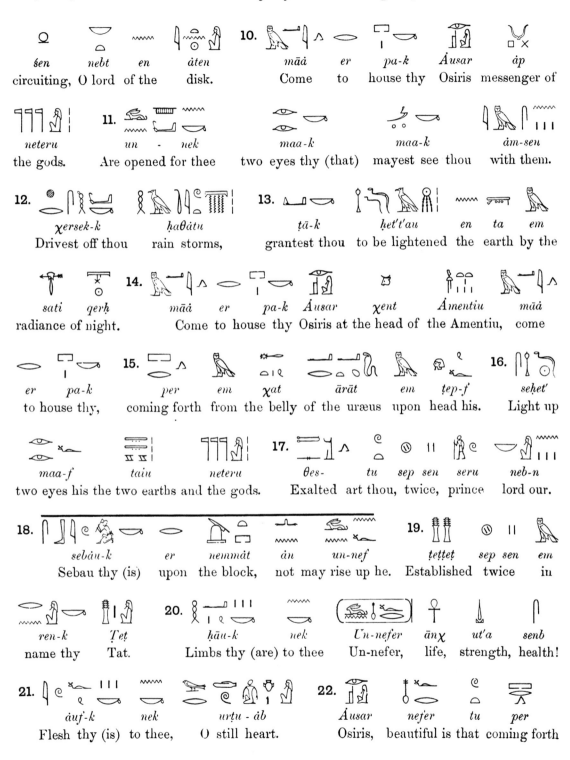

23. 24.
àm-k *Hu* *pu* *ṭep-re-k* *Tatanen* *àtf-k*
from thee. Hu to wit (is) utterance thy. Tatanen father thy (is)

25. 26.
ḥer *uθes* *pet* *er* *χent-k* *ḥer* *fṭu-s* *āpi*
for bearing up heaven for walking thy over four (quarters) its. Flies

27.
ba-k *em* *àbt* *un-nek* *em* *senen* *en* *Rā*
soul thy on the left hand, risest thou in the image of Rā.

28. 29.
seśep-tu *àmu* *ṭuaut* *em* *ḥāā* *neka-nek*
Receive thee those who are in the underworld with exultation. Opens a passage for thee

30. 31.
Seb *àm-f* *iu-sen* *nek* *em* *ḥetep* *māi - nek*
Seb through it. Come they to thee in peace, comest thou

em *ḥetep* *er* *Ṭeṭṭu*
in peace to Tattu.

Column XVII.

1. 2. 3.
θes - tu *erek* *Àusar* *θes - tu* *sep sen* *em* *ḥetep* *iu-nek*
Exalted art thou therefore Osiris. Exalted art thou, twice, in peace. Comes to thee

4.
Àuset *nebt* *χut* *mà* *utet-s* *uā* *sem* *neteru* *àu-s*
Isis lady of the horizon as engendered has she the ONE, the guide of the gods. Is she

5. 6.
àu *net'ti-k* *àu-s* *àu* *net'* *ḥrà-k* *net'ti-s* *ḥrà* *en* *Ḥeru*
for avenging thee, is she for avenging thee. Avenges she Horus,

10. *mut-k Nut iu-s nek em ḥetepet* 11. *qeṭäu -s-tu*
Mother thy Nut comes she to thee with peace offerings. Builds up she thee

em ānχ en χat-s 12. *ba-tu sep sen ṭeṭtu sep sen*
with the life of body her. Endowed with soul art thou, twice, established art thou, twice.

13. *ba nek sam t'a nebt ḥemt beti er šennu-k em*
A soul is to thee, phallus, impregnator, lord of women. (There is) unguent upon hair thy in

iu-k en Neter tatet 14. *beti er šennu-k ānti per t'esef*
coming thy to the Divine land. The unguent upon hair thy is *ānti* coming forth of itself.

15. *per māā em ḥetep sep sen* 16. *net äθi māā em ḥetep*
O coming one, proceeding in peace, twice! King, sovereign, come in peace.

17. *nebt Sau āāiu-s erek* 18. *Šenθit äb-s rer nek*
lord of Sais, two hands her (are) to thee, Senthit, heart her turns to thee.

19. *äuk em neter per em neter* 20. *mākaθä äu än un ḥrä*
Art thou like a god coming forth like a god . . . . never has been to the face of

χi-f 21. *šennu-k em māfek em t'et-f em iu-k em*
baby his. Hair thy (is) of emerald upon body his (*sic*) in coming thy into

seχet māfek 22. *šennu-k em χesbet nes χesbet* 23. *äs-k*
the fields of emerald. Hair thy (is) of blue appertaining to lapis lazuli, for thou art

24.
χesbet àu ḥer šennu-k ànememu-k ḥāu-k nek
blue above hair thy. Skin thy and limbs thy (are) to thee

25. 26.
em bàa qemāt qesu-k nubàu em ḥet′ mà nuk em
of steel southern. Bones thy (are) moulded of silver, as I am from

27. 28.
χi θesti-k nek em māfek ki t′eṭ sti er
a babe. Teeth thy (are) to thee of emerald, otherwise said, the unguent from

šennu-k em ānti per t′esef
hair thy (is) of *ānti* coming forth of itself.

Column XVI.

1. 2.
ḥeru ṭep-k em χesbet Seb fa - f nek em
The top of head thy (is) of lapis lazuli. Seb loaded (is) he for thee with

3. 4.
ḥetepu seχenti-f neter per em fent-f āuāā
peace offerings. Conveys he the god coming forth from nose his. Heir

5. 6.
ur per em Rā sems seru nefer ḥrà ba
mighty coming forth from Rā. Eldest one, prince, beautiful of face. Soul

7.
ānχ enti Àstennu χi per em maa setem
living of Àstennu. Babe coming forth from the god of seeing and hearing.

8. 9.
sems seru àturti āu en Seb ṭā-f nek
Eldest one, prince of the two regions, heir of Seb. Gives he to thee

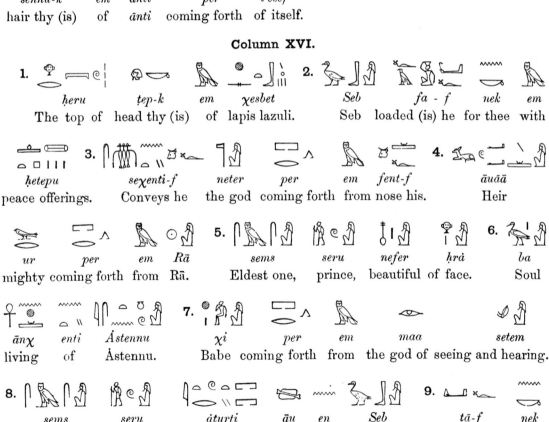

7. *set àri t'a en àtf-s* 8. *Nebert'er per em*

the woman acting as engenderer of father her, Nebert'er coming forth from

ma Ḥeru šepset betu em Rā 9. *per em t'efet'*

the eye of Horus. The venerable one advancing like Rā, coming forth from the pupil

em mat Àtmu 10. *t'er uben Rā em sep ḥetepi iu-f pu*

of the eye of Àtmu when rose Rā for time first. Gone out has it.

COLOPHON.

1. . . . . . *àu em* . . . . *m* . . . . *u*[a] 2. *neter ḥen en neter ḥet en*

. . . . prophet of the temple of

Ḥet 3. *nāuu en Àmen* 4. *en sa χemt neter ḥen Nesi-Àmsu*

Het, the scribe of Àmen of the order third, prophet Nesi-Àmsu

5. *se en neter ḥen* 6. *Pe-ṭā-Àmen-suten-taiu* 7. *àrit en àḥi*

son of the prophet Pe-ta-Àmen-suten-taiu, born of the sistrum bearer

en Àmen-Rā 8. *Ta-šere en ta mut-set* 9. *Nesti-tuurā*

of Àmen-Rā, Ta-šere, mother her was Nesti-tuurā.

10. *nāuu en renpit met' sen àbeṭ ftu še en P-āa ānχ ut'a*

Written in year twelve month four of the sowing season of the King, life, [strength,

senb 11. *Àrksantrs se en Àrksantrs* 12. *ḥā neter àtf*

health,] Alexander the son of Alexander. First divine father,

[a] The transcription of this line is very doubtful.

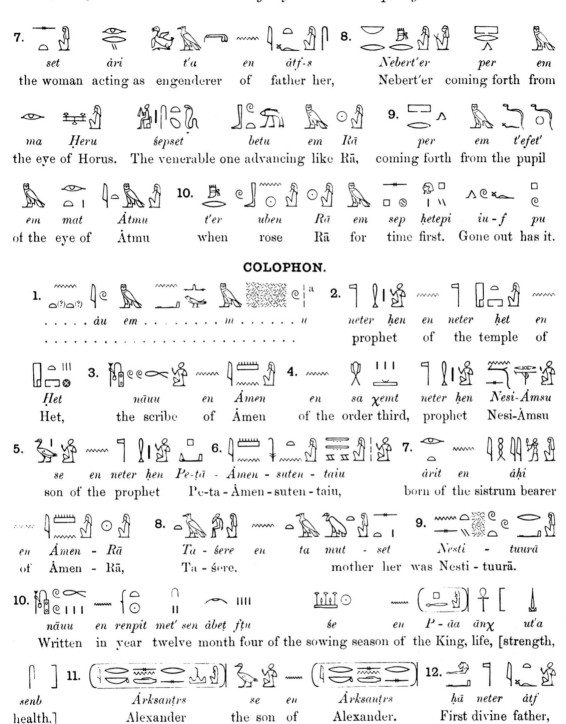

neter ḥen en Åmen-Rā suten neteru neter ḥen 13. *en Ḥeru p Rā*
prophet of Åmen-Rā king of the gods, prophet of Horus the Sun,

pa śere āaā ur ḥetep en Åmen neter ḥen 14. *en Åmen*
the child great very first of Åmen, prophet of Åmen

sept ābu neter ḥen en χensu ḥer åb Benent 15. *neter ḥen*
provided with two horns, prophet of Chonsu within Benenet, prophet

en Åusar ur pa åśta neter ḥen en Åusar ḥer åb
of Osiris, great one of the persea trees, prophet of Osiris within

16. *Åśer neter ḥen en Åmen-qa-åuset ḥer åb Åpi* 17. *āb*
Åśer, prophet of Amen exalted of throne within the Apts, priest

en p Rā ḥetep ḥet en pa Åmen ḥer sa sen 18. *nāuu*
of the Sun, first one of the temple of the house of Amen in order two, scribe,

neter net en Åmen ḥer sa sen åtennu 19. *en Åmen en*
inspector of Åmen of order two, vicar of Åmen in

sa sen sa ftu neter ḥen en Nefer-ḥetep pa neter 20. *āaā*
order two and order four, prophet of Nefer-ḥetep the god great,

neter ḥen en Nefer-ḥetep pa śere neter ḥen en Åusar Ḥeru
prophet of Nefer-ḥetep the child, prophet of Osiris, Horus,

21. *Ȧuset Nebt-ḥet en neter ḥet en Ḥet neter ḥen en Ȧmsu*
Isis, Nephthys of the temple of Het, prophet of Ȧmsu,

neter ḥen en 22. *Ȧtmu nebt Ḥet-seχem ȧtennu en Nefer-ḥetep en pa ftu*
prophet of Atmu, lord of Ḥet-sechem, vicar of Nefer-ḥetep of the four

23. *sa neter ḥen en ḥetep en Nefer-ḥetep neter ḥen en na neteru*
orders, prophet first of Nefer-ḥetep, prophet of the gods.

THE LITANIES OF SEKER.

Column XVIII.

1. *entāu en ȧn en Seker er ḥer šetai t'eṭtu*
The litanies which brought in Seker in addition to the mysteries recited.

2. *ȧ seṭennu per em χat* 3. *ȧ se semsu nu*
Hail prince coming forth from the womb. Hail son eldest of the

paut ḥetepi 4. *ȧ nebt ḥrȧu āšt χeperu* 5. *ȧ rer*
cycles first. Hail lord of faces many and becomings. Hail circle

en nub em er - pau 6. *ȧ nebt āḥā ṭāt renpit* 7. *ȧ nebt ānχ*
of gold in the temples. Hail lord of time, giver of years. Hail lord of life

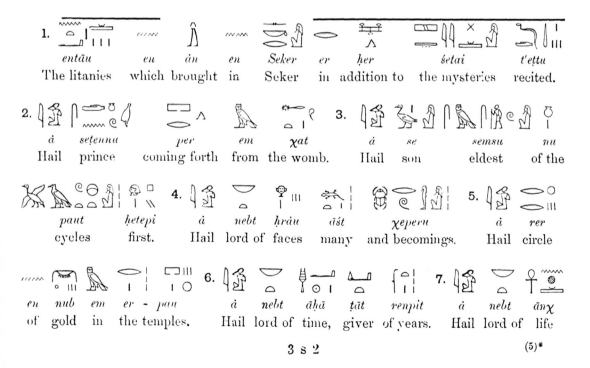

er neḥeḥ 8. *ȧ nebt ḥeḥ āšt ḥefnu* 9. *ȧ pesṭ*
for ever. Hail lord of millions many and myriads. Hail shining

ḥer uben ḥetep 10. *ȧ senet'em nef ȧḥeti* 11. *ȧ pa*
in rising and setting. Hail makes pleasant he throats. Hail the

nebt senṭet āāi setet 12. *ȧ nebt ḥrȧu āšt ārāt* 13. *ȧ*
lord of terror, great of trembling. Hail lord of faces many and uraei. Hail

χā em ḥet' nebt urerer 14. *ȧ pa sefi*
crowned with the white crown, lord of the *urerer* crown. Hail the baby

šeps nu Ḥeru ḥekennu 15. *ȧ se en Rā em uȧa*
venerable of Horus, praise. Hail son of Rā in the boat

ḥeḥ 16. *ȧ semi ḳaḥu māā er šetatet-k*
of millions. Hail guide of rest, come to secret places thy.

17. *ȧ pa nebt senṭeti χeper t'esef* 18. *ȧ urṭu - ȧb*
Hail the lord of fear self - produced. Hail still heart,

māā er nut-k 19. *ȧ ȧri hai māā er nut-k*
come to town thy. Hail making acclamation, come to town thy.

20. *ȧ pa meriti en na neteru neterit* 21. *ȧ s-*
O the Loved One of the gods and goddesses, O making

meḥ - f *māā* *er* *ḥet-k* 22. *ȧ* *ȧm* *ṭuaut*
to plunge himself, come to temple thy. Hail thou who art in the under world,

māā *er* *ābtu - k* 23. *ȧ* *māket* *su* *māā* *er*
come to offerings thy. O protector of them come to

ḥet-k 24. *ȧ* *rut* *kenkenememti* *er* *seśep* *ȧten*
temple thy. Hail growing moon-god for illuminating the disc.

25. *ȧ* *kektu* *śeps* *nu* *ḥet* *āat* 26. *ȧ* *nāi* *ennuḥ*
Hail flowers venerable of the temple great. Hail bringing the cordage

śeps *nu* *sektet* 27. *ȧ* *pa* *nebt* *ḥennu*
venerable of the Sekti boat. Hail the lord of the *ḥennu* boat,

renp - tu *em* *śetait* 28. *ȧ* *na* *baiu* *ȧker* *enti* *em*
becomest young thou in the secret place. Hail the souls perfect who are in

neter *χertet* 29. *ȧ* *pa* *sȧp* *śeps* *nu* *qemāt* *meḥit*
Neter - χert. Hail the visitor venerable of the south and north.

30. *ȧ* *pa* *ȧmen* *ȧn* *reχ* *su* *reχit* 31. *ȧ*
Hail the hidden one, not known (is) he to mankind. Hail

nememes *pa* *enti* *em* *ṭuaut* *er* *maa* *pa* *ȧten*
lightener of him who is in the under world to see the disc.

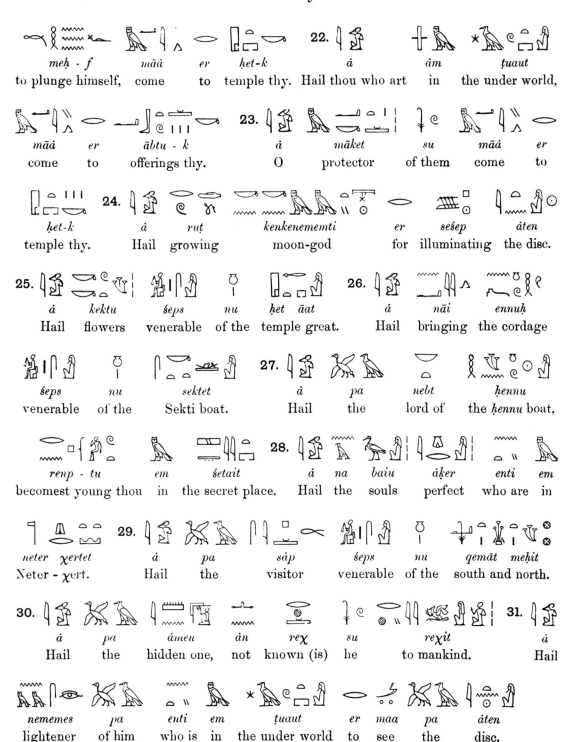

Column XIX.

1\. *à pa nebt atf ur em Ḥet - suten - ḥenen*
Hail the lord of the *atf* crown, great one in Ḥet - suten - ḥenen.

2\. *à āā šefi ermā nārt*
Hail great of might near Nārt.

3\. *à un em Uast*
Hail rising in Thebes,

aχaχ er neḥeḥ
flourishing for ever.

4\. *à Àmen Rā suten neteru sruṭ*
Hail Àmen - Rā king of the gods, making

ḥāu-f em uben ḥetep
to grow limbs his in rising and setting.

5\. *à ḥetep . . . . mennu ḥetepu em Re-stau*
Hail . . . . oblations offerings in Ru-stau.

6\. *à ṭāt àārāt ḥer ṭep neb-s*
Hail placing the uræus upon the head of lord its.

7\. *à smen ta*
Hail stablisher of the earth

ḥer àuset-f
upon seat its.

8\. *à un re en pa fṭu neteru āā enti em*
Hail opener of the mouth of the four gods great who (are) in

neter χertet
Neter - χert.

9\. *à ba ānχ en Àusar χā - f en Àāḥ*
Hail soul living of Osiris, crowner (is) he of the moon.

10\. *à àmen t'et-f em šetait āat em Ànnu*
Hail hiding body his in the coffin great in Heliopolis.

11\. *à*
Hail

netrà àmen Àusar em neter χertet 12. *à ḥetep ba - f en*
powerful one, hidden one, Osiris in Neter-χert. Hail uniting soul his to

pet àu χeft-f χer 13. *t'eṭ-nek Àuset neterit χeru*
heaven, is enemy his fallen. Says to thee Isis goddess crying,

hai em àtur 14. *peχχa àbṭ āb em ḥāt*
"Hail from the river separating the *àbṭu* fish pure from the front

15. *uàa en Rā nebt àp χeper em θeḥḥutu*
of the boat of Rā, lord of excretion turning into the rejoicing gods.

16. *suḥt χeper em ḥen ḥesq ṭepu* 17. *nu χak-en-àbu*
The egg becoming Ḥen, cutting off the heads of the rebels

em ren-s pui nebt Ṭep-àḥet 18. *nebt àp ī-tu em*
in name her that of lady of Tep-àḥet. Lady of excretion, comest thou in

ḥat ṭepu em ren-s pui 19. *en Ḥet-ḥert nebt māfek*
front of the heads in name her that of Hathor lady of emerald,

nebt Uast 20. *ī-tu em ḥetep em ren-s pui en Ḥet-ḥert*
lady of Thebes. Comest thou in peace in name her that of Hathor

nebt Uast 21. *ī - tu em ḥetep Tait em ren-s pfi en*
lady of Thebes. Comest thou in peace Tait in name her that of

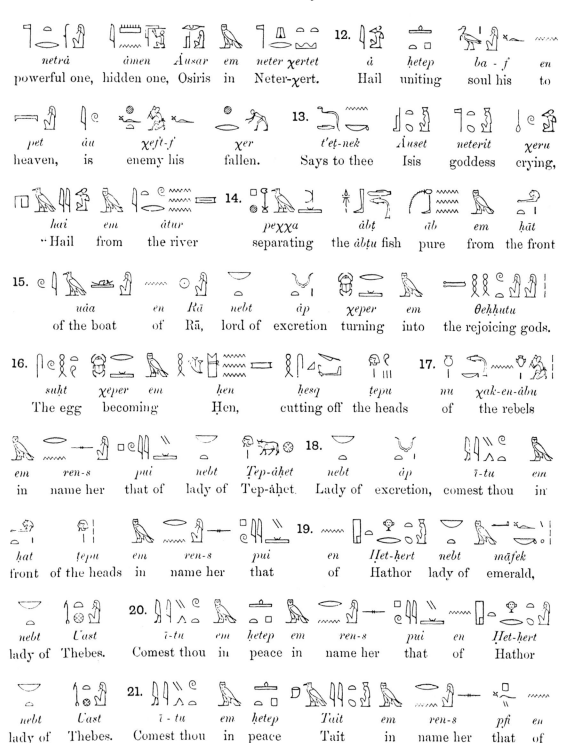

22. *nebt ḥetep ı-tu em ḥāt er seχer χeft-s* 23. *em ren-s*
lady of peace. Comest thou in front to overthrow enemy her in name her

pfi en Ḥet-ḥert nebt Ḥet-suten-ḥenen 24. *Nub ī - tu em*
that of Hathor lady of Ḥet-suten-ḥenen. Golden one, comest thou in

ḥetep em ren-s pfi en Ḥet-ḥert 25. *nebt Àneb*
peace in name her that of Hathor lady of Memphis. . . . .

ḥetep-tu ermā Neb-er-t'er em rent pui en Ḥet-ḥert nebt
restest thou near Neb-er-t'er in name thy that of Hathor lady of

šet ṭešer uben nub ermā àtf-s 26. *em ren-s*
water red. Rises the golden one near father her, in name her

pui Bast šem em ḥeru 27. *pau ermā pau ur em*
that of Bast, advancing above the houses near the great double house in

ren-s pui en Sati 28. *Uat' taui sem*
name her that of Sati. Verdifier of the two lands, leader

neteru em ren-s pui Uat'it 29. *seχem Ḥet-ḥert*
of the gods in name her that of Uat'it. Gains the mastery Hathor

em Sebàu en àtf - s em ren-s pfi en Seχet 30. *seχem*
over the Sebau of father her in name her that of Seχet. Gains the mastery

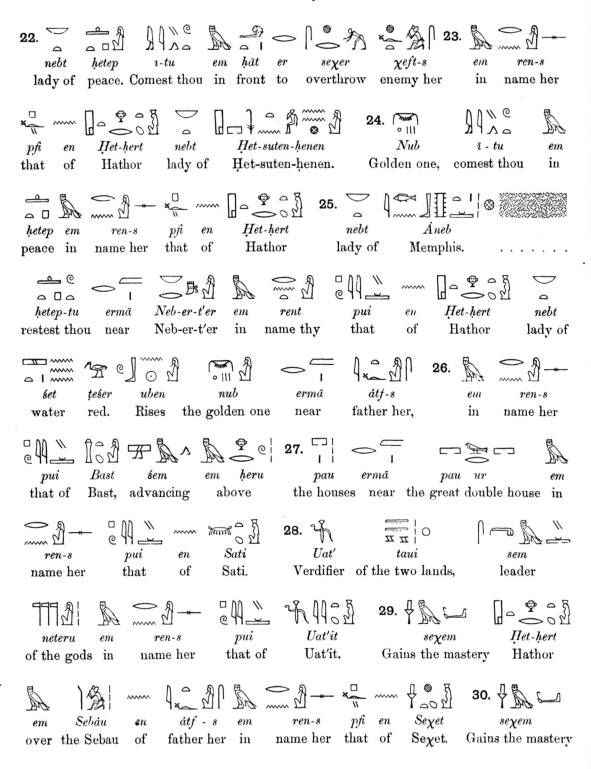

Uat'it em neferi em ren-s pți en nebt Ámmu

Uat'it over the fire in name her that of lady of Ammu.

31.

ānti em țep samu-s em ren-s pți en Nit

Perfume (is) upon head and hair her in name her that of Neith.

Column XX.

1. … 2.

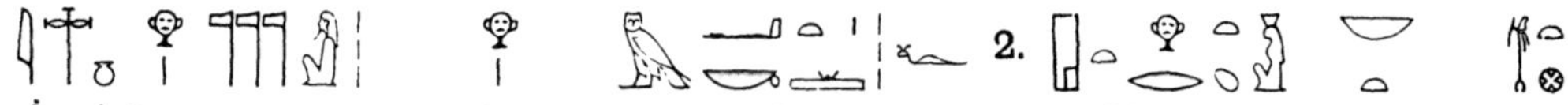

Ánet' ḥrȧ neteru her mȧket-f Ḥet-ḥert nebt Uast

Hail gods on account of virtues his! Hathor lady of Thebes.

3. … 4. … 5.

Ḥet-ḥert nebt Suten-ḥenen Ḥet-ḥert nebt Țep-ȧhet Ḥet-ḥert

Hathor lady of Suten-ḥenen. Hathor lady of Țep-ȧhet. Hathor

6. … 7.

nebt Nehȧu Ḥet-ḥert nebt Reḥsau Ḥet-ḥert nebt

lady of Nehau. Hathor lady of Reḥsau. Hathor lady of

8. … 9.

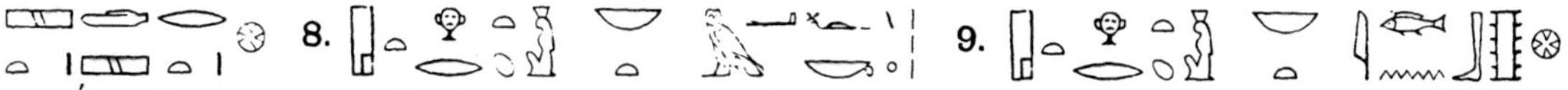

Śet-țeśert Ḥet-ḥert nebt Mȧfek Ḥet-ḥert nebt Áneb

Śet-Țeśert. Hathor lady of Emerald. Hathor lady of Memphis.

10. … 11. … 12.

Ḥet-ḥert nebt Uaua Ḥet-ḥert nebt Ámmu Ḥet-ḥert

Hathor lady of Uaua. Hathor lady of Ammu. Hathor

13. … 14.

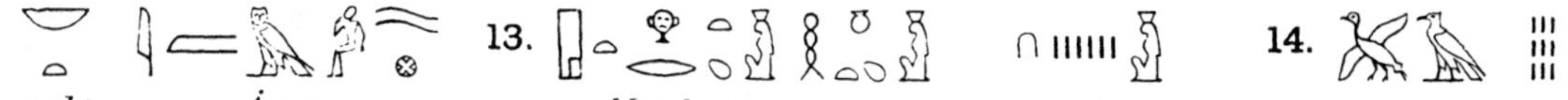

nebt Ámem Ḥet-ḥert ḥent XVI pa paut

lady of Amem. Hathor lady of Sixteen (Lycopolis). O ye nine

15.

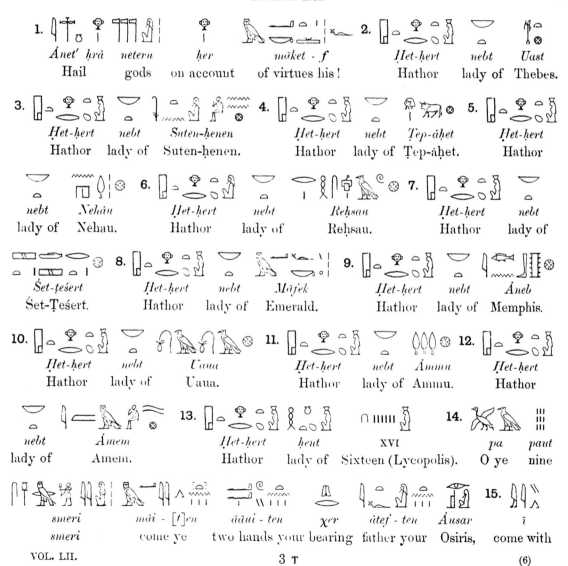

smeri māi-[t]en āāui-ten χer ȧtef-ten Ásar ī

smeri come ye two hands your bearing father your Osiris, come with

16.

neter *sa - ta* *sep* *ftu* *à* *seχet* *ḥeb* *sep sen* *àθi*
divine adorations. Times four. Hail crown of the festival, twice, sovereign.

17. 18.

à *net'em-tu* *χenemem* *mer-k* *à* *ānχ tu* *sep sen* *er* *neḥeḥ*
Hail rejoicest thou the nurses whom lovest thou. Hail livest thou, twice, for ever.

19. 20.

à *ḥeb - k* *en* *t'etta* *à* *senà* *ta* *ābba*
Hail makest festival thou for ever. Hail smeller of the earth advancing along

21. 22.

uat *à* *ṭeṭṭeṭ-θ* *em* *Ṭeṭṭeṭ* *ḥert* *à* *neter* *setem-k*
the ways. Hail established art thou in Tattu upper. Hail god hearest thou

sa-ta *hai* *setem-k* *sa-ta* *em* *re* *en* *neter* *septu*
adoration, hail hearest thou adoration from the mouth of the divine nomes.

23. 24.

à *bes* *em* *maatu-f* *se* *neter* *ḥen* *à* *setep*
Hail coming forth from two eyes his, son of the prophet. Hail protected

25.

sa *χeft* *t'eṭ-k* *à* *māku - à* *P-āa* *ḥer* *àri* *mer-k*
by amulets when speakest thou. Hail protect me O king to do pleasure thy.

26. 27.

à *māku-à* *P-āa* *ḥer* *àri* *ḥesu-k* *à* *ḥems* *māà*
Hail protect me O king to do will thy. Hail rester comes

28.

erek *urṭu* - *àb* *pu* *à* *se* *neter* *ḥen* *šeṭ* *nef*
to thee the resting of heart to wit. Hail son of the prophet, recited is for him

ḥeb 29. *à* *ṭeṭṭeṭ* *ren* *em* *Ṭeṭṭeṭ* *ḥert* 30. *à* *net'emi*
the festal ritual. Hail established is (thy) name in Tattu upper. Hail pleasant

sti *em* *Ṭeṭṭeṭ* *ḥert* 31. *à* *māà* *ṭer* *sebàu*
of odour in Tattu upper. Hail coming to destroy Sebau.

32. *à* *māà* *ṭūau* *neχen*
Hail coming to extol the Baby.

Column XXI.

1. *à* *ṭāṭ* *senṭet - f* *em* *χakàbu* 2. *à* *àr* *bakàu*
Hail giving of terror his in the evil-minded. Hail (thou) who art at work

šes *neb-f* *àn* *neter* *ḥen* *Bast* *àm-f* 3. *à* *χakàbu*
following lord his. not a prophet of Bast in him (*sic*). Hail evil-minded

mesṭ *neter* *ḥet* *ḥu* *menànàu* *er* *χeχ-f* 4. *à* *ī* *en*
hating the temple striking death from throat his. Hail cometh the

nebt *Ṭeṭṭeṭ* *ḥert* *ḥu - nef* *χakàbu* 5. *t'eṭṭu* *sep* *met' sas*
lord of Tattu upper, repulsed has he the evil-minded. Said times sixteen

sešep *ṭeχenu*
(by) players on tambourines.

6. *iu-f* *pu*
Gone out (is) it to wit.

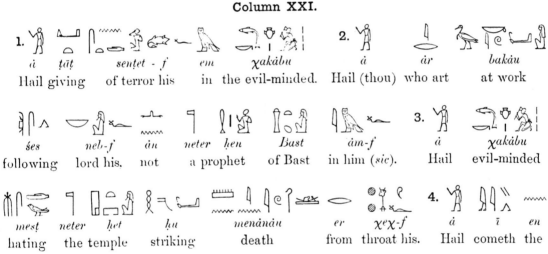

COLOPHON (*continued from page* 491).

The following fifteen lines are written in the same hand as the part of the colophon which gives the date, and appear to have been added some time after the other parts of the work were written.

1.
àu ren - sen men uaḥ àn sek er neḥeḥ embaḥ
Are names their established and increased, not destroyed for ever before

2.
Àusar Ḥeru Àuset Nebt-ḥet neteru neterit àpu enti ḥer šāt
Osiris, Horus, Isis, Nephthys, the gods and goddesses these who are upon book

3.
pen embaḥ neteru neterit er āu sen enti em neter
this in presence of the gods and goddesses whosoever are they who are in Neter

4.
χertet, sebχetu šetet āā àmu ṭūaut àu àri sen
χert, and the pylons secret great which are in the Nether-world. Are made they

5.
ha ren àpu àm ṭūaut àqert nàs-tu er sen
to come forth names these in the Nether-world mighty. Proclaimed art thou by them

6.
em uàa en Rā àu erṭā en sen per χeru ḥer āb en
in the boat of Rā, are given by them sacrificial meals upon the table of the

neter āā em χertu ent hru neb àu erṭā en sen qebḥ
god great in the course of day every. Are given by them fresh water

7.
sentrā mà suteniu net àqert àmu
and incense as to the kings of north and south mighty who are in the

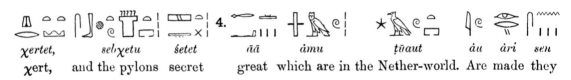

8\.
neter χertet àu erṭā sen per hi em χer ḥesiu
Neter χert. Is given by them coming forth and advancing among the obedient ones

9\.
ent Àusar χent Àmentiu àu erṭā sen hi sati àten
of Osiris at the head of the Àmentiu. Is given by them the falling of the rays of the disc

10\.
ḥer χat - sen hru neb àr se nebt en set nebt en
upon body their day every. Should person any of foreign land any whether

Neḥes Kaś χar menmen śāt pen
Black, Ethiopian, Syrian, remove book this, (or)

11\.
ruàa - f seḥen àn āb - tu χat - sen àn ṭāt - sen
carry off it a thief, not may approach body their, not may they give themselves

12\.
em qebḥ àn seseni-tu nefu àn āḥā-un se set
in the cool, not may breathe they breezes, not may arise for them a son or a daughter

13\.
er sati - un àn seχau-tu ren-sen ḥetep ta
for seed their, not may be remembered for them name their upon earth

14\.
àu mesu àn maa-u sati àten àr se nebt maa
for children, not may see they beams of the disc! Should person any see

śāt pen àri nef men ka ren - à χer
book this, and should work he that may be established *ka* my and name my among

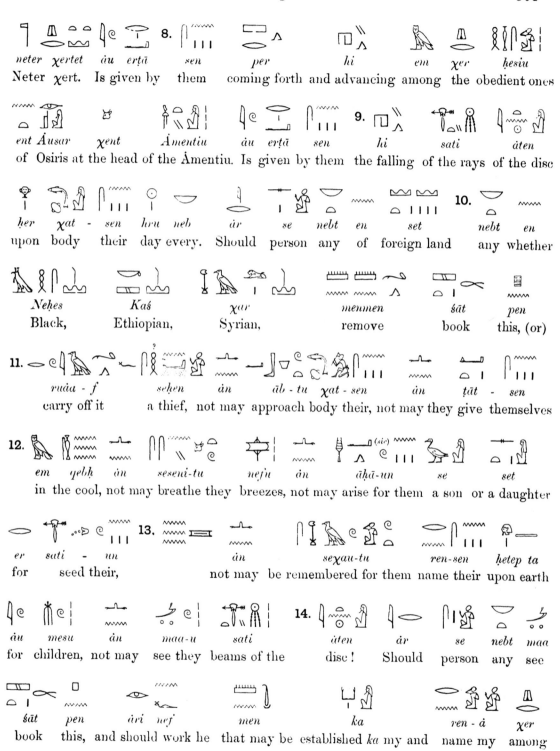

15. *ḥesiu* *àri* - *nef* *màtet* *emχet* *menànàu* (sic) - *f* *em*
the favoured ones, may there be done for him likewise after death his in

ṭebu *àru* *àri* - *nef* *nà*
retribution for what done has he for me.

THE OVERTHROWING OF ĀPEPI.

Column XXII.

1. *ḥā* *em* *šāt* *ent* *seχer* *Āpepi* *χeft* *nu* *Rā* *χeft*
Beginning of the book of overthrowing Apepi the enemy of Rā, the enemy

nu *Un-nefer* *ānχ* *ut'a* *senb* *māt-χeru* *àrit* *en* (sic) *pa* *Àmen* - *Rā*
of Un-nefer, life strength, health, triumphant, made for the temple of Amen-Rā

neb *nest* *taiu* *χent* *Àpit* *em* *χert*
lord of the thrones of the two lands, at the head of the Apts in the course

ent *hru* *neb*
of day every.

2. *Re* *en* *peḳas* *er* *Āpepi* *t'eṭtu* *ṭep-k* *Āpepi*
Chapter of spitting upon Apepi. Say, "Be spit upon thou Apepi.

sep *ftu* *àu* *enen* *en* *Rā* *ḥnā* *ka* - *f* *àu* *enen* *P-āa* *ḥnā*
Times four. Is resting Rā with *ka* his, is resting P-aa with

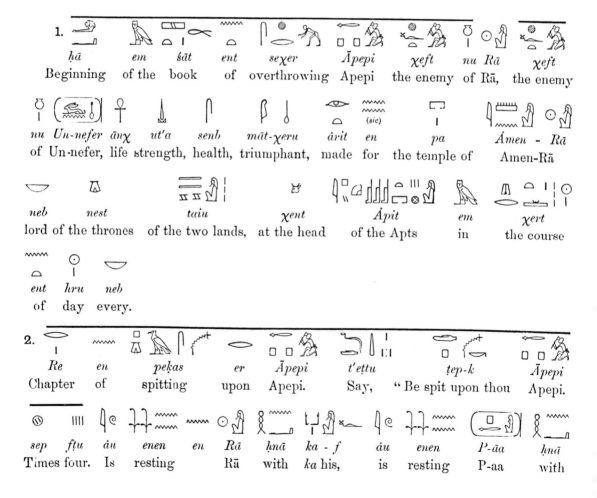

ka-f ī en Rā user ī en Rā 3. *neχt ī en*
ka his. Cometh Rā mighty, cometh Rā victorious, cometh

Rā qa ī en Rā sept ī en Rā em ḥāā
Rā exalted, cometh Rā dowered, cometh Rā with acclamation,

ī en Rā em nefer ī en Rā em suten ī en
cometh Rā in beauty, cometh Rā as king of the north, cometh

Rā em net ī en Rā em neteru 4. *ḥetepu ī en Rā*
Rā as king of the south, cometh Rā with divine oblations, cometh Rā

em mātχeru māā ȧrek en P-āa ānχ ut'a senb ṭer-k
with triumph, cometh then P-āa life, strength, health. Destroyed hast thou

nef χefti-f neb mā seχer-f nek Āpepi beḥen-f nek
for him enemies his all as overthrows he for thee Apepi, slays he for thee

Qeṭṭu ṭā-f ȧau en peḥti-k 5. *suaś-tu-f em*
Qettu, gives he adoration to might thy. Adores thee he at

χāu-k neb uben-k nef ȧm-sen mā seχer-f nek
risings thy all, risest thou for him in them as overthrows he for thee

χefti-k neb em χert ent hru neb
enemies thy all in the course of day every."

Re en sȧn Āpepi em ret ȧb t'eṭtu θes - tu ȧrek Rā
Chapter of defiling Apepi with the foot left. Say, "Exalted art thou therefore Rā,

6. *ṭer χefti-k pesṭ ȧrek Rā χefti-k χer māk*
destroyed are enemies thy, shine therefore Rā, enemies thy (are) fallen. Verily has

ṭer nek P-āa ānχ ut'a senb χefti-k neb Rā ṭer-k
destroyed for thee P-āa, life, strength, health, enemies thy all Rā, destroyed for thee are

χefti-k nebt em mit em ānχ māk Rā seχem-f ȧm-k Āpepi
enemies thy all in death in life. Verily Rā prevails he over thee Apepi,

7. *neśeni nesert - f erek seχem-s ȧm-k sept*
bristles flame his against thee, prevails it over thee turning

heh-s erek hi set-s er χefti nu Rā sep ftu
flame its against thee; falls flame its against the enemies of Rā. Times four.

hi set er χefti neb nu P-āa ānχ ut'a senb seχem
Falls the flame against enemies all of P-aa life, strength, health! Prevails

erek 8. *Rā ȧu χefti-k stutu er-k Rā em χut-k*
then Rā, is enemy thy trampled upon by thee, O Rā, in horizon thy.

ṭūau-tu ȧmu sekti rer - nek ȧḥiti uāa - k
Adore thee those who are in the *sekti* boat, go round thee the *ȧḥiti* and boat thy

em ḥāā nem-k χā em neteru - ȧbu em χennu
with acclamation, renewest thou festival in the valiant hearted within the

māāti 9. *ȧaut - nek Rā Ḥeru-χuti sep ftu*
māāt boat. Adoration to thee Rā Harmachis"! Times four.

Re en seśep māb er ḥu Āpepi t'eṭtu seśep en Ḥeru
Chapter of taking a lance to smite Apepi. Say, "Receives Horus

māb-f en bȧa qenqen – 10. *nef ṭepu χefti nu Rā seśep*
lance his of steel, shatters he the heads of the enemies of Rā. Receives

en Ḥeru māb - f en bȧa qenqen - nef ṭepu χefti nu P-āa
Horus lance his of steel, shatters he the heads of enemies of P-āa

ānχ ut'a senb māk Ḥeru seśep nef māb-f en bȧa ḥu -
life, strength, health. Verily Horus takes he lance his of steel, smites

11. *nef ṭepu Sebȧu em-baḥ uȧa-f θes-tu erek Rā*
he the heads of Sebȧu in front of boat his. Exalted art thou then, Rā,

sesunnu Sebȧu - k ȧru śāiṭ em Āpepi χer
hooked is Sebȧu thy; is made a slaughter of Apepi, fallen has

sami ent Qeṭtu θes - tu P-āa 12. *sesunnu*
the devil of the Fiend. Exalted art thou P-āa, hooked is

Sebȧu-k ȧri šāṭ em χefti-k χer Semi - f
Sebau thy, is made a slaughter of foes thy, fallen has Fiend his.

māā ȧrek Rā em χut-k šes-tu ent em kerȧut - sen
Come then Rā in splendours thy, follow thee those who are in shrines their,

ṭūau en sen tu 13. *em neferu - k uben - k pesṭ - k ȧn*
adore they thee in beauties thy, risest thou, shinest thou without

χefti-k ḥekau-k em sa ḥāu-k P-āa ṭūau-f
foes thy; words of power thy are as protectors of limbs thy. P-aa adores he

Rā ṭāt-f māb-f er Āpepi sešep-f besu ṭā-f set
Rā, gives he lance his against Apepi, takes he flame, gives he flame

ȧm-f 14. *sesunnu - f χat ent χefti-k set ȧm-k*
upon him, hooks he the accursed body of enemies thy; fire upon thee,

nesert ȧm-k set en ȧm-ten χefti nu P-āa[a] ānχ ut'a senb
flame upon thee, fire upon you enemies of P-aa life, strength, health,

ȧm - s - ten θes - tu ȧrek Rā sesunnu Sebȧu-k erṭā set
devours it you. Exalted art thou then Rā, hooked are *Sebau* thy, given is fire

15. *em Āpepi peshu - f em qeb ent pesṭ - f ȧhai*
upon Apepi, bites it into the bend of backbone his. Hail

[a] The signs in the cartouche are omitted on the papyrus.

set em Āpepi àu Rā em māu en māu seśep
fire upon Apepi! Is Rā in the breezes of the north winds, receive them

àqṭiu - f neteru àbu àmu χut 16. *ḥāā - tu em maa - f*
punters his the valiant hearted who are in the horizon and who exult at the sight of him.

seχer nef Sebàu seχem set em Āpepi hemhemti
Overthrows he Sebau, prevails the flame over Apepi, roars

Qeṭṭu ben set em ḥetep sep sen Rā Ḥeru-χuti àmmā ḥrà-k
Qettu, not are they in peace. Twice. O Rā - Harmachis give face thy

nefer en P-āa ānχ ut'a senb 17. *ṭer-k nef χefti-f*
beautiful to P-aa life, strength, health! Destroy thou for him enemies his

neb ṭūau - f Rā em un māt mātχeru Rā er Āpepi sep ftu
all, adores he Rā in very truth. Triumphs Rā over Apepi, times four,

mātχeru P-āa er χefti-f sep ftu
triumphs P-aa over enemies his, times four."

Re en qaàs Āpepi t'eṭtu 18. *qaàs qaàsu*
Chapter of binding Apepi. Say, "Fetter O fetterers,

qaàs Āpepi χeft pfi en Rā àm-k reχ àri nek Āpepi
fetter Apepi enemy that of Rā, not do thou know what is done to thee Apepi,

χesef àrek meter àm-k à ḥem em at-f neken-
meets therefore justice thee. O going back at season his, destroys

19. *f su t'esef serq àḥetit-f sau qaàs qaàs*
he him himself opening throat his holding firm the fetter. Fettering

ten àn Ḥeru netet - ten àn Rā àn benben - ten àn
to you cries Horus, tying to you cries Rā, not emission to you, not

tata - ten àn 20. *ḥeru-ten χer t'ebāu-f nàk-*
erection to you, not depart ye from under fingers his; be damned

ten àn Rā netet - ten àn Ḥeru àm χent àn maa
to you cries Rā, tying to you cries Horus in invisibility."

Re en seśep ṭes àu ḥu Āpepi t'eṭtu net'eràu
Chapter of taking a knife to smite Apepi. Say, "May have the mastery

sep sen menḥu 21. *seχer χeft nu Rā em ṭes-k*
twice the slaughterer and the overthrowing of the enemy of Rā with knife thy;

net'eràu sep sen menḥu seχer χeft nu P-āa em
may have the mastery twice the slaughterer and the overthrowing of the enemy of P-āa with

ṭes - k ṭepu - ten enen Sebàu t'at'anut - k pfi enen Āpepi
knife thy, heads of yours those O Sebau, and head thy that that of Apepi

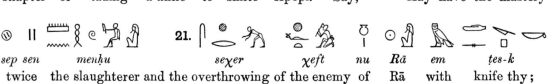

em *śāiṭ* **22.** *ābau* *ā* *em* *ṭes - f* *sept*
with slaughtering and fighting the hand with knife his. O providing

Septet *nesert* *Asbit* *ḥer* *tekau* *seχer - ten*
Septet flame; and Asbit presiding over the spark, overthrow ye

Qeṭṭu *em* *ṭes - ten* *beḥen - ten* *Unuti* **23.** *em* *ṭes - ten*
Qettu with knife your, slay ye Unuti with knife your,

śāiṭ - ten *ḥer* *ṭu - ten* *beḥen - ten* *ḥer* *ȧrit* *en*
slay ye because of injury your, slay ye because of what has been done

ten *meter* *en* *ȧm - ten* *ȧri - ten* *ḥer* *buṭu* *ȧru - en - ten*
to you; be there justice from you, do ye (it) because of the evil done to you.

mātχeru - Rā *er - ten* *Ḥeru* *beḥen - f - ten*
Triumphs Rā over you, Horus hacks in pieces he you."

Re *en* **24.** *erṭā* *set* *ȧu* *Āpepi* *t'eṭtu* *set* *ȧm - k* *Āpepi*
Chapter of placing fire against Apepi. Say, "Fire upon thee Apepi

χeft *pfi* *en* *Rā* *seχem* *ȧrek* *maa* *Ḥeru* *em* *ba* *em*
enemy that of Rā, prevails then the eye of Horus over the accursed soul and

χebit *en* *Āpepi* *qaqa* *χut* *maa* *Ḥeru* *em* *χeft*
shade of Apepi, gnaws the flame of the eye of Horus into enemy

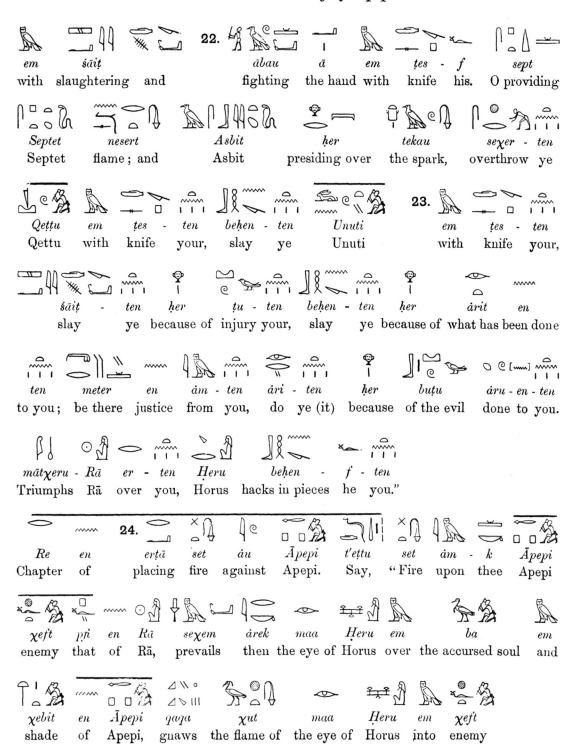

Column XXIII.

1. 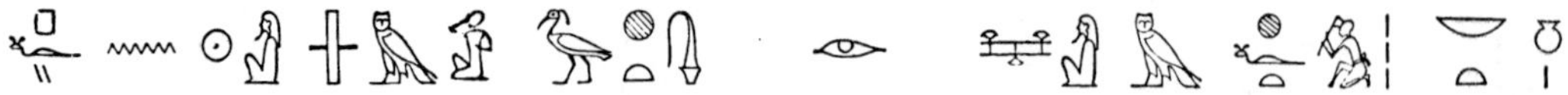

pfi en Rā àm χut maa Ḥeru em χefti nebt nu

that of Rā, eats the flame of the eye of Horus into enemies all of

P-āa ānχ ut'a senb em mit em ānχ t'eṭ - ten em ḥekau χeft

P-āa, life, strength, health, in death in life." Speak ye with [these] words of power when

erṭā Āpepi àu set t'eṭtu tep - k tem - tu Āpepi 2. *χet*

is given Apepi to the flame, and say, "Be tasted thou, death to thee Apepi, going back,

ḥem χeft en Rā χer senb ḥem ḥa - k

retreating, enemy of Rā falling down, being repulsed, going back retreatest thou;

àu χet - nà-tu àu beḥen - nà-tu mātχeru Rā erek Āpepi sep fṭu

driven back have I thee, cut asunder have I thee, triumphs Rā over thee Apepi. Times four.

tep-k Āpepi sep fṭu 3. *ḥa-k Sebàu tem erek*

Be tasted thou Apepi. Times four. Back thou Sebàu, an end to thee

àu eref sennu - χet - nà - tu àu eref seḥetem - nà - tu

is therefore, driven flame have I at thee therefore, made to be destroyed have I thee,

sàpi - nà - tu ṭu tem tem-k tep-k tem - tu àn

reckoned up have I thee for evil; an end, an end to thee, be tasted thou, an end to thee, not

un - nek 4. *tem tem-k tem erek tep-k tem*

rise thou. An end, an end to thee, an end to thee, be tasted thou, come to an end.

[a] The signs in the cartouche are omitted on the papyrus.

àu seḥetem - nà Āpepi χeft en Rā mātχeru Rā erek Āpepi
Destroyed have I Apepi the enemy of Rā. Triumphs Rā over thee Apepi.

sep fṭu mātχeru P-āa er χefti - f sep fṭu 5. *àr emχet sàn*
Times four. Triumphs P-āa over enemies his. Times four." And afterwards shall be defiled

χer-k Āpepi sep fṭu em reṭ-k àb t'eṭ χer-k àu χeft en
by thee Apepi times four with foot thy left. Shall be said by thee when the countenance of

Rā er āāiu-k χabu emχet uben - f mātχeru Rā erek
Rā is upon both sides thy bending after rises he, "Triumphs Rā over thee

Āpepi sep fṭu 6. *s - mātχeru Rā erek Āpepi em un māt*
Apepi. Times four. Triumphs Rā over thee Apepi in very truth."

seḥetem Āpepi t'eṭtu re pen ḥer Āpepi nāuu ḥer šuu
To cause the destruction of Apepi, say chapter this over Apepi written upon papyrus

nemau em rei uat' ḥnā àru Āpepi em menḥ 7. *χat*
new with colour green, together with figure of Apepi in wax cut

mātennu ren - f ḥer - f em rei uat' erṭāt àu set
and inscribed accursed name his upon it in colour green, lay it upon the fire (that)

amem - f χeft Rā ṭā - f su em ṭūau em āḥā màtet
may devour him the enemy of Rā. Puts one it at dawn, at noon, likewise

em *māšer* *χeft* *Rā* *ḥetep* - *f* 8. *em* *ānχtet* *àu* *unnut* *sas*
at eventide when Rā sets he in the land of life, at hour six

ent *ḳerḥ* *àu* *unnut* *χemennu* *ent* *hru* *er* *peḥ* *ruhau*
of the night, at hour eight of the day, at the arrival of evening

neferit (sic) *er* *unnut* *nebt* *ent* *hru* *ent* *ḳerḥ* *em* *hru* *enti* *ḥeb*
up to hour every of the day and of the night, on the day of festival,

9. *em* *hru* *em* *àbṭu* *em* *sas* *enti* *ḥeb* *met' ṭua* *enti* *ḥeb* *màtet*
by day by month, by sixth day of festival, fifteenth day of festival likewise

hru *neb* *seχer* *Āpepi* *χeft* *nu* *Rā* *em* *χat-pet* *χer* *pesṭ*
day every. Overthrown is Apepi the enemy of Rā in the shower, for shines

Rā *seχer* *Āpepi* *em* *un* *māt* 10. *sennu-χet* *pu* *em* *χet* *ent*
Rā and overthrown is Apepi in very truth, burnt to wit in a fire of

χessau *erṭāt* *sepu-f* *er* *χāā* *χer* *useš* *smen* *em*
dried grass. (?) Are placed remains its to be mixed with excrement and set in

χet *uā* *àru* *χer* - *k* *màtet* *enen* *àu* *unnut* *sas* *ent* *ḳerḥ*
fire one. Is to be done by thee the like of this at hour six of the night,

11. *àu* *ḥet'* *met' ṭua* *ent* *hru* *erṭāt* *Āpepi* *er* *set* *peḳaàs*
at daybreak of fifteen of day, is given Apepi to the flame, spits (one)

ḥer - f āšt sep sen em ḥāṭ unnut nebt ent hru neferit
upon him many times, twice, at the beginning of hour every of the day until

er rer χebit àr emχet enen ḥet' sas **12.** *ent hru ertāt*
turns round the shadow. After this at daybreak of six of day is given

χer - k Āpepi àu set peḳàs ḥer - f sànt em reṭ - k àb
by thee Apepi to the fire, spit upon him defiling with foot thy left,

χesef hemhemti ent ḥau - ḥrà àrit en χer - k
repulsed are the roarings of the 'backward face.' Done is by thee

màtet enen **13.** *àu ḥet' met'-ṭuau ent hru χesef Āpepi àm - f*
the like of this at daybreak fifteen of day, repulsed is Apepi by it

ṭebṭeb er sekti - k àru[a] *χer - k màtet enen χeft pesàu*
and slain before *sekti* boat thy. Is done by thee the like of this when boil

šenreā em àbtet ent pet χeft Rā ḥetep-f **14.** *em*
tempests in the eastern parts of the sky when Rā sets he in the

ānχtet er tem ertāt χeper ṭešertu em àbtet ent
land of life, so as not to let become threatening red in the eastern parts of the

[a] *ertāt* is written in the text, and *àru* just above it.

pet ȧri χer-k mȧtet enen āšt sep sen ȧu tem erṭāt
sky. Is done by thee the like of this many times, twice, so as neither to let

χeper χaθ em pet tem erṭāt χeper 15. *qerȧu*
become a shower in the sky, nor to let become a rain storm

em pet ȧri χer - k mȧtet enen āšt sep sen er χa-pet
in the sky. Is done by thee the like of this many times, twice, against the shower

er pesṭ ȧtennu seχer Āpepi em un māt χut en
for the shining of the sun's disk. Overthrown is Apepi in very truth. Good is it to

ȧri-s her hetep ta χut 16. *nef em neter χertet erṭāt peḥti en*
do it upon earth, good for one in the nether world, is given power to

se pen er ȧaut ent ḥer-f neḥem-f pu mā
person this for dignities which are above him, delivered is he to wit from

χet nebt bu-ṭu em un māt ȧu maa - nȧ χeper mā - ȧ
things all evil in very truth. "May see I it happen to me."

šāt 17. *ḥetep ent seχer Āpepi χeft nu Rā*
Book first of overthrowing Apepi the enemy of Rā.

t'eṭtu χer ḥer ḥrȧ-k Āpepi χeft pfi en Rā ḥem ḥa - k
Say, "Down upon face thy Apepi enemy that of Rā, go back, retreat thou

18.

χeri Sebȧu ȧt āāiu - f ȧt reṭṭu - f
enemy, Sebau without arms his and without legs his,

šāiṭ χenti - k ȧu χet ḥer - k ȧuk χer - tu
split up is snout thy, are things upon thee. Art thou fallen thou,

seχer-tu seχer en tu Rā Ḥeru - χuti ṭer-nef-tu nȧk-nef-tu
overthrown thou, overthrows thee Rā - Harmachis, destroys he thee, damns he thee,

19.

sesunnu - tu ȧrit - f en t'et - f ȧuk χer - tu en set
hook thee does he body his. Art thou thrown down thou by the flame,

per ȧm - s nesert per em heh - s per em at - s
comes forth from it fire proceeding from flame its, comes forth at moment its

heh - s erek χesef at - k ȧn Ȧuset em χu
flame its against thee. Repulsed is crocodile thy, says Isis with the strength of

20.

ṭep - re - s beḥen ba - k āu θest - k uṭ en
utterance her, is cut in pieces soul thy, severed are vertebræ thy, inflicts

Ḥeru set'ebu - k Ḥeru mesu ḥer sau - k seḥetem - tu
Horus blows thy, the Horus children are for smashing thee, destroyed art thou

en at - sen ḥem ḥem - k χet χet - k χer - tu
at season their. Back, back thou, retreat, retreat thou, fallen art thou,

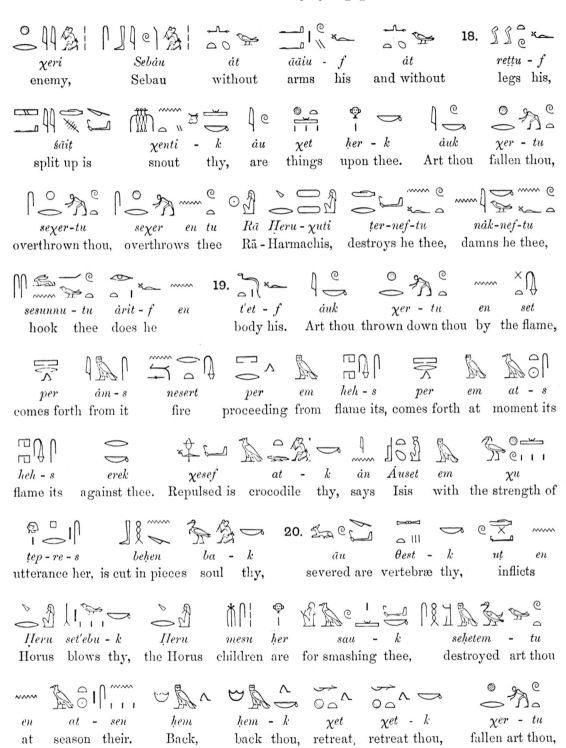

χet *ḥem - tu* *Āpepi* 21. *seχetχet - tu* *paut* *neteru* *āat*
retreating, going back thou Apepi. Makes to turn back thee the cycle of the gods great

ȧmu *Ȧnnu* *seḥem* *en* *Heru* *at - k* *sȧaṭ* *en*
who are in Heliopolis, makes to go back Horus crocodile thy, paralyses

Sut *at - k* *χesef - tu* *Ȧuset* *beḥen - tu* *Nebt - ḥet* *seχetχet - tu*
Sut moment thy. Repulses thee Isis, cuts asunder thee Nephthys, makes to go back thee

paut *neteru* *āat* 22. *ȧmu* *ḥāt* *uȧa* *en* *Rā* *māta*
the cycle of the gods great who are in the front of the boat of Rā. The chain

en *Sut* *ḥer* *neḥbt - k* *ṭāt* *Heru* *mesu* *māb - sen* *ȧm - k*
of Sut is upon neck thy, give the Horus children spears their into thee,

χesef - tu *neteru* *ȧpu* *saa* *nu* *sebeχtu* *šetaut*
repulse thee gods those the guardians of the portals secret.

23. *per* *heh - sen* *er - ek* *em* *set* *ȧ* *χet* *ḥem* *en*
Comes forth flame their against thee from the fire. O going back, retreating from

heh - sen *em* *nesert* *per* *em* *re - sen* *ȧ* *χer* *senb*
flames their of fire coming forth from mouths their! O falling one, wriggler,

Āpepi *ȧ* *χet*
Apepi, O going back,

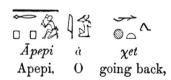

Column XXIV.

1. 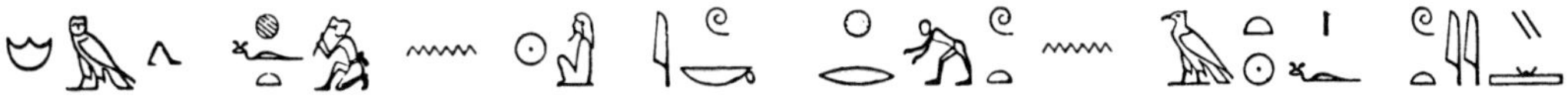

ḥem χeft en Rā àuk χer - tu en at - f tui

retreating, enemy of Rā, art thou fallen thou at moment his this!

seχer - tu àmu uàa - f ḥa - k er - ek àuk

Have overthrown thee those who are in boat his, back thou for thee. Art thou

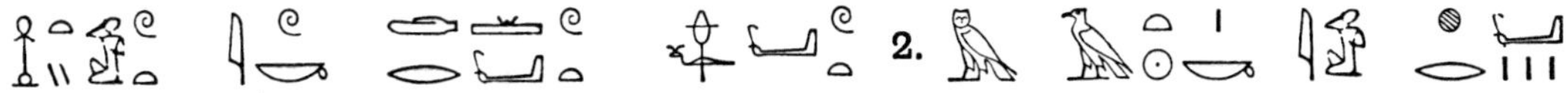

šenti - tu àuk ṭer - tu χesef - tu 2. *em at - k à χer*

cursed thou, art thou destroyed thou, repulsed thou at moment thy. O trippings up

erek àuk ḥem - tu ba - k ḥem - tu ṭeṭ àuf - k

to thee! Art thou turned back thou and soul thy, turned back art thou, carried off is flesh thy,

uṭ set'ebu - k àru āṭ - k šāiṭ - k ṭer

inflicted are blows thy, is made cutting thy and slaughter thy, destroyed is

3. 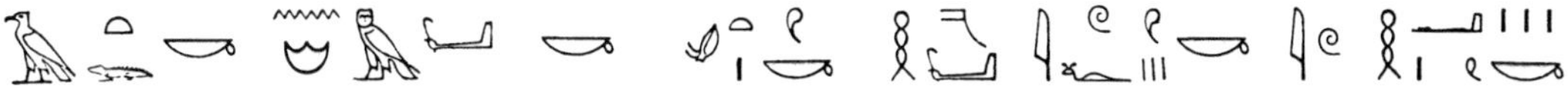

at - k neḥem - k mest'er-k ḥu àuf - k àu ḥāu - k

crocodile thy, deprived art thou of ear thy, struck is flesh thy from limbs thy.

setenemem ba - k er χebit - k sek ren - k ṭer

turned back is soul thy from shade thy, destroyed is name thy, made nothing

ḥekau - k 4. *seḥetem - tu χer seχer - tu àn*

are enchantments thy, destroyed art thou, pierced, overthrown art thou, not

per - k em χebt - k tui er neḥeḥ ḥnā t'etta ṭāṭ set'ebu - k

mayest come forth thou from cavern thy that for ever and ever. Given are blows thy

nem qaȧs - k sau - tu em sau mertu
a second time, fettered art thou and beaten by the beaters cruel,

χesef at - k neḥem at - k neḥem Rā mest'er-k
is repulsed moment thy, is turned back crocodile thy, seizes Rā ear thy,

seḥem - tu em ȧuset - k tui χer seχetχet - tu
making to go back thee upon seat thy that, upset and made to go back art thou,

sȧp - tu en ṭu sau sau - tu - f ȧn per
condemned art thou for crime, beating, beats thee he, not coming forth

sep - f tem ba - k seḥetem χebit - k sȧp - tu en
luck his. Damned is soul thy, destroyed is shade thy, condemned thee has

maa Ḥeru seχem - s ȧm - k ȧm - s ȧm - k er t'er
the eye of Horus, prevails it over thee, eats it into thee to the fulness

en ḥrȧ - s ȧ tem erek Āpepi sati - nes-tu ḥem - nes-tu
of face its. O an end to thee Apepi, shoots it thee, turns back it thee,

seḥetem - nes-tu tem - nes - tu t'eṭṭu ṭeṭṭeṭ em re
destroys it thee, makes an end it of thee." Say firmly with the mouth,

χer ḥer ḥrȧ - k Āpepi χeft en Rā per set er - ek
"Down upon face thy Apepi enemy of Rā! Comes forth the flame against thee

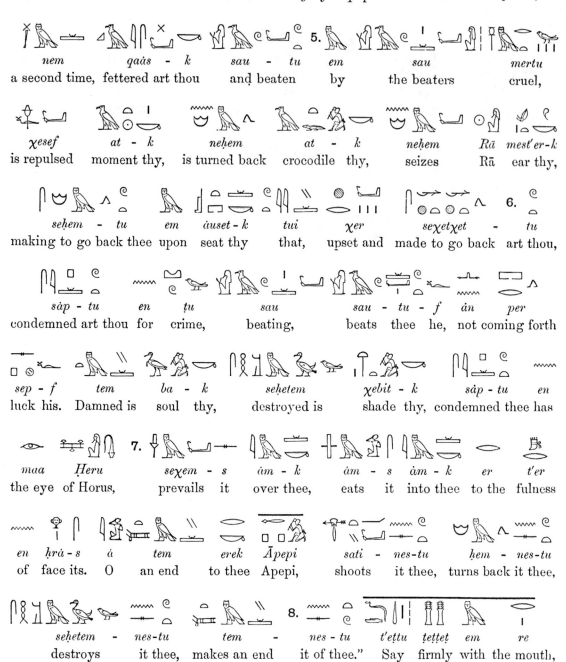

9.

per em maa Ḥeru per nebȧt ur er - ek per em

coming forth from the eye of Horus, comes forth fire great against thee, coming forth from

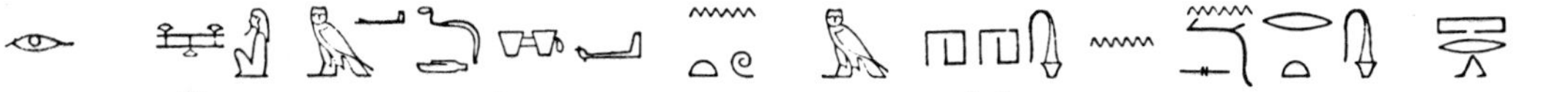

maa Ḥeru māt'eṭ - en - tu em heh en nesert per

the eye of Horus. Thrust down art thou into the flame of fire, comes forth

χet erek mer nesert - s ȧu ba - k χu - k

the flame against thee, deadly is flame its to soul thy, χu thy,

10.

ḥekau - k χat - k χebit - k nebt amem

words of power thy, body thy, shade thy. The mistress of fire

seχem - s ȧm - k sesunnu heh - s em ba - k tem - s

prevails it over thee, hooks flame it into soul thy, makes an end it

11.

ȧru-k sesunnu - s χeperu - k ȧuk χer - tu en

of what is to thee, hooks it forms thy. Art thou fallen through

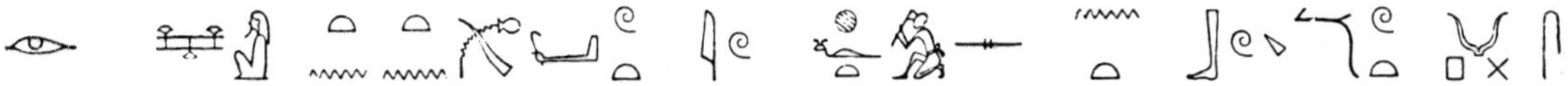

maa Ḥeru tenten - tu ȧu χeft - s ent bu - nes - tu ȧp - s

the eye of Horus, powerful against enemy its, which devours thee, leads it

12.

set ur seχem maa Rā ȧm - k ȧm - tu ȧmi

the fire mighty, prevails the eye of Rā over thee, devours thee the flame,

ȧt sepi en χer mā - s ḥem ereḳ ȧuk beḥen - tu

not remains what falls from it. Back to thee, art thou cut asunder,

ba - k uśer χenȧ ren - k χer ȧrek ren - k χer
soul thy is parched, buried is name thy, silence therefore is to name thy, fallen

ȧrek ren - k χem - tu χesef - tu χem - k
therefore is name thy, finished art thou, repulsed art thou, forgotten, forgotten, forgotten art thou.

χet erek ḥem erek ȧuk beḥen-tu ḥerȧu - tu ȧu
Retreat to thee, back to thee, art thou cut in pieces, removed art thou from

ȧmu kerȧut - f ȧ sek sek tem tem - k Āpepi
those in shrine his. O ground up, ground up, end, end to thee, Apepi,

χeft en Rā ȧn un - nek ȧn un ba - k ȧuk maa Ḥeru
enemy of Rā! Not rising to thee, not rising to soul thy, thou the eye of Horus

seχem - s ȧm - k ȧm - tu-s hru neb mȧ utu en Rā ȧru
prevails it over thee, eats thee it day every as decreed Rā to be done

erek Āpepi ȧuk χer - tu en set χet qeqa uaua
to thee Apepi. Art thou fallen thou into fire and flame, feeds the flame

ȧm - k sȧp - tu ent ȧmit maa Ḥeru χut ent
upon thee, condemned art thou to the fire of the eye of Horus, the fire which

bunes - nes-tu ȧm - s ba - k χut - k χat - k χebit - k
eats it thee, eats it soul thy, χu thy, body thy, shade thy;

àn benben - k àn tata - k 17. *en t'et t'etta mātχeru Rā*
not erections to thee, not emissions to thee of body for ever and ever. Triumphs Rā

erek Āpepi sep fṭu mātχeru Ḥeru er χefti sep fṭu mātχeru
against thee Apepi. Times four. Triumphs Horus over the Enemy. Times four. Triumphs

P-āa er χefti - f sep fṭu χet erek ḥem erek en
P-āa over enemies his. Times four. Back to thee, retreat to thee at

18. *ḥekau pen per em re-à ḥer P-āa t'etta*
word of power this coming forth from mouth my on behalf of P-āa for ever.

ṭer - k ḥekau pen àn ī - k sep - f t'etta Āpepi
Destroys thee word of power this, not comes to thee fate his for ever. O Apepi

χeft en Rā ṭep-k 19. *χeri Sebàu sep fṭu t'eṭtu*
enemy of Rā, taste thou enemy, Sebau. Times four. To be said

àn sa āb tur às àru nek ren en Āpepi nāu
by a person clean, purified. Now may be made by thee the name of Apepi written

ḥer šuu nemau erṭā 20. *- f er χet χeft Rā ṭā - f*
upon papyrus new, and place it upon the fire when Rā gives he

su χeft Rā em āḥā χeft Rā ḥetep - f em ānχ-let em
himself, when Rā is in culmination, when Rā sets he in the land of life, on

seχef hru em hru em unnut nebt ent hru neb em àbṭu em sas enti
seven of day, by day, at hour every of day every, by month, on sixth day

ḥeb em 21. *met' ṭua enti ḥeb màtet hru nebt en seχer χeft*
festival, on fifteenth day festival, likewise day every for overthrowing enemies

nu Rā Ḥeru-χuti
of Rā - Harmachis.

ḥet meḥt sen ent seχer Āpepi χeft nu Rā
Book second of overthrowing Apepi the enemy of Rā.

χer ḥer ḥrà-ten χeft nu Rā Sebàu 22. *nebt χeft mesu*
Fall upon faces your, enemies of Rā, Sebau every, enemies, children

beteš χak-àbu àpu Sebàu àt ren-sen χebti àri
of inertness, rebels these, Sebau, without name (are) they, sinners. Are made

χebti - sen utut àru āṭi χak - àbu 23. *kauti*
caverns their as decreed to be made, tied fast are the rebels, the katui,

Sebàu tennu χeriu àri χenen χer àref-ten
and the Sebau; how many are the enemies! Is made your overthrowing, fall therefore ye,

χer-ten em at ent Rā tem - ten χer-f-ten
fall ye at the moment of Rā, an end to you, throws down he you.

Column XXV.

1\.

χer - f țepu - ten ḥer ḥrà - ten às pu ḥetem - f ten su

Casts down he heads your upon faces your, and so destroys he you, is he

àri šāț - ten à tem - tu tem - ten seḥetem - ten

making slaughter your. Oh destruction an end to you. Be destroyed you,

àt - ten àntu - ten àn χeper - ten àn un-ten țer

annihilated you, eclipsed you. Not may become you, not may exist you, be destroyed

țepu-ten 2. *senàt ḥāt - ten ḥesq θesu - ten uț set'ebu*

heads your, be cut throats your, be severed vertebræ your, be inflicted blows

àri šāț - ten χer en maa Ḥeru sepț nesert - s er-ten

making slaughter your. Falls the eye of Horus dowered with flame its against you,

seχem heh - s àm-ten χāt maa Rā er ten 3. *ḥu*

obtains the mastery flame its over you. Rises the eye of Rā against you, smites

user - f en àm - ten seχem maat - f en àm - ten

power his at you, obtains the mastery eye his over you,

àm - s - ten sesunnu - s - ten em ren - s pui en àmi

eats it you, hooks it you in name its that of Àmi (eater),

seχem - s en àm - ten em ren - s pui Seχet χer - ten en

obtains the mastery it over you in name its that of Seχet. Overthrow you

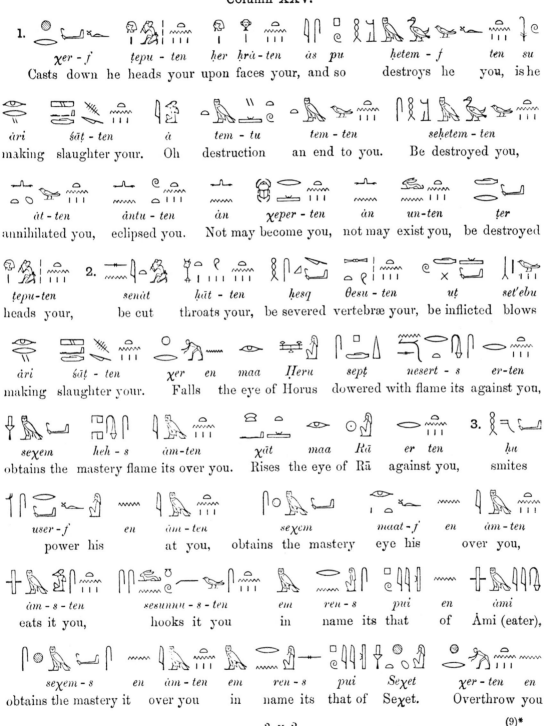

4.
heh - s mer nesert set per em heh-s à
flame its cruel, and the flame and burning coming forth from fire its. O

seksek - s - ten à sek sep sen per set er ten χeft
destroys it you, O destroying, comes forth the fire against you enemy

nu Rā Sebàu nu Ḥeru àu ba - ten χat - ten χebit - ten
of Rā and Sebau of Horus, against souls your, bodies your and shades your.

5.
per set peses - ten χenfi χenfi - s - ten ubti
Comes forth fire roasting you, frizzling frizzles it you, scorching

ubti - s - ten Àp - s - ur àp - s - ten àm - s - ten ..... nesbu - s - ten
scorches it you. Àp-s-ur judges she you, devours she you, consumes she you,

seḥetem - s ba - ten sesunnu - s heh-s em χebit - ten
destroys she souls your, hooks she fire her into shades your.

6.

à tem tem - ten àu - ten ṭer - tu sep sen useḥ - ten
O an end, an end to you. Are ye destroyed, twice, cut asunder are you,

māṭes - ten àri āṭi - ten sàpi - ten en uaua
hacked in pieces are you, is made slaughter your, judged are you by the fire and

nesert āat nebt rekeḥu àm χut - s em ba - ten
the flame great lord of blazing. Eats fire its into souls your,

7.

sesunnu heh-s em χat-ten māt'eṭ-s - ten em nebȧṭ-s
hooks flame its into bodies your, binds it you with fire its,

ur ṭes-s-ten em ṭes-s ṭenṭennu-s-ten em ṭenṭennu-s
the fire cuts it you with cutting its, pierces it you with piercing its,

[a] 8.
qaqa-s em nebȧt-s nesert-s-ten em nesert-s haut-s-
consumes it with fire its, burns up it you with burning its, parches it

ten em haut-s rekeḥu-s-ten em rekeḥu-s amem-s-ten
you with heat its, consumes it you with burning its, devours it you

9.
em amem-s set-s-ten em ren-s pfi en set
with devouring flame its, bites it into you in name its that of "Set" (Fire),

ȧpt-s-ten em ren-s pui en ȧpt-s-ur χer-ten en
judges it you in name its that of 'Ȧpt-s-ur.' Overthrows you

nebȧṭ-s sepṭ nesert ur ȧm heh-s ȧm-s χut-s em
fire its provided with flame great in fire its, eats it fire its into

10.
ba-ten ȧ χer χer - ten χer ȧref-ten ȧu-ten
souls your. O fall, fall ye, fall therefore ye! Are ye

χer-tu seχertu χer-ten en Rā χer-ten en ṭenṭen en
fallen, overthrown. Overthrows you Rā, fall ye by the impact of

[a] This word is written twice in the papyrus.

at - f *tem - ten - nef* *tem - ten* *seḥetem - f - ten*

moment his. Makes an end to you he, come to nought ye, destroys he you,

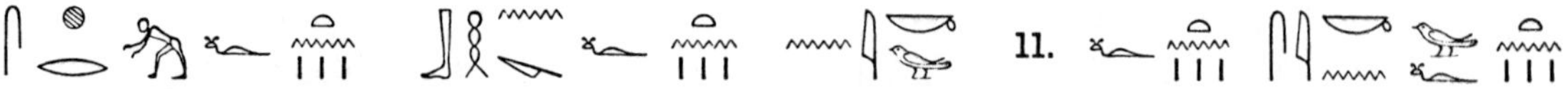

seχer - f - ten *beḥen - f - ten* *nȧk* - 11. *f - ten* *sȧken - f - ten*

overthrows he you, cuts asunder he you, annihilates he you, ruins he you.

sek - f *ren - ten* *beḥen - f* *ba - ten* *χenfȧ - f - ten*

Destroys he name your, hacks in pieces he souls your, roasts he you,

ḥetem - f - ten *reṭḥu - f - ten* *sesunnu - f - ten*

finishes he you, hooks he you, hooks he you,

χer - f - ten *χer - ten* *en* *ȧmi - s* *ḥetem - s* - 12. *ten* *ȧm*

overthrows he you. Fall ye by flame its, destroys it you, be not

ten *un* *ȧ* *tem* *tem - ten* *sep sen* *tem* *ȧref - ten*

to you existence. O an end, an end to you, twice! An end therefore to you,

tem - ten *tem* *ba - ten* *tem - ten* *tem* *χat - ten*

an end to you. An end to soul your, an end to you. An end to body your,

tem - ten *tem* *χebit - ten* *tem - ten* *ȧn* *un - ten* *ȧn*

an end to you. An end to shade your an end to you. Be not existence to you, be not

un 13. *ba - ten* *ȧn* *un - ten* *ȧn* *un* *χat - ten*

existence to soul your. Be not existence to you, be not existence to body your.

àn un - ten àn un χebit - ten àn un - ten àn
Be not existence to you, be not existence to shades your. Be not existence to you, be not

un ānχ - ten àn un ten àn un nehep - ten àn
existence to life your. Be not existence to you, be not existence to defence your. Be not

θes ṭep - ten em ḥāu - ten 14. *χet àref - ten nef ḥem*
fastened heads your upon limbs your. Retreat therefore ye before him, go back

àref - ten Sebàu àm - ten un-un en Teḥuti àref - ten em
therefore ye Sebau. Be not ye waking up Thoth therefore ye with

ḥekau - f neter āa user - f er ten rethu - nef - ten
magic words his. The god great victorious is he over you, hooks he you,

ṭā - f àritu mest - ten per set ṭep 15. *- re - f er - ten*
gives he to be done to you what hate ye. Comes forth the fire of utterance his against you,

amem àref - ten Sebàu àm unun en Teḥuti àref - ten
be consumed therefore ye Sebau; be not waking up Thoth therefore ye

em ḥekau - f seχer - f - ten beḥen - f - ten seḥetem - f - ten
with magic words his. Overthrows he you, hacks in pieces he you, destroys he you,

sàpi-f - ten en maa Ḥeru per em maa Ḥeru qaqa - s -
judges it you the Horus fire coming forth from the eye of Ḥorus, devours it

16. *ten er t'er en ḥrà-s seḥetem - s-ten em āā*
you to the whole of face its (*i.e.*, entirely). Destroys it you with the might

afit - s àn χesef - tu - s em at mertu àb - s em
of flame its, not repulsed is it at the moment wished by heart its in

ren - s pfi en Mert tem àref - ten nes ḥem àref - ten
name its that of Mert. An end therefore to you before it, retreat therefore ye

nes ḥem àref - ten nes 17. *neχt àref - ten nes χeft nebt*
before it, go back therefore ye before it, withdraw therefore ye before it, enemy every

nu Rā χeft nebt nu Ḥeru sati - s àref - ten ḥem - s - ten
of Rā, and enemy every of Horus. Shoots it therefore you, drives back it you,

seḥetem - s - ten tem àref - ten - nes sek àref - ten nes
destroys it you, an end therefore to you before it; destruction therefore to you before it

àm - ten ben ben àm - ten 18. *tata en t'et t'etta*
be not to you erections, be not to you emissions of body for ever!

àu Rā semātχeru - f māāt àref - ten Āpepi mesu beṭeś
Rā makes to triumph over him justice, therefore you, O Apepi and children of inertness,

uru beṭeś mātχeru Rā er χefti - f sep ftu mātχeru Ḥeru
great ones of inertness. Triumphs Rā over enemies his. Times four. Triumphs Horus

er χefti - f sep fṭu mātχeru Ȧusar 19. *χent Ȧmentiu er χefti - f*

over enemies his, times four; triumphs Osiris at the head of the Amentiu over enemies his.

sep fṭu mātχeru P-āa[a] ānχ ut'a senb er χefti - f sep fṭu

Times four. Triumphs P-āa, life, strength, health, over enemies his. Times four.

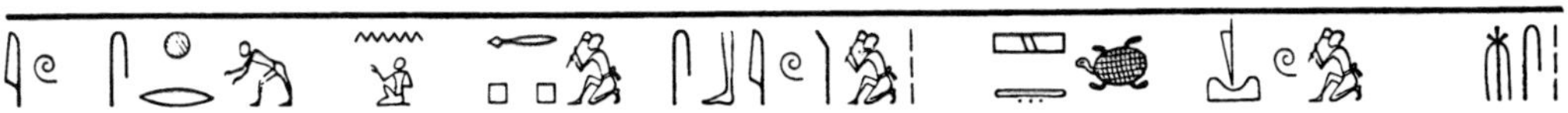

ȧu seχer - nȧ Āpepi Sebȧu šeta Qeṭṭu mesu

Overthrown have I Apepi, the Sebȧu, the Tortoise, Qeṭṭu and the children

beṭeš em ȧuset - sen nebt em bu nebt enti ȧu - sen ȧm

of inertness in station their every, in place every which are they there.

20. *er seχer - nȧ χefti nebt nu Rā em ȧuset - sen nebt em*

Overthrown have I enemies all of Rā in station their every, in

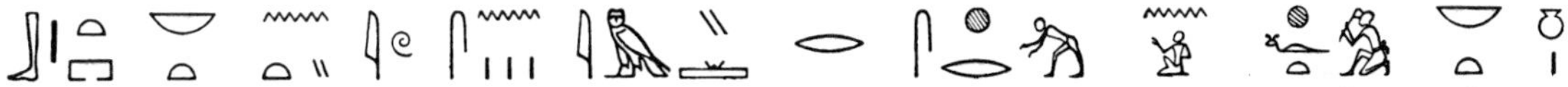

bu nebt enti ȧu - sen ȧm er seχer - nȧ χeft nebt nu

place every which are they there. Overthrown have I enemy every of

Ḥeru em ȧuset - sen nebt em bu nebt enti ȧu - sen ȧm

Horus in seat their every in place every which are they there.

ȧu seχer - nȧ χeft nebt nu Ȧmen - 21. *Rā neb nest*

Overthrown have I enemy every of Ȧmen - Rā lord of the thrones

taiu χent Ȧpit em ȧuset - sen nebt em bu

of the two countries at the head of the Apts, in station their every and in place

[a] In the papyrus the cartouche is empty.

nebt enti àu - sen àm àu seχer - nà χeft nebt nu Ptaḥ
every which are they there. Overthrown have I enemy every of Ptah

Qemā Ȧnbu-f nebt taiu em àuset - sen nebt em bu nebt
of Memphis, lord of the two countries, in station their every in place every

enti àu - sen àm 22. *mà enti er ḥāt χeft nebt nu Ȧtmu*
which are they there: likewise before enemy every of Ȧtmu,

màtet χeft nebt nu Teḥuti nebt χemennu màtet χeft nebt
likewise enemy every of Thoth lord of Chemennu, likewise enemy every

nu Iusāset neb Ȧnnu Ḥet-ḥert nebt Ḥetep-Ḥemet χebit Ȧtmu
of Iusaset lady of Heliopolis, Hathor lady of Ḥetep-Ḥemet and the shade of Atmu;

χeft nebt nu Ḥeru χent χaṭθà nebt Ka-kamit χeft nebt
enemy every of Horus prince of Chatta, lord of Ka-Kamit; enemy every

23. *nu χuaut neter ṡes (?) χeft nebt nu Bast āat nebt Bast χeft*
of χuaut .... enemy every of Bast, great one, lady of Bast; enemy

nebt nu Ȧusar nebt Ṭeṭṭuṭ χeft nebt nu Ba nebt Ṭeṭṭu neter āa
every of Osiris lord of Tettut; and enemy every of the ram lord of Tettut, god great,

ānχ en Rā àu seχer - nà χeft nebt nu Ȧn - ḥer Ṡu
the life of Rā Overthrown have I enemy every of Ȧn - ḥer - Shu

24.

se Ḥeru - Ṭemam χeft nebt nu Ȧmen - Rā neb
the son of Horus the concealed; enemy every of Amen - Rā lord of

Sam - beḥutet χeft nebt nu Ȧnpu nebt Sauti χeft nebt nu
Sam - beḥutet, enemy every of Ȧnubis lord of Siut, enemy every of

Ḥeru nebt ȧbtiu χeft nebt nu Ḥeru maa nebt Śeṭennu
Horus lord of the easterns; enemy every of "Horus the Double-eyed," lord of Śeṭennu;

χeft nebt nu Ḥeru ȧm
enemy every of Horus in ....

Column XXVI.

1. *χeft nebt nu Ḥeru Sam taiu nebt χaṭeṭ χeft*
enemy every of Horus the Pilot of the two earths, lord of χateṭ; enemy

nebt nu Ḥeru em Pe Uat'it em Tep χeft nebt nu Ḥeru uru
every of Horus in Pe and Uat'it in Tep; enemy every of Horus, the aged,

nebt Qemāt em ȧuset - sen nebt em bu nebt enti ȧu - sen ȧm
lord of Qemā in station their every, in place every which are they there.

ȧu seχer - nȧ χeft nebt nu Seb 2. *em ȧuset - sen nebt em bu*
Overthrown have I enemy every of Seb in station their every, in place

nebt enti ȧu - sen ȧm t'eṭtu ȧn sa āb tur ȧs ȧru-nek
every which are they there. Said by a person washed and clean, "Now art done for thou

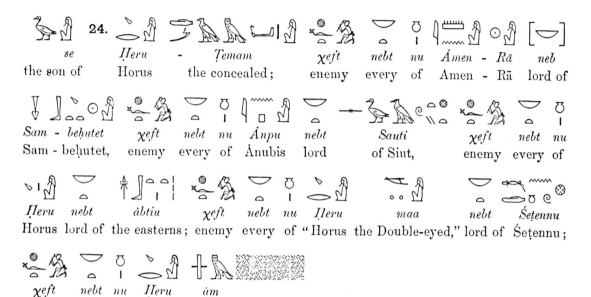

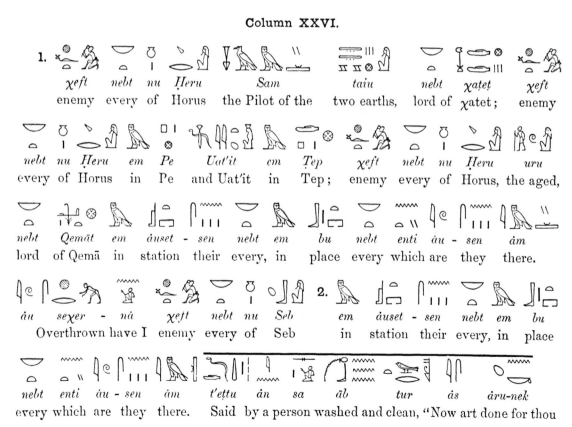

χeft nebt nu Rā χeft nebt nu P-āa ānχ ut'a senb em mit
enemy every of Rā, enemy every of P-āa life, strength, health, in death

em ānχ ḥnā seχeri nebt enti em ȧb - f ren en
in life together with designs all which are in heart his. The name of

ȧtf - sen mut - sen 3. *mesu - sen em ȧbt nebt nāu em*
father their, mother their, children their upon (leg) left every shall be written with

rii uat' ḥer śuu nemau māṭennu ren - sen ḥer śenbt-
colour green upon papyrus new; inscribed shall be names their upon bodies

sen ȧru em menḥ mātet senḥu em śenti ent mennu kam
their made of wax and likewise tied up with hair of colour dark;

peḳaȧs ḥer sen 4. *sȧn em ret ȧbt seχer em māb*
spit upon them and spurn (them) with the foot left; pierce with a lance

em ṭes erṭāt ḥer χet em ment ent mābti (?) ḥer sa
of stone; put (them) upon the flame of fire of the burners (?) upon the

ren en Āpepi sennu χet em χet ent χessau χeft Rā
name of Apepi. Kindle a fire with the flame of χessau grass when Rā

ṭā - f su χeft Rā em āḥā 5. *χeft Rā ḥetep - f em*
gives he himself; when Rā (is) in culmination; when Rā sets he in

ānχtet unnut ḥetepi ent hru ent ḳerḥ em unnut sen ent ḳerḥ
the land of life; hour first of day of night; at hour (?) second of night

neferit er unnut χemet enti ḳerḥ àu ḥet' ta màtet unnut
until hour three of night until lightens the earth; likewise hour

nebt enti ḳerḥ unnut nebt ent hru em pautta em sas enti ḥeb
every of the night; hour every of the day of the new moon feast; on sixth of festival;

em 6. *met' ṭua enti ḥeb màtet àbṭu seχer χeft nu Rā*
on fifteenth of festival; likewise of the month. Overthrown is the enemy of Rā,

seχer Āpepi em un mā̆t àu seχer χeft nu Rā àu ta (sic)
overthrown is Apepi in very truth, overthrown is the enemy of Rā." Is

àrutu šāt ten em sem pen enti em nāuu χeft t'at
made book this after copy this which (is) in writing when goes forth

àṭep er seχer χeft 7. *nu Rā χeft nebt nu Ḥeru - maa*
the boat to overthrow enemy of Rā, enemy every of Horus of two eyes

em Āat - peḳa χut en se šenti - nef šāt ten embaḥ
in Aat - Peḳa. Good (it is) for a person (when) recites he book this before

neter pen šeps em šes māāt ḥeḥ en sep
god this venerable with rope of law, (*i.e.*, regularly,) thousands of times.

šāt ent seχer χeft nu Rā em χerti ent hru neb
The book of overthrowing the enemy of Rā in the course of day every.

8.
t'eṭtu χer ḥer ḥrȧ - k Āpepi χeft en Rā harp
Say, "Down upon face thy Apepi enemy of Rā! plunge,

sep sen per em χemt senb sep sen sȧn - tu sȧn
twice, coming out from unknown place. Turn back, twice, quickly, quickening

em sȧn - f āq - f per - f seχer erek ȧu šet
as hastens he (when) enters he and comes forth he. Overthrowing to thee at the sea

9.
Nu Rā pu utut ȧru šāiṭ ȧu χā
of Nu! Rā it is (who) has commanded to perform slaughter. Rises

nesert ur erek sept per em Ȧpt-ḥekau un maa
the flame great against thee, provided coming forth from Ȧpt-ḥekau, open of two eyes

tu petrȧ taiu perti ḥekau ur erek em
thou looking upon the two earths, comes forth the spell great against thee from

10.
seḥ en ȧm kerȧut - f per bȧak erek
the closet which is in shrine his. Comes forth the hawk against thee,

ṭenṭennu ȧārāt per χet erek em re en
present themselves the uræi, comes forth flame against thee from the mouth of

sau nu sebχet šeta tem χeft Sebȧu
the guardians of the pylons secret. An end [to thee] enemy, Sebȧu,

taȧr Āpepi ḥetep Rā ḥer ȧa - f em χennu kerȧut - f
be fettered Apepi, rests Rā upon station his within shrine his.

11. *ȧnet' ḥrȧ-k Rā ḥer ȧb meḥenet - f ȧu χeru - k mātχeru er*
Hail to thee Rā within diadem his! Is voice thy triumphant over

Āpepi sep fṭu ȧu χeru - k māt er χefti - k sep fṭu ȧu
Apepi. Times four. Is voice thy law against enemies thy. Times four. Is

χeru P-āa ānχ ut'a senb mātχeru er χefti - f sep fṭu
the voice of P-āa, life, strength, health, triumphant over enemies his. Times four.

šep - k Āpepi sep fṭu šāt ent **12.** *seḥem Āpepi χeft ur*
Be spit upon thou Apepi. Times four." The book of turning back Apepi enemy great.

šāt ȧru em trȧ en ṭūau t'eṭtu šep - k Āpepi χeft
Recitation (?) made at the season of dawn. Say "Be spit upon thou Apepi enemy

en Rā sep fṭu ka ḥeru - tu er ȧm kerȧut - f
of Rā. Times four! O turned back from (him that is) in shrine his,

tem - tu Sebȧu χer-tu ḥer ḥrȧ - k šep-k ḥrȧ - k ḥem
an end to thee Sebȧu, fallen art thou upon face thy. Be spit upon face thy, retreat

13. *tu em àuset - k ṭebu māṭennu - k šerău uat - k*
thou into place thy, be impeded roads thy, be stopped paths thy,

mas - k em àuset - k ent sef àn peḥti - k àahau
be confined thou in place thy of yesterday. Not strength to thee, feeble

àb - k ḥāu - k em qemtu àuk sàati - tu àn un
heart thy, limbs thy in torpidity, art thou annihilated, not be

pert - k àuk utut en 14. *àmu nemmat menḥu sepṭ*
exit thy. Art thou decreed to those at the block and the slaughterers provided with

ṭes senà - sen ṭep - k āu - sen neḥeb - k àri - sen tu
knives; cut off they head thy; chop they neck thy, do for they thee

em nem sep sen ha - sen - tu àu set ṭenṭen - tu ḥerău -
a second time, twice; throw they thee to the flame; goading thee terrify

sen tu er nesert em at - s 15. *seχem - s àm - k*
they thee more than the flame at moment its. Gains the mastery it over thee;

àm - s ḥāu - k qeq - s ķesu - k sesunnu - s āt - k tet
eats it limbs thy; devours it bones thy; hooks it members thy; carries off

χnum mesu - k er nemmat - f ḥāu - k em sebu en set
Chnumis children thy to block his. Limbs thy are transferred to the flame;

sesunnu - s ba - k ȧn šaȧs - f ḥer ta ȧn 16. *χeper*
hooks it soul thy; not may pass it over earth; not may become

āāu - k em ta pen Āpepi χeft en Rā seḥetem - tu Ḥeru
arms thy on earth this, Apepi enemy of Rā. Destroys thee Horus

uru se Ȧuset ȧn āuur - k ȧn mestu - nek ȧn
the aged son of Isis; not be conception to thee; not birth to thee; not

nememti ba - k em s-θes Šu ȧn maa - k ȧn
may reach out soul thy to (what) supports Shu; not mayest see thou; not

ḳa - k ȧuk seḥetem - tu 17. *ȧn un χebit - k Āpepi χeft*
mayest look thou; art destroyed thou; not may be shade thy Apepi enemy

en Rā šep-k Sebȧu tem ren - k ȧn seχau - tuk
of Rā. Be spit upon thou Sebȧu; an end to name thy; not be remembrance to thee;

ȧri net'erȧu - k pekas - tu ḥer - k tennu seχau - tuk
be made mastery thy; be sick thou over thyself at each remembrance of thine;

ḥu Rā set'ebu - k qaȧs - tuk en Ȧuset 18. *senḥu - tuk*
inflicts Rā blows thy; tied up art thou by Isis; bound art thou (by)

Nebt - ḥet χut en Teḥuti er ḥetem - tuk ȧn un ba - k
Nephthys; the virtues of Thoth are for destroying thee. Not may exist soul thy

mā baiu ȧn un χat - k χenti χatu peshu - tuk
among the souls; not may be body thy with carcases; may bite thee

χet ȧm - tu nesert ȧri uaua ḥetep-s ḥer - k 19. *Āpepi*
the fire; may devour thee the flame making burning; may rest it upon thee, Apepi

χeft en Rā ȧu Rā em ḥāā Ȧtmu em āu ȧbu
enemy of Rā. Is Rā rejoicing, Is Tmu in heart pulsings of delight,

Ḥeru uru ȧb-f net'em Āpepi mes en set
Horus the elder heart his (is) glad; Apepi is transferred to the flame

nekȧu mes en χet ȧn un res ȧn un
and Nekau is transferred to the fire. Not may exist at all, not may exist

χebit - f em pet em ta Āpepi 20. *χeft en Rā šep - k*
shade his in heaven, or in earth. Apepi enemy of Rā, be spit upon thou,

tem Āpepi sep fṭu t'eṭtu ḥer Āpepi ȧru em menḥ χa
an end to Apepi. Times four." Say over Apepi made of wax, inscribed

mȧtet nāu ḥer šuu nemau ṭā er χet ȧu χeft
likewise written upon papyrus new, and put upon the fire in the presence

en Rā hru neb mȧtet hru uā ȧbṭu hru sas enti ḥeb
of Rā day every, likewise day first of the months, and day sixth of festival

met' ṭua *enti* *ḥeb* 21. *seχer* *Āpepi* *ḥer* *māu* *ḥer* *ta*
and fifteenth of festival. Overthrown is Apepi by water, by land,

ḥer *àχemu*
by the stars.

šāt *enti* *reχ* *χeperu* *nu* *Rā* *seχer* *Āpepi*
Book of knowing the evolutions of Rā and overthrowing Apepi.

t'eṭṭu *Neb-er-t'er* *t'eṭ-f* *emχet* *χeper-f* *nuk* *pu* *χeper* *em*
Words of Neb-er-t'er. Says he after became he, "I am to wit the becomer as

χeperà *χeper-nà* *χeper* 22. *χeperu* *χeper* *χeperu* *neb* *emχet*
χeperà. Became I the becoming of becomings, the becoming of becomings all after

χeper-à *āšt* *χeperu* *em* *per* *em* *re-à* *àn* *χeper*
becomings my many, and the evolutions coming forth from mouth my. Not had become

pet *àn* *χeper* *ta* *àn* *qemam* *seta* *t'etfet* *em*
heaven, not had become earth, not were created ground objects and reptiles in

bu *pui* *θes-nà* *àm-sen* *em* 23. *nu* *em*
place that. Raised I them out of the watery mass from

enenu *àn* *qem-nà* *bu* *āḥā-nà* *àm* *χut-nà*
inertness. Not found I a place could stand I there. Strong was I

(11)*

em ȧb - ȧ senti - nȧ em śu ȧri - nȧ ȧru nebt uā - k[uȧ] ȧn
in heart my, founded I Shu, made I attributes all. Alone was I, not

ȧśeś - nȧ em Śu ȧn tef - nȧ em Tefnut ȧn χeper ki
evacuated had I Shu, not had spit up I Tefnut. Not became other

24. *ȧri - nef ḥnā - ȧ senti - nȧ em ȧb - ȧ t'es - ȧ χeper āśt*
worked he with me. Laid foundation I in heart my own, became many

χeperu nu χeperu em χeperu nu mesu em χeperu nu
the becomings of the becomings out of the becomings of births from the becomings of

mesu - sen ȧnuk pu hat - ȧ em χefā - ȧ tataȧt - nȧ
births their. I to wit cohabited I with fist my, copulated I

Column XXVII.

1. *em χebit - ȧ χer - nȧ em re - a t'es - ȧ ȧśeś - nȧ em Śu*
with shade my, poured liquid I into mouth my own, evacuated I Shu,

tefnut - nȧ em Tefnut ȧn ȧtf - ȧ Nu s - atet - sen
spit up I Tefnut." Says father my Nu, "Eclipse they

mat - ȧ em sa - sen t'er ḥenḥen uau - sen er - ȧ emχet
eye my behind them, since for centuries proceeded they from me after

χeper - ȧ em neter 2. *uā neter χemet pu er - ȧ χeper - nȧ em ta*
became I from god one gods three to wit from me, became I in land

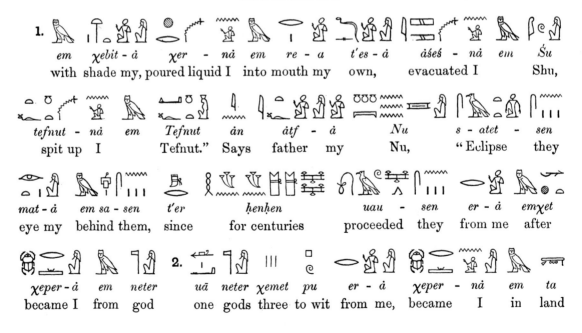

pen ḥāā áref Śu Tefnut em enenu un - sen
this. Rejoiced therefore Shu and Tefnut in the inert watery mass were they

án - f án - sen ná mat - á emχet - sen emχet áref
in it, and bring they to me eye my after them. After therefore

sam-ná āt - á rem - ná ḥer - sen χeper 3. *reθ pu*
gather up I limbs my, weep I over them, become men and women to wit

em remu per em mat - á χāru - s er - á emχet
from the tears coming out from eye my, growls it at me as

ī - s qem - s ári - ná ket em áuset - s ṭebi - s em χut
comes it finds it made have I another in place its restoring it with splendour

áru - ná s - χenti áref áuset - s em ḥrá - á emχet áref ḥeq - s
made have I approaching therefore place its in face my, afterwards therefore rules it

4. *ta pen er t'er - f χer en at - sen áu uabu - sen*
earth this whole of it. Fall destinies their upon plants their,

ṭebu - ná tet - s ám - s per - ná em uabu
restore I (what) carries away it from it. Come forth I from the plants,

qemam - ná t'etfet nebt χeper nebt ám - sen mesu án
create I reptiles all becomes all from them. Give birth

Šu Tefnut 5. *ḥnā Nut mesu ȧn Seb Nut Ȧusar Ḥeru*
Shu and Tefnut to Nut, giving birth to Seb and Nut Osiris, Horus

χent-ȧn-maa Sut Ȧuset Nebt-ḥet em χat uā em-sa uā ȧm-sen
χent-an-maa, Sut, Isis, Nephthys at birth, one after the other of them,

mesu-sen āšt-sen em ta pen t'eṭtu urt-ḥekau ka
children their multiply they upon earth this. Says Urt-ḥekau the genius

pu ḥekau 6. *utut-sen er ḥetem χefti em*
namely of enchantments, fated are they for destroying the enemies by

χut ṭep-re-sen ȧu utut enen χeper em ḥāu-ȧ
the force of utterance their. Is fated what become has of limbs my.

ȧu seχer χeft pui ṭu χer su en set Āpepi ṭes
Is fallen enemy that evil, fallen has he into flame Apepi, a knife (is)

ḥer ṭep-f 7. *beḥen mest'er-f ȧn un ren-f em ta pen ȧu*
on head his, cut off (is) ear his, not exists name his upon earth this. Is

utut-nȧ ḥu set'ebu er-ef sesunnu-nȧ ḳesu-f
fated for me to inflict blows upon him. Grip I bones his,

seḥetem-nȧ ba-f em χerti ent hru neb āuu-nȧ
destroy I soul his in the course of day every, sever I

θesu - f er neḥeb - f set em ṭes 8. *āṭ àuf - f*
vertebræ his from neck his cutting with flint cuttings from flesh his,

tebteb ḥer meseq - f erṭāt - f en set seχem - s
stabbing through hide his. Given is he to the fire, obtains mastery it

àm - f em ren - s pui en Seχet χut - s àm - f em
over him in name its that of 'Seχet,' has power it over him in

ren - s pui en χut - ubti - χeft sesunnu - k ba - f
name her that of 'Eye burning the enemy,' grippest thou soul his,

9. *sennu χet ḳesu - f āt - f mes en set àu utut iu en*
burnt are bones his, flesh his (is) transferred to the fire. Has decreed [him] to come

Ḥeru àref āā peḥti em ḥāt uàa en Rā māta -
Horus therefore, great of strength in front of the boat of Rā. Ties up

nef su māta - f en bàa àru - f ḥāu - f em tem un
he him [with] bond his of steel, makes he limbs his not to rise up,

χesef at - f emχet 10. *aṭ - f ṭāt - f qāu - f em*
stopping opportunity his, following eclipse his, gives he vomit his from

ḥati - f àuf sau senḥu netet neḥem Aker
stomach his. Is he fettering, binding, tying, taking away Aker

peḥti - f er āuu - nȧ ḥāu - f er ḳesu - f er sau - nȧ
strength his that may sever I flesh his from bones his, that may fetter I

ret - f ȧu šāiṭ - nȧ āāui - f ȧu 11. *χetem - nȧ re - f*
feet his, that may cut off I two hands his, that may shut up I mouth his

septu - f ȧu χeba - nȧ ȧbeḥu - f er ḥesq - nȧ nest - f
and lips his, that may break I teeth his, that may cut out I tongue his

er ḥenḳeḳ - f er tet - nȧ t'eṭtu - f ȧu šep - nȧ maa - f ȧu
from throat his, that may seize I words his, that may block up I eyes his, that

neḥem - nȧ mest'er ȧref ȧu šeṭ - nȧ 12. *ḥāti - f en ȧuset - f*
may carry off I the ear therefore, that may tear out I heart his from place its

nest - f pu āḥā - f ȧru-ȧ su em tem un
and throne its, that is to say, station its, that may make I him in condition of non-existence

ȧn un ren - f ȧn un mesu - f ȧn un - nef ȧn
Not may exist name his; not may exist what is born to him, not may exist he, not

un hennu - f ȧn un - nef ȧn un rei - f ȧn un - nef
may exist kinsfolk his, not may exist he, not may exist neighbour his, not may exist he;

ȧn un āuāā - f 13. *ȧn ruṭ suḥt - f ȧn θes*
not may exist heir his. Not may grow egg his, not may be established

metu-f θes rer àn un ba-f χat-f χut-f
seed his, on the other hand, not may exist soul his, body his, χu his,

χebit-f ḥekau-f àn un ḳesu-f àn un ànememu-f
shade his, words of power his. Not may exist bones his, not may exist skin his,

àuf χer seχer àn un-nef χer-s en śet 14. *enti*
let him fall and be overthrown; not may be he. Let grip it the flame of

maa Ḥeru en ḥenti en àmenḥui χer ṭes
the eye of Horus, and of the striker, and of the sacrificers having the knife;

temi àri-sen entā-sen àm-f àuf χer en
the cutting perform they, knives (?) their are in him, he falls by the

ḥu set'ebu pui ṭu utut-nà àref em χerti
inflicting of blows those evil. Decreed have I therefore in the course

15. *en hru neb ḥer qeten-f pui ṭu χer-s ḥer-f em ṭes*
of day every upon form his that evil. Falls it upon him with a knife

temi ḥesq ṭep-f àu neḥebt-f śeṭ Seχet ḥāti-sen
cutting, hacking head his from neck his, tears out Seχet hearts their

ṭāt set ḥer tekau ḥer ret-s ṭāt-s en śet nesert-
placing them upon the fire with leg her, places she [them] on the fire, burns

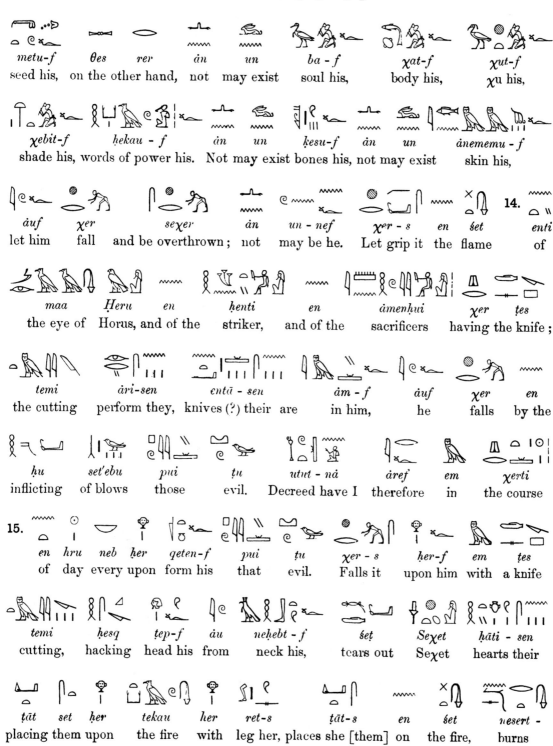

16.

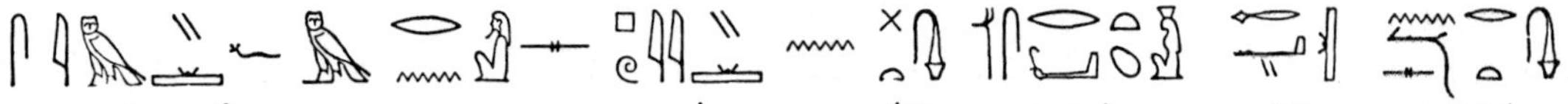

s *àm - f* *em* *ren - s* *pui* *en* *śet - usert - āā* *nesert -*

she into him in name her that of "Fire powerful, great one," burns

s *àm - f* *setenemem - s* *ba - f* *àu* *χat - f* *seχem - s*

she into him, drives back she soul his from body his. Obtains mastery she

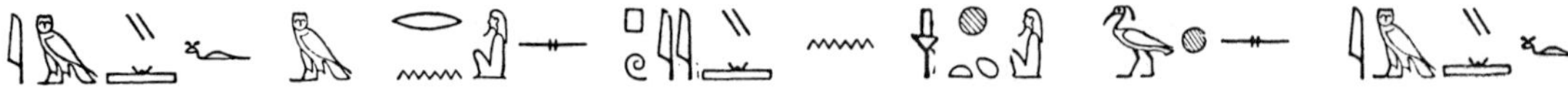

àm - f *em* *ren-s* *pui* *en* *Seχet* *χu-s* *àm - f*

over him in name her that of Seχet, overpowers she him

17.

em *ren - s* *pfi* *χut - Nebàt* *àm - s* *ḥāti - f*

in name her that of "Eye flaming," eats she heart his,

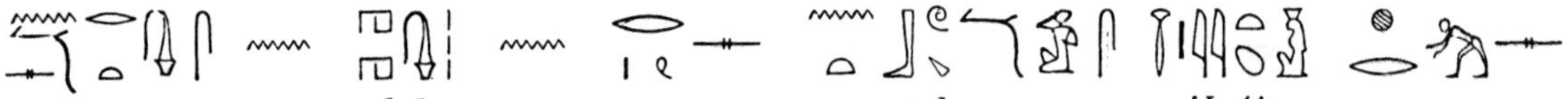

nesert - s *en* *heh* *en* *re-s* *netebu - s* *Uat'it* *χer-s*

burns she with flames of mouth her. Devours she Uat'it, falls she

er *χebt - f* *àn* *per-f* *àm-s* *er* *neḥeḥ* *ḥnā* *t'eṭta* *sau - s*

upon cavern his, not may come forth he from it for ever and for ever. Constrains she

18.

àmu *sau* *ḥesq - sen* *ba - f* *χat - f* *χebit-f*

those who have fetters, cut in pieces they soul his, body his, shade his,

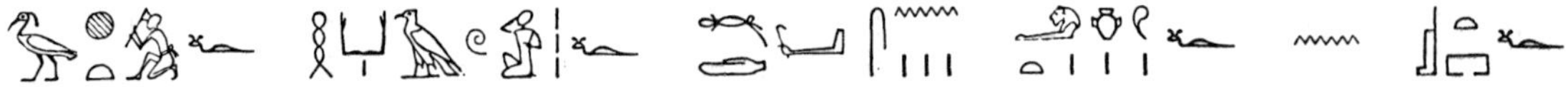

χut-f *ḥekau - f* *śeṭ - sen* *ḥāti - f* *en* *àuset-f*

χut his, words of magic his, tear out they heart his from place its,

(sic)

sàn *ren-f* *àuf* *χer* *àn* *un-nef* *er* *utut-nà*

destroying name his. Is he fallen, not may be he, for decreed have I

uśer - f *uśer* 19. *ba - f* *àn* *un* *nest-f* *àn* *un*
annihilation his, the annihilation of soul his; not let exist throne his, not let exist

àuset-f *net'erȧu - nes* *śemert* *en* *Śu* *àu* *māk* *ent* *àm*
seat his. Seized has she the bows of Shu at the store-house of the eater

uat'etu *ṭāt-s* *peχat* *en* *nest-f* *sepṭ* *seḥetem*
of limbs (?). Granted has she the splitting of tongue his, providing destruction

Sat *en* *at* *ṭenṭen - s* *ṭā - s* *Seχet* 20. *àu* *nesert*
Sat at the moment of strength her. Gives she, Seχet, into the flame

ṭep-re-s *ḥāti - f* *χer* *em* *śāāṭ - s* *śep - f* *χer*
of mouth her heart his. Falls [he] by slaughter her, stopped up is eye his, gripped,

seχer *Āpepi* *seχer - s* *Rā* *t'esef* *semātχeru* *Rā* *er* *Āpepi* *embaḥ*
overthrown is Apepi. Overthrows he Rā himself, triumphs Rā over Āpepi before

paut *neteru* *āat* *un* *ṭes* 21. *men* *em* *ṭep-f* *embaḥ* *Rā*
the cycle of the gods great, being a knife stuck in head his before Rā

hru *neb* *seχer-s* *neteru* *qemāu* *seχer-s* *neteru* *meḥtetu* *seχer-s*
day every. Overthrow him the gods southern, overthrow him the gods northern, overthrow him

neteru *Àmentetu* *seχer-s* *neteru* *Àbtetu* *senḥu-s* *saḥu*
the gods western, overthrow him the gods eastern; tie up him the starry gods of Orion

22.

en pet qemāu mesenḥ su mesχet em pet meḥtetu

of the heaven southern; turns back him the Great Bear in heavens northern,

netet-s āmu χaabeset šenti-s χet ām-s nesert

tie up him those who are in the decans. Eats it flame, devours it fire,

23.

sesunnu-s ḳesḳesu-f šennu-f ses-s ḥāu-f ubti-s

grips it bones his, hair his, burns up it limbs his, shrivels up it

ānememu-f seχer-s ḥer āāui neteru ān un ren-f

skin his, overthrown is it by the hands of the gods. Not may exist name his

em re en reθ ān seχaut-tuf em āb en neteru

in the mouth of men, not may be remembered it in the heart of the gods.

24.

peḳas-tu ḥer-f tennu seχau-tuf ḥu en Rā

May be spit upon face his each time mentioned is he! Inflicts Rā

set'ebu-f tem su sep sen χer-s sep sen Āpepi χer

blows his, annihilated is he, annihilated is he, gripped is he, gripped is he, Āpepi. Grips

su en šet χer-s en Ḥenbu ān χāru-f

him the flame, grips it Ḥenbu, not let breathe him,

sep sen ān ṭepā-tuf nifu sep sen āuf en šet

not let breathe him; not let smell him breezes, not let smell him breezes. Is he to the fire.

25.

heh-s en maaut-f semam χet-s ȧmtu ȧpt-f neteru
burns it two eyes his, slays flame its eating up forehead his. The gods

ȧmu uȧa-f mertu teken ȧm-f remu
who are in boat his desire to advance against him; the tears

per em mat-ȧ er ten ḥu-ten-set'ebu ten eref ḥer
coming forth from eye my [are] against you. Inflict ye blows your upon him upon

26.

qeṭeu-f pui ṭu maa-ten neteru ȧn ṭāt-ten
form his that evil. Look ye gods, not grant ye,

neteru un em ȧuset-f pu māḥā-f ȧn ṭāt-ten neteru un
O gods, existence in seat his to wit tomb his, not grant ye, O gods, to exist

ren-f ȧn ṭāt-ten neteru un ba-f χu-f χebit-f
name his, not grant ye, O gods, to exist soul his, χu his, shade his,

ḳesu-f šennu-f ȧn ṭāt-ten neteru useχt āāiu-f
bones his, hair his, not grant ye, O gods, the space of two hands his.

Column XXVIII.

1.

ȧn χeper mesu-f āā-f ȧn ṭāt-ten neteru ȧn
Not may become children his heirs his, not grant ye, O gods, not

(*sic*)

ruṭ metut-f ȧn θes-s ḥeḥet-f ȧn ṭāt-ten neteru χeper
may grow seed his, not may prick up it ears its, not grant ye, O gods, to become

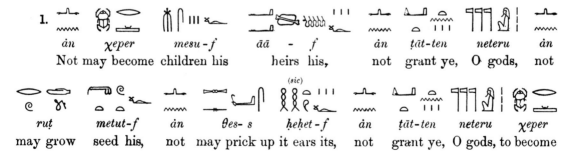

ḥekau - f *àn* *ṭāt-ten* *neteru* *un - nef* *em* *pet* *un - nef*
words of magic his, not grant ye, O gods, that may be he in heaven or may be he

em *ta* *àn* *ṭāt-ten*[a] *neteru* *un* - 2. *nef* *em* *qemāu*
upon earth. Not grant ye, O gods, to be him among the southern ones,

meḥtetu *Àmentetu* *Àbtetu* *àn* *ṭāt - ten* *neteru* *un - nef* *em*
northern ones, western ones, eastern ones, not grant ye, O gods, to be him among

tememu *àuf* *en* *šet* *en* *χut* *tui* *ent* *Ḥeru*
mortals. May be he in the fire of eye that of Horus,

seχem - s *àm - f* *em* *χerti* *ent* *hru* *neb* *un - nes*
may obtain mastery it over him in the course of day every. May be it

àm - f *àn* *āχem - s* *àm - f* *er* *neḥeḥ* 3. *t'etta*
in him, not may be quenched it in him for ever and ever,

neḥem - s *at - f* *χesef-s* *aṭ - f* *ses - f*
may seize it moment his, may repulse it {crocodile / eclipse} his, may burn he,

tem - f *un - nef* *χer - s* *Āpepi* *χer - s* *en* *šet*
may come to an end he, may be it to him. May grip it Āpepi, may overthrow it flame,

seχer - s *Rā* *t'esef* *mātχeru* *Rā* *erek* *Āpepi*[b] *māk*
may overthrow it Rā himself, triumphs Rā over thee Āpepi. Verily

[a] Written above the line.

[b] This should be written in red in the MS.

beḥen - nȧ - tu *māk* *sȧn - nȧ* *ren - k* 4. *ertā* *entuk*
slain have I thee, verily erased have I name thy. Given art thou

en *śet* *hru* *neb* *mȧ* *utut* *en* *Rā* *ȧri* *erek* *maa* *ȧrek*
to the flame day every as decreed Rā to do to thee. Look then

Rā *setem* *ȧrek* *Rā* *māk* *ṭer - nȧ* *χefti - k* *sȧn* -
Rā, hear then Rā, verily destroyed have I enemies thy, wiped out

nȧ - s *em* *ret* *peḳaȧs - nȧ* *ḥer - f* *semātχeru* *Rā* *erek*
have I it with the feet, spit have I upon him. Triumphs Rā over thee,

ki *t'eṭ* *er* *χefti - f* *nebt* *χer* 5. *ȧn* *un - sen* *ubti*
otherwise said, over enemy his every. Falling down not may be they, burnt be

ren - f *er* *ṭer - nȧ* *ȧuset - f* *nest - f* *pu* *māḥā - f*
name his because destroyed have I seat his, throne his, to wit, sepulchre his.

ȧu *ḥetem - nȧ* *ba - f* *χut - f* *χat - f* *χebit - f*
Destroyed have I soul his, *χu* his, body his, shade his,

ḥekau - f *mettu - f* *suḥt - f* *ḳesu - f* *śennu - f* *ṭāt*
words of power his, seed his, egg his, bones his, hair his, given [is he]

en *śet* *hru* *neb* *ȧu* *utut* 6. *en* *Rā* *ȧru - nef* *ṭer*
to the flame day every. Has commanded Rā to be done to him destruction

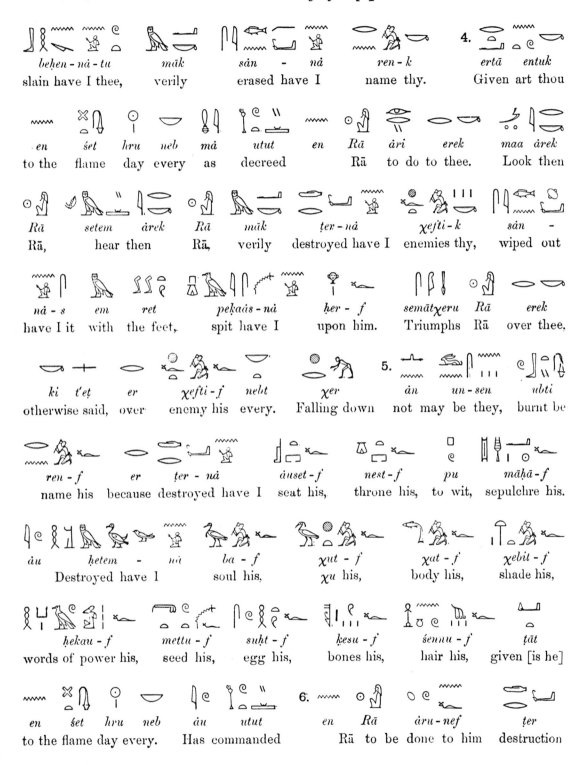

ȧrek sesunnu ȧrek ubti χefti nebt en P-āa ānχ ut'a
therefore, seizure therefore, and burning enemies all of P-āa, life, strength,

senb em mit em ānχ ȧmmā seṭef - tu ȧuf - sen
health, in death in life. May be cut in pieces members their,

ṭebṭeb ḥer mesq - sen ȧru χet ȧm-sen nebu
may be torn out of skin their, may make property of them the lords of

Ȧnnu seḥetem 7. *embaḥ-k Rā hru neb ses en ȧm-ten*
Heliopolis, destroying before thee, O Rā, day every; fire upon you.

ȧn un ba - sen χut - sen χat - sen χebit-sen ḥekau - sen
Not may be soul their, χut their, body their, shade their, words of power their,

ḳesu - sen śennu-sen χut - sen ṭep-re - sen t'eṭtu-sen ȧm ȧn un
bones their, hair their, strength their, voice their, words their there. Not may be

8. *ȧst - sen pa-sen baba - sen māḥā - sen*
graves their, house their, caverns their, sepulchre their

ȧm ȧn un seχet-sen neh - sen ba - sen ȧn
there. Not may be field their, sycamore their, bushes their, not

un māu - sen ta - sen tekau - sen nebȧt - sen ȧm ȧn
may be water their, bread their, fire their, flame their there. Not

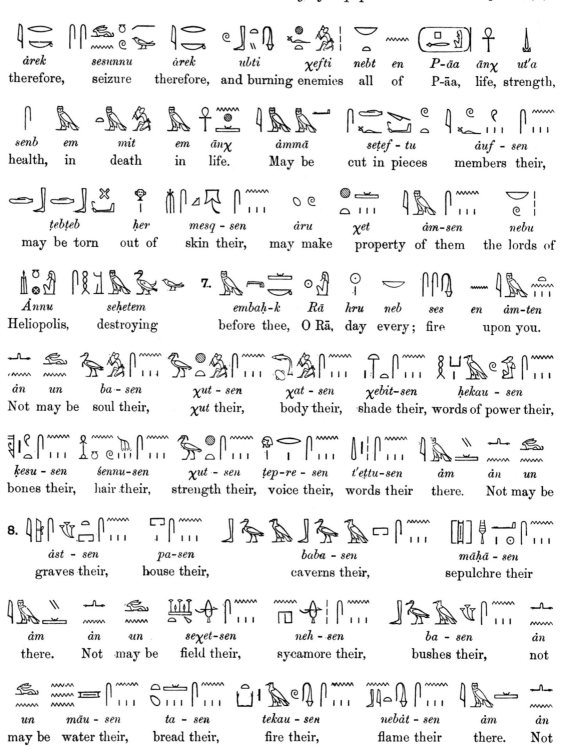

9.

un mesu - sen hennu - sen āāut - sen uḥsȧ - sen
may be children their. posterity their, heirs their, families their,

ȧm ȧn un ṭep-sen āāut-sen rettu-sen mest'er-sen mettu-sen
there. Not may be head their, hands their, feet their, ear their seed their

ȧm ȧn un nest-sen ḥeru ta - sen ȧm ȧn sati - tu
there. Not may be seat their upon land their there. Not let be poured out

10. *en sen māu em ta pen emmā ānχiu em neter-χertet*
for them water in land this, among the living in Neter-χertet,

emmā χut mitu utut-k sen ȧu nemmat en Seχet
among the χu the damned. Decreest thou them to the block of Seχet

en Āat - nebt - Ȧśer seχer-k sen em at en
in Āat - nebt - Ȧśer. Overthrown hast thou them at the moment of

11. *ḥunnu ur sȧp - k set en ȧmu sau er*
the babe mighty, judged hast thou those who guard before

Ȧmentiu ȧn ertā per ba - sen em ṭūaut ȧn
those in Ȧmenti. Not may be given coming forth to soul their from the *tūat*, not

unenu emmā ānχiu ḥer ḥetep ta ȧn ṭeka - sen Rā hru neb
may be they among the living upon earth, not may see they Rā day every.

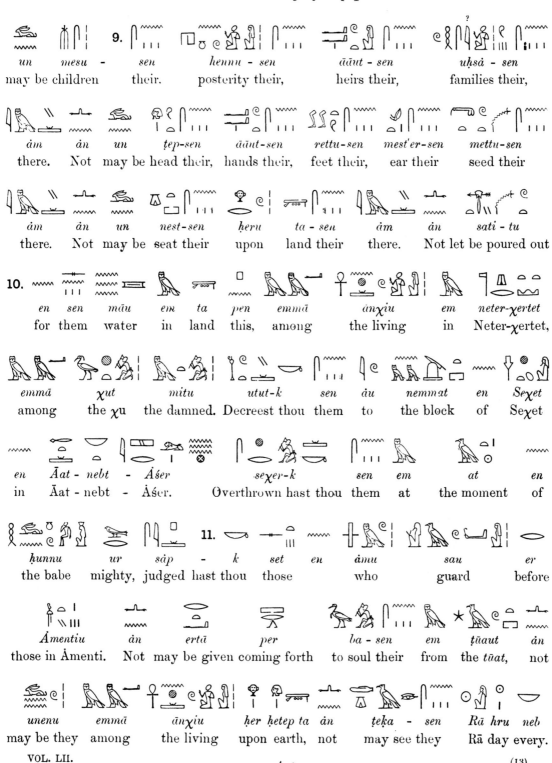

un-sen senḥu netet em χebt 12. *em ṭūaut χert ȧn*
May be they fettered and tied in the cavern in the *tūat* lower, not

ertā per ba - sen ȧm - sen er neḥeḥ ḥnā t'etta
may be granted exit to soul their among them for ever and ever.

utut erek pu χeper er sen er šennu - sen Rā em kerȧut - f
Decree thy is it to happen to them for cursing their Rā in shrine his.

neteru ȧmu - f meter er sen nes - set āāiu ent Āpepi
The gods within it do justice to them, catch hold they the two hands of Apepi.

13. *maa Ḥeru seχem - s ȧm - sen ubti - sen ḥer χau*
The eye of Horus obtains mastery it over them, burn they upon the altars

en Seχet ḥer māket ent ām uat'ti sesunnu
of Seχet and upon the brazier which devours limbs and seizes

embaḥ - k Rā hru neb mȧ utut en neter āā ȧru er sen
in presence of thee Rā, day every as decreed god great to be done to them,

Rā ȧu neḥeḥ sep sen un-nek em kerȧu - k 14. *nāi - k em*
O Rā, for ever and ever. Art thou in shrine thy, comest thou in

sekti ḥetep - k em āṭi t'a - k petpet - k em ḥetep
the *sekti* boat, restest thou in the *āṭi* boat, traversest thou two heavens thy in peace.

seχem - k *ānχ - k* *senb - k* *suaḥ - k* *χut - k*
Obtainest mastery thou, livest thou, strong art thou, increasest thou strength thy,

ṭer - k *χeft - k* *nebt* *em* *utut - k* *àu* *àru* *enen* *bu* *ṭu* *àu*
destroyest thou enemy thy every by decree thy. Is done that wrong to

P-āa *ānχ* *ut'a* *senb* 15. *em* *māb* *neb* *ṭu* *em* *se* *neb* *set neb*
P-āa, life, strength, health, with spears all evil by man every, woman every,

mit *neb* *χu* *neb* *āb - reu* *àbtiu* *nu* *set* *nebt* *χeft*
damned person every, *χu* every whatsoever, easterns of countries all, enemy

neb *en* *P-āa* *ānχ* *ut'a* *senb* *em* *mit* *em* *ānχ* *ṭer - nà*
every of P-āa, life, strength, health, in death in life. Slain have I,

seḥetem - nà *sep - k* *χer - tu* *Āpepi* *mātχeru* *Rā* *erek*
destroyed have I vomit thy, fallen art thou Āpepi! Triumphs Rā over thee

Āpepi *sep* *fṭu* *mātχeru* *P-āa* *ānχ* *ut'a* *senb* 16. *er* *χefti - f*
Āpepi. Times four. Triumphs P-āa, life, strength, health, over enemies his.

sep *fṭu* *t'eṭtu* *re* *pen* *ḥer* *Āpepi* *nāuu* *ḥer* *šuu*
Times four. Say chapter this over Āpepi written upon papyrus

nemau *em* *rei* *uat'* *ertā* *em* *χennu en* *nest* *àru* *ren - f*
new with colour green, placed inside a covering (?) made name his

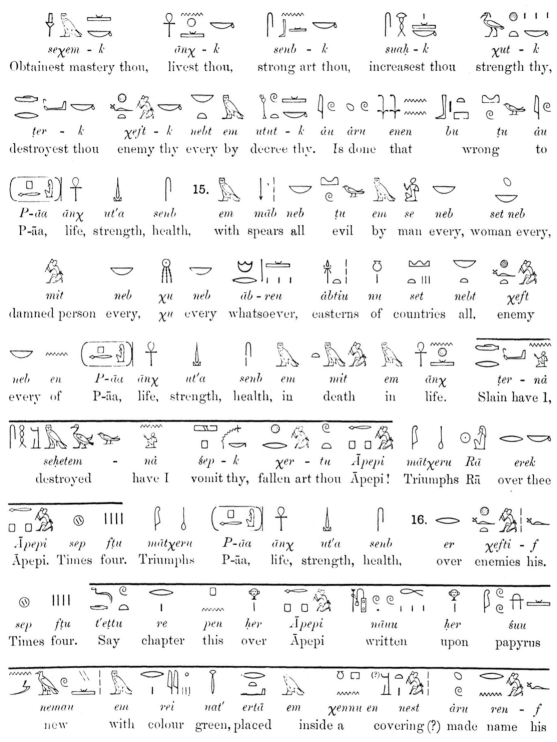

ḥer - f senḥu netet ṭā en χet hru neb sȧn em
upon it [and] bind it up and tie it up, give it to the fire day every, spurning with

ret-k ȧbt pekas 17. *ḥer - f sep fṭu em χert ent hru neb*
foot thy left, spit upon it times four in the course of day every.

t'eṭ χer - k ṭā - k su en šet mātχeru Rā erek Āpepi
Said by thee placest thou it in the fire, "Triumphs Rā over thee Āpepi.

sep fṭu mātχeru Ḥeru er χeft - f sep fṭu mātχeru P-āa ānχ ut'a
Times four. Triumphs Horus over enemy his. Times four. Triumphs P-āa, life, strength,

senb er χefti - f sep fṭu ȧsk nāu - nek enen ren
health over enemies his. Times four." Now thou writest thou that name of

seχti nebt seχti 18. *nebt senṭeti āb-k er sen em*
seχti male all, *seχti* female all, fears heart thy with reference to them,

χeft neb en P-āa ānχ ut'a senb em mit em ānχ ren en
enemies all of P-āa, life, strength, health, in death in life, name of

ȧtf - sen ren en mut - sen ren en mesu em χennu en
father their, name of mother their, name of children [their] inside

nest ertāt en ȧru menḥ ertāt ḥer χet ḥer sa ren en
the covering (?), place it in work of wax, place it upon the fire, in addition to name of

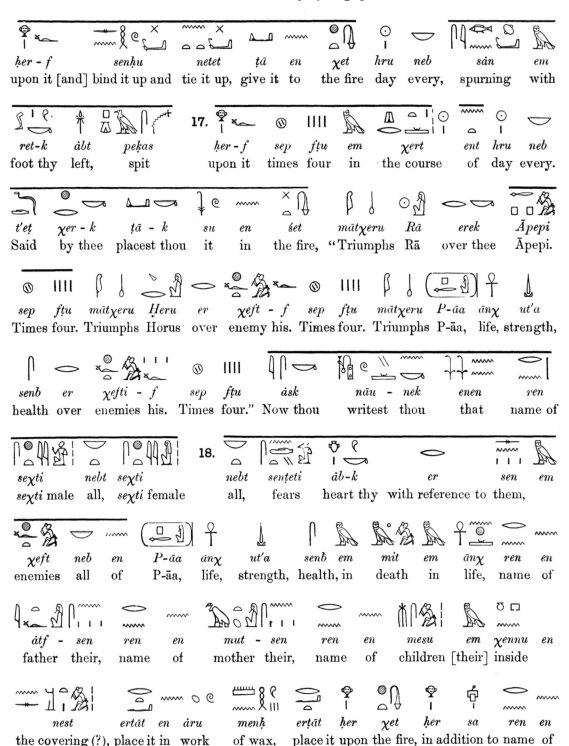

19.

Āpepi *àm* *χeft* *Rā* *ṭā - f* *su* *ka* *ki* *sep* *ḥetepi* *em*

Āpepi, burn it when Rā gives he himself. Repeatest thou time first at the

āḥā *en* *hru* *χeft* *Rā* *ḥetep - f* *em* *ānχtet* *àu* *śuu* *ḥer*

noon of the day, when Rā sets he in the land of life, whilst [it is] light upon

uār *en* *ṭu* *àu* *χut* - *nek* *enen* *àu* *semi* *nebt* *em*

the foot on the mountain. Shalt recite thou this over picture every in

20.

un *māt* *χut* *àru-s* *ḥer* *ḥetep* *ta* *em* *neter χertet*

very truth; great power [is] the doing of it upon earth [and] in Neter-χertet.

śāt *ent* *reχ* *χeperu* *nu* *Rā* *seχer* *Āpepi*

The book of knowing the becomings of Rā [and] overthrowing Āpepi.

t'eṭtu *Neb-er-t'er* *t'eṭ - f* *χeper-à* *χeper* *χeperu* *χeper-kuà*

The words of Neb-er-t'er. Says he, "Became I the becoming of becomings, become have I

em *χeperu* *en* *χeperà* *χeper* *em* *sep* *ḥetepi* *χeper-kuà* *em*

in the becomings of χeperà, becoming at time first. Become have I in

21.

χeperu *en* *χeperà* *χeper-à* *χeper* *χeperu* *pu* *en*

the becomings of χeperà. Became I the becoming of becomings to wit

pa - nà *àu* *paut* *àru - nà* *pa - nà* *em* *paut*

produced myself I from the matter [which] made I. Produced myself I in the matter

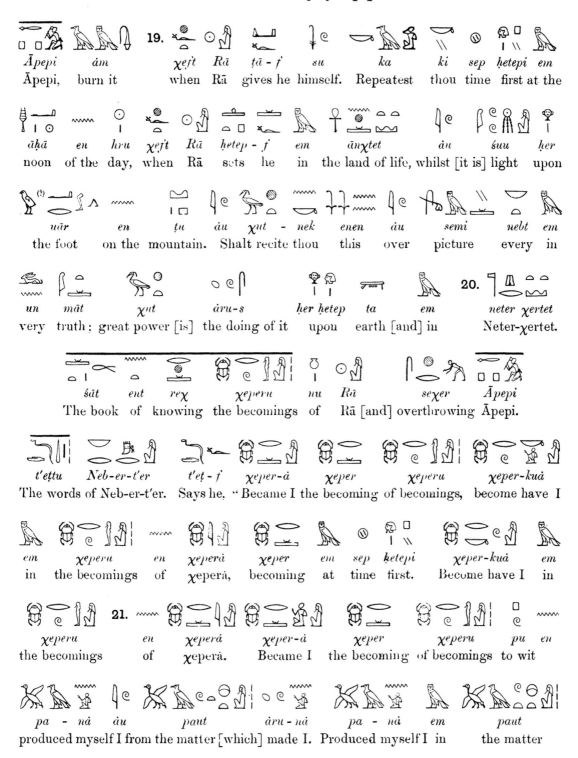

pa ren - à Àusàres paut pautti àri - à
[in] name my Ausares (Osiris?), matter of matter. Done have I

mertui 22. *nebt em ta pen useχt - nà àm - f θes - nà*
will [my] all in earth this. Spread out have I in it, raised have I

ṭet - à uāu - kuà àn mesu - sen àn àśeś - nà em Śu
hand my. Alone was I, not born were they; not had evacuated I Shu,

àn ṭāf - nà em Ṭāfnet àn - nà re - à t'es - à ren - à pu
not had spit up I Ṭāfnet. Spake I with mouth my my own name my, to wit,

ḥekau ànuk pu χeper 23. *nà em χeperu χeper - kuà*
word of power. I, to wit, became I in becomings. Become have I

em χeperu en χeperà χeper - nà em pautti
in the becomings of χeperà, became I out of the primeval matter

χeper āśt χeperu em ḥetep-ā àn χeper χeperu nebt
becoming many becomings from the beginning. Not had become becomings any

em ta pen àri - nà àri nebt uā - kuà àn χeper 24. *ki en*
in land this. Made I makings all. Alone was I, not was another

àru-nef ḥnā - à em bu pui àri-à χeperu àm
worked he with me in place that. Made I becomings there

em *ba* *pui* *θes* - *nà* *àm* *em* *Nu* *em*
by means of soul that [which] raised up I there out of Nu from

enen *àn* *qem* - *nà* *but* *āḥā* - *nà* *àm* *χut* - *nà*
inactivity. Not found I place [where might] stand I there. Strong was I

em *àb-à* *senti* - 25. *nà* *em* *ḥrà* - *à* *àri* - *nà* *àri* *nebt*
in heart my, laid foundation I for self my, made I makings all.

nāu - *k[uà]* *senti* - *nà* *em* *àb-à* *qemam* - *nà* *ki*
Alone was I, laid foundation I for heart my. Created I other

χeperu *āšt* *χeperu* *nu* *χeperà* *χeper* *àn* *mesu* - *sen*
becomings numerous, the becomings of χeperà. Became children their

em *χeperu* *nu* *mesu* - *sen* 26. *ànuk* *pu* *àšeš* - *nà* *em*
out of the becomings of children their. I, to wit, evacuated I

Šu *ṭāf* - *nà* *em* *Ṭāfnet* *χeper* - *nà* *em* *neter* *uā* *neter* *χemet*
Shu, spat up I Ṭefnut: became I out of god one, gods three

pu *er* - *à* *χeperitu* *em* *ta* *pen* *ḥāā* *àref* *Šu*
to wit from myself, becoming in land this. Rejoiced therefore Shu

Ṭāfnet *em* *Nu* *unen* - *sen* *àm* *àn* *maa* - *à* *àn* - *nà*
and Ṭefnut in Heaven, (sky) rose they there. Says eye my, {"Brought / commanded} I

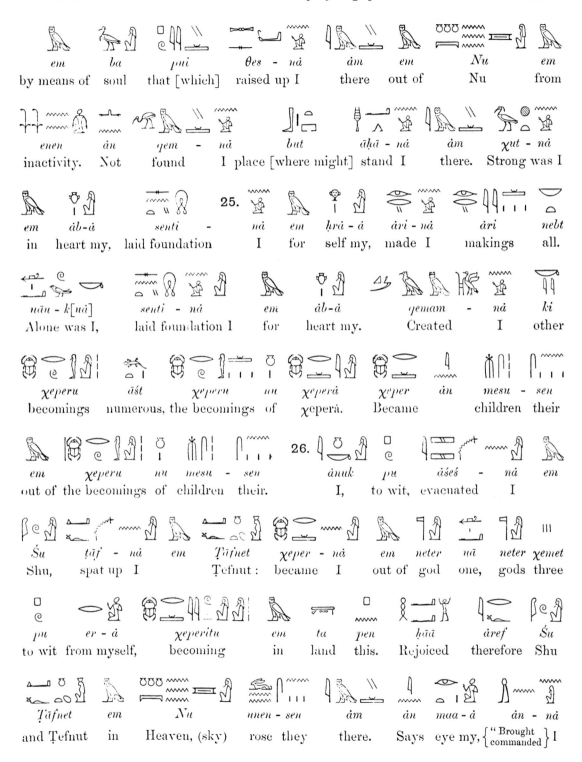

27. *sen emχet ḥennu uau - sen er - ȧ sam-nȧ em*
them, after centuries, came they to me." Collected I

ātu - ȧ per - sen ȧm t'es-ȧ emχet hat - nȧ em χefā - ȧ
limbs my came forth they there from myself after had commerce I with fist my,

ī - nȧ ȧb-ȧ em ṭet-ȧ āāaā χer em re - ȧ
came to me heart my out of hand my of the seed (?) [which] fell from mouth my.

ȧśeś - nȧ
Evacuated I

Column XXIX.

1. *em Śu tāf - nȧ em Ṭāfnet χeper - nȧ em neter uā neter χemt*
Shu, spat up I Ṭefnut, became I from god one gods three

pu er - ȧ χeperitu em ta pen ḥāā ȧref Śu
to wit from myself, becoming in land this. Rejoiced therefore Shu

Ṭāfnet em Nu unen - sen ȧm - f ȧn mat - ȧ ȧn - nȧ
and Tefnut in the watery mass rose they in it. Says eye my, {"Brought / commanded} have I

en sen emχet ḥennu **2.** *uau - sen er - ȧ sam-nȧ em*
them, after centuries came they to me." Collected I

āt per - sen ȧm t'es - ȧ emχet hati - nȧ em
limbs [my] came forth they there from myself after had commerce I with

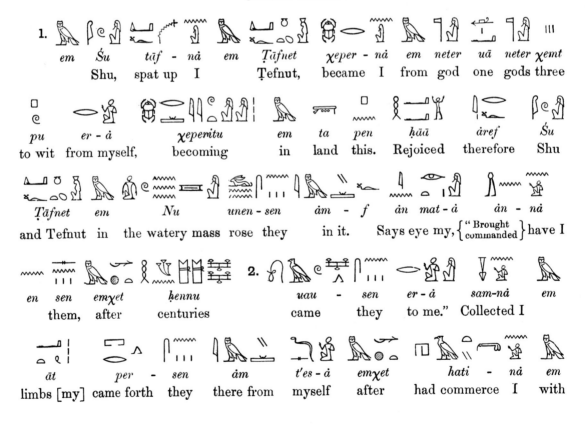

χefā - à *ī - nà* *àb-à* *em* *ṭet - à* *āāaā* *χer* *em*

hand my. Came to me heart my out of hand my of the seed falling out of

re - à *àśeś - nà* *em* *Śu* *ṭāf - nà* *em* *Ṭāfnet* *àn* *àtf -*

mouth my. Evacuated I Shu, spat up I Tefnut. Says father

3. 

à *Nu* *ati - sen* *mat - à* *emsa - sen* *uabu* *sep sen*

my Nu, "Eclipse they eye my behind them, for numbers, numbers

ḥennu *uabu* *ḥefi* *em* *rem* *em*

of centuries; numbers of reptiles from Rem, from

rem - θ *er - à* *ka* *em* *mat - à* *χeper* *ret* *pu*

the crying . . . . . my." Called out eye my became men to wit.

4. 

ṭebu - nà *su* *em* *χut* *χāru - nes* *er - à* *emχet* *ī - s*

Filled I it with power, growled it against me, after came it

ket *reṭ* *em* *χennu en àuset* *seχer* *en* *ṭenṭen - s* *àu*

another growth within the place. Fell force its upon

uabu - s *ḥer* *uabu* *ṭebu - nà* *àm-s* *nāā*

masses (?) its, upon the masses [which] accumulated I in it, putting order

5. 

àm - s *χenti* *àref* *àuset - s* *ḥer - à* *ḥeq - nes* *ta* *t'er - f*

in it: approaching therefore place its before me rules it earth all of it.

mes en *Shu* *Ṭāfnet* *Nut* *Ȧusar* *Ḥeru* *χenti - ȧn - maa* *Sut*
Give birth Shu and Tefnut to Nut, Osiris, Horus χenti - ȧn - maa, Sut,

Ȧuset *Nebtḥet* *ȧn* *mesu - sen* *qemam - sen* *χeperu* 6. *āšt*
Isis, Nephthys. Behold children their create they becomings many

em *ta* *pen* *em* *χeperu* *nu* *mesu* *em* *χeperu* *nu* *mesu -*
in earth this from the becomings of children, from the becomings of children

sen *šennut - sen* *ren - ȧ* *seχer - sen* *χefti - sen* *qemam - sen*
their. Invoke they name my, overthrow they enemies their, create they

ḥekau *en* *seχer* *Āpepi* *ȧuf* 7. *ḥer* *sau* *ḥer*
words of power for overthrowing Apepi. Is he for being bound by the

āāui *en* *Aker* *ȧn* *un* *āāiu - f* *ȧn* *un* *ret - f*
two hands of Aker, not may be two hands his, not may be legs his,

satet - f *en* *ȧuset* *uā* *mȧ* *ḥu* *Rā* *set'ebu - f* *utut - nef*
may be fastened he to place one as inflicts Rā blows his decreed for him.

ȧu *seχer - tuf* *ḥer* *sati - f* *pui* *ṭu* 8. *senpu* *ḥrȧ - f* *ḥer*
Is overthrown he upon back his that evil, to cut face his for what

ȧri - nef *men* *su* *ȧu* *sati - f* *pui* *ṭu* *mesu* *ḥer*
done has he. Remains he upon back his that evil. The children are for

seχer - tuf ḥer tenemem ba - f àu χat - f χebit - f
overthrowing him, to turn away soul his from body his and shade his,

reχi χet àmu uàa rerem ent mat - à ḥer
the learned ones who are in the boat, *i.e.*, the tears of eye my are

merà 9. *teken àm - sen utut set'ebu - f àn àri - nef χert - f*
desiring to enter into them. Decreed [are] blows his, not may make he courses his

em ta pen en mertu - f śer - f śer ba - f
in earth this according to will his. Annihilated is he, annihilated is soul his,

seχer - s àmu qemāu seχer - s àmu meḥtet
overthrow it those among the southern ones, overthrow it those among the northern ones,

seχer - s àmu 10. *àmentiu seχer - s àmu àbṭiu*
overthrow it those among the western ones, overthrow it those among the eastern ones,

reχ χet àmu ta pen paut neteru χeperu em àḥā - à
and the sages who are in earth this. O cycle of the gods [who] became from limbs my

res - ten ḥer seχer Āpepi śenti - s ṭer ren - f seχer
watch ye to destroy Āpepi! may curse they to destroy name his and may overthrow

su ermen - ten 11. *àm - ten ertā useχt ren - f àn*
him two arms your which are with you. Is granted to be scattered name his, not

χeper mesu - f àn χeper nest - f àn ba - f χat - f
may become children his, not may become seat his, not soul his, body his,

χut - f àuf en maa Rā seχem - s àm - f àm - s
χu his. Is he to the eye of Rā, obtains mastery it over him, eats it

àm - f ànuk utut (sic) er seχer - tuf ṭer ren - f
into him. I [am] commanded to overthrow him, to destroy name his,

12. *sesunnu ren - f ḥekau - f utut - nà s en nesert*
to lay hold of name his and words of power his. Decreed have I it to the flame,

sàp - nà - s en tau erṭā - nà - s en maa Rā χut ent
decreed have I it to the fire, given have I it to the eye of Rā, the eye that

bunes - nes àmu - nes ba - f χut - f χat - f χebit - f
shall eat it and devour it, soul his, χu his, body his, shade his,

13. *ḥekau - f àn tata - f àn benben - f en*
and words of power his. Not may have emission he, not may have erection he of

t'et t'etta t'eṭtu ḥer Āpepi ent àri en menḥ nāu ren - f
body for ever! To be said over Āpepi which is made of wax inscribed name his

ḥer - f em rei uat' ḥnā àru - f ḥer šuu nemau
upon it with colour green, and made it upon papyrus new

ḥnā àru ren en χeft neb en P-āa 14. *em mit em ānχ*
and made name of enemy every of P-āa in death in life,

em menḥ nāu ren en sen ḥer en sen em rei uat′
in wax written name of them upon them with colour green,

senḥu em χennu en nesu peḳaȧs ḥer - sen sȧn em
tied up within coverings. Spit upon them and defile with

rettu-k àbt àru āṭi - sen em ṭes ṭā er χet 15. *en*
feet thy left, make cuttings their with a stone knife, place upon a fire of

χessau āχem em māt ent āmāt ḥnā nāu
χesau grass, quench with the urine of a crocodile, and paint

ren en Āpepi χeft neb en P-āa ānχ ut′a senb em
the names of Āpepi and enemy every of P-āa, life, strength, health, in

mit em ānχ em . . . . . . ḥer seta sȧn em ret - k
death in life, on a slab (?) upon the ground; defile with leg thy

àbt em mȧ māāt χut en se 16. *reχ - nef sem*
left like the reality of the χu of a person. Knows it image

pen Rā χeperu - f semātχeru - f er χeft - f šāt pu
this Rā and becomings his, triumphs he over enemies his. Book is it

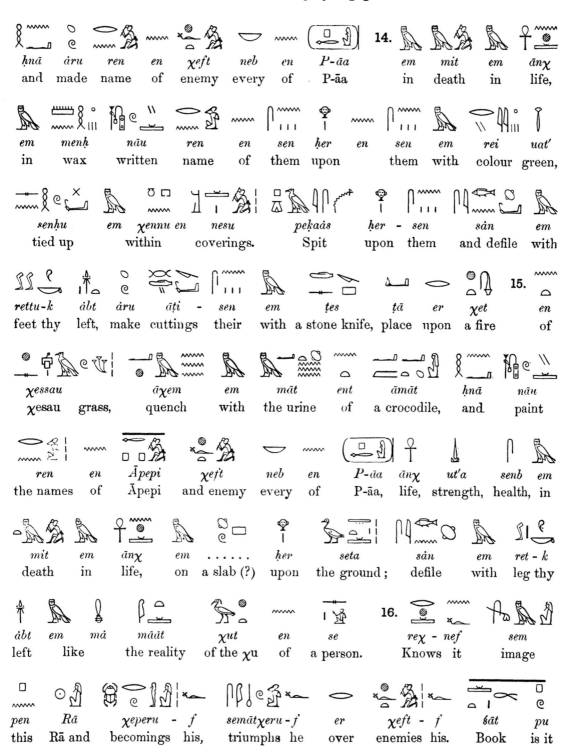

šeta em seḥ ȧn maa-s mat nebt šāt šeta ent
secret in the chamber, not let see it eye any the book secret of

seχer Āpepi
overthrowing Āpepi.

ṭhet ḥekau ren-sen 17. *ṭer Āpepi beḥen semi-f*
Chapter of magical words, name their destroys Āpepi, cutting off demons his.

semātχeru Rā er χefti-f erṭāt nāāi uȧa en Rā em
Triumphs Rā over enemies his, is granted to advance the boat of Rā in

ḥetep erṭāt χetχet Āpepi en šet erṭāt šem-f er
peace, is granted to turn back Āpepi to the fire, is granted to advance he to the

neter nemmat ȧu ṭer ḥau ḥer at 18. *em un māt erṭāt*
divine block, is beaten the filth into nothingness. In very truth is granted

χetχet ba-f χat-f χut-f χebit-f mesu-f
to turn back soul his, body his, χu his, shade his, children his

. . . . *u-f uḥi-f māhau-f āuāā-f*
[kinsfolk] his, family his, relatives his, heirs his,

ȧnememu-f ȧru-f χeperu-f t'et-f suḥt-
hair his, belongings his, becomings his, body his, egg his,

19.

ren - f - pautti f āāiu - f rettu-f saȧs - f

name his, substance his, two hands his, feet his, {speech / teeth} his,

ḥekau - f χut - f ȧuset - f tepḥut - f pu māḥā - f

words of power his, strength his, seat his, cavern his, to wit tomb his,

āāiu - f seχer - tuf pu neḥem mest'er-f ȧm - f tebteb

two hands his; overthrown is he, to wit, taken away is ear his from him. Comes

en sekti - k 20. *erṭāt seχem tes ȧm - f embaḥ*

along *sekti* boat thy, is granted to obtain mastery the flint knife which is in it before

Rā hru neb se-neteru ȧbu - f setem - nef šāt ten erṭāt

Rā day every. Fortified of heart is he who hears he book this. Is granted

nāi uȧa en Rā em ḥetep ṭer Āpepi em ren - f

to come the boat of Rā in peace, destroyed is Āpepi in name his

nebt ṭuau neter seχeper peḥti - f qaȧs 21. *nāu*

every. Glorified is the god making to become strength his! Tied up is the writing,

beḥen Nekȧu Qeṭṭu ḥāā neter em χeperu ȧn Ȧuset t'eṭ

cut asunder are Nekȧu and Ḳettu. "Rejoices the god in becomings," says Isis. Says

en Rā setenemem sebȧu šep maatu-f er sešeta

Rā making to retreat Sebȧu, "Blinded are two eyes his from covering up

ḥer en pet em un mā̆t sesunnu ba - f χat - f
the height of heaven in very truth. Gripped is soul his and body his,

22. *seḥem ḳesu - f erṭāt en śet erṭāt peshu - f en àuf - f*
turned back bones his, given to the fire, given bite his into flesh his

t'es - f erṭāt entuf en ṭet χait nu Rā erṭāt senb -
his own. Given is he into the hand of the executioners of Rā, given to turn back

entuf T'eṭṭu ḥa - k Āpepi nepet pui en Rā ḥa - k qebt
is he." To be recited. Back thou Āpepi, sole[a] that of Rā, back thou claw

pui 23. *en māχaṭi χer Sebàu àt āāiu - f àt*
that of strife, enemy, Sebàu without arms his, without

rettu-f mesu settu per em χennu en tepḥut - f nepet
legs his, [whose] children are destroyed coming forth from within cavern his, the sole

ḥem en Rā àuà reχ-kuà ṭu àru - nek śāt
turned back by Rā. I know, I, the evil wrought hast thou, cut off

ṭep-k àru śāṭ - k 24. *àn fa ḥrà - k er*
is head thy, wrought is slaughter thy, not lift up face thy against

neter āa tekau em ḥrà - k χet em ba - k seti
the god great. Fire upon face thy, flame upon soul thy, may destroy

[a] *I.e.*, that upon which Rā treads.

nemmat āat em àuf - k χenemem - k em šāiṭ en neter
the block great flesh thy, mayest smell thou the slaughter of the god

25.

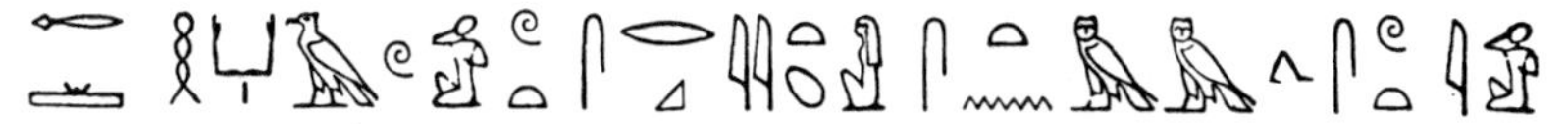

āa ḥekau - tu Serqit setenemem - s-tu à āq sep sen
great, curses thee Serqet, turns back she thee. O entering, entering.

χer - tu sep sen em ḥekau pen em re - à erṭāt-tu
fallen art thou, fallen art thou by curse this from mouth my. Given art thou

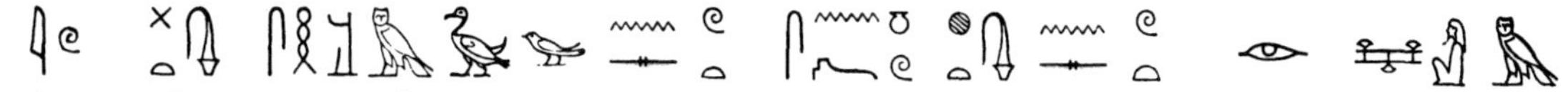

àu šet sehetem - nes - tu sennu - χet - nes - tu maa Ḥeru em
to the flame, destroyed it thee, throws fire it at thee the eye of Horus on

àpt - k χer ḥer ḥrà - k seχer - tu ba - k seχem maa
brow thy, fall upon face thy, overthrown is soul thy, obtains mastery eye

26.

Rā àm - k àuk χertu sep sen senbet - tu sep sen
of Rā over thee, art fallen thou, art fallen thou, fallen, fallen.

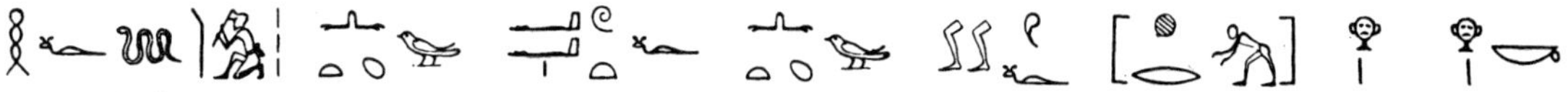

ḥefiu àt āāiu - f àt rettu-f χer ḥer ḥrà - k
O serpent without two arms his, without legs his, fall upon face thy,

àn un māḥā - k āq - k àu āχ en šet seχer - tu
not may be sepulchre thy. Enterest thou into the brazier of fire. Overthrows thee

27.

neter āa χeper t'esef sehetem - tu àmu uàa - f
the god great becoming of himself, destroy thee those who are in boat his

[a] In the MS.  is written twice.

em χut en ṭep - re - sen em ḥekau ȧmu χat - sen

with the might of utterance their, with the words of power from within interior their,

erṭāt-tu ḥer pesṭ - k śāiṭ qebt - k χait nu

placed art thou upon back thy, cut is throat thy, the executioners of

Seχet ḥer semam - k

Seχet are for slaying thee.

Column XXX.

1. 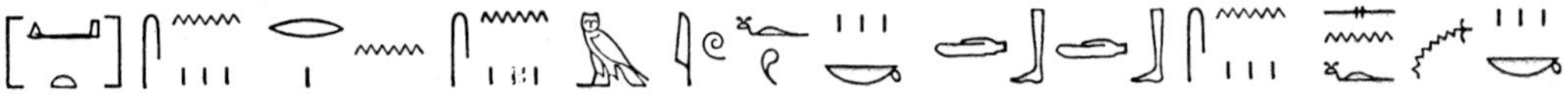

ṭāt - sen re en sen em ȧuf - k ṭebṭeb - sen senf - k

Give they mouth their in flesh thy, spill they blood thy

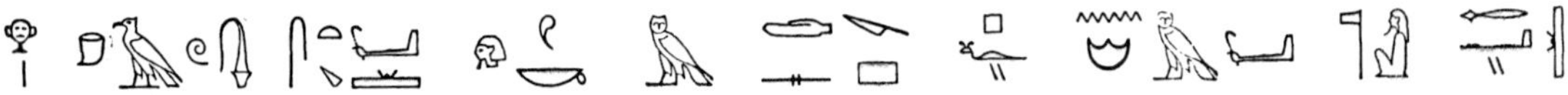

ḥer tau set ṭep-k em ṭes pfi neḥem neter āā

upon the fire, breaking head thy with flint knife that, takes away god great

mest'er-k χetχet sep sen ḥem sep sen χer - tu ṭer - tu

ears thy, retreat, retreat, go back, go back, overthrown art thou, destroyed thou

ȧrek 2. *ḥem er - ek ȧu śaȧsi - k neḥem neter āā*

therefore. Back to thee from journeys thy, removes god great

rettu - k per Rā χā Ḥeru ur ḥekau - sen erek

legs thy, comes Rā, rises Horus, great one, curse they thee.

mātχeru Rā erek Āpepi ṭep - k χeri beḥen - tu Rā

Triumphs Rā over thee Apepi, spit upon art thou O enemy, slays thee Rā,

šep - k *χer tu* 3. *tem - tu en Teḥuti em maa - k*
spit upon art thou, fallen art thou, annihilated art thou. Thoth [blinds] two eyes thy,

ḥekau - f ḥer net'erău - f ām-k tem-k χeperu - k
utters words of power he that may seize he thee. Finished are for thee becomings thy,

seḥetem āru - k tem χat - k ṭer χebit - k
destroyed belongings thy, finished body thy, destroyed shade thy,

ḥekau - k ārek neḥem - f ānχ - k ān un ṭep - k
[finished] words of power thy for thee. Takes away he life thy, not may be spittle thy

4. *nifu sep sen χer erek tem erek χenen ārek*
and breath, twice, falling to thee, annihilation to thee, seizure to thee.

Sebāu en neter āuk sāpi-tu en šāiṭ āat ṭer
O Sebau, by the god! Art thou decreed for slaughter great, destroyed are

- k ḥer ḥetep - sen ān nek āāiu - k ān nek rettu-k
. . . . . thy before them. Not to thee are arms thy, not to thee legs thy,

ān χut en āb - k āu āuset - f 5. *beḥen - tu sep sen ḥem*
not is the strength of heart thy in place its. Cut asunder art thou, twice, retreat,

sep sen senb erek per māb Ḥeru erek mātau
twice, back to thee. Comes forth the dagger of Horus against thee, the chain

en Sut erṭāt em ȧpt - k seḥetem - entu Rā t'esef ṭer
of Sut is put upon forehead thy; destroys thee Rā himself. Destroyed is

χeru - k ȧn un sebeḥu - k ȧhai ȧuk ṭer - tu
voice thy, not may be imprecations thy. O art thou destroyed,

6. *tem - tu ȧn un χeperu - k ȧuk en maa Ḥeru seχem - s*
annihilated, not may be becomings thy, art thou to the eye of Horus, obtains mastery it

ȧm-k em χert en hru neb Āpepi χeft en Rā ṭer - tu
over thee in the course of day every. O Apepi, enemy of Rā, destroys thee

Rā ḥem - tu Ȧtmu em χut ṭep-re - sen setem - k
Rā, turns back thee Atmu with the might of utterances their. Hearest thou

ḥekau - ȧ 7. *. . . . . en set . . mȧ utut en Rā ȧru erek*
words of power my, ... as commanded Rā to be done to thee.

χeft en Rā reχ - nȧ ȧri nek māā ḥem - tu ḥer sep - k
O enemy of Rā, know I what is done to thee. Come turn thou in turn thy

ṭu ȧuk χer - tu en at - k bȧn āḥā ȧrek šenti - tu Rā
evil. Art thou fallen at moment thy evil, stoppage to thee. Curses thee Rā,

ȧu paut neteru āa meter 8. *Āpepi χeft en Rā ȧuk*
is the cycle of the gods great judging Apepi the enemy of Rā. Art thou

χer - tu seχer - tu χeru àrek en at Āpepi tui erṭā-
fallen, overthrown, seizures to thee at the moment, O Apepi, that. Given

entu en ṭes seχem - f àm - k mā ṭesi àpu
art thou to the knife, obtains mastery he over thee with knives those which

àmu uàa - f àuk en śet seχem - s àm - k
are in boat his. Art thou to the fire, obtains mastery it over thee

9. *em χert ent hru neb àuk en nemmat ḥrà - k eres*
in the course of day every. Art thou to the block, face thy is to it,

seχer - tu Àuset em ḥekau - s àuk en maa Ḥeru
overthrows thee Isis with words of power her. Art thou to the eye of Horus.

usert ubti ubti - s ba - k àuk en Ḥeru āāiu
Usert, the burning one, burns she soul thy. Art thou to Horus and the two arms

en neter āā per māb - f àm ā - f er - ek àuk en
of the god great, comes dagger his in hand 10. his against thee. Art thou to

Sut se Nut sau - f θes - k āu - f neḥbet - k
Sut the son of Nut, smashes he backbone thy, cuts he neck thy,

mātau - tu - f en mātau - f tui neχt àm
chains up thee he with chain his that victorious [which] is in

āāiu - f *àuk* *en* *maa* *Rā* *maa* *Ḥeru* *uśā - tu*
hands his. Art thou to the eye of Rā, flames Horus biting into

11. *χat - k* *àuk* *en* *àqṭi* *Rā* *en* *χennu* *Rā* *uaḥ - sen*
body thy. Art thou to the rowers of Rā, to the sailors of Rā, place they

ṭep-k *er* *ta* *àuk* *en* *Ḥeru* *χent - àn - maa* *ḥaṭek -*
head thy upon the earth. Art thou to Horus dwelling in darkness, cut in pieces

tu *em* *baḥennu-f* *tui* *àm* *seχem* *àuk* *en* *sau*
art thou by knife his that which is in Seχem. Art thou to the keepers

nu *sebeχet* 12. *śetau* *per* *heh - sen* *tekau - sen* *erek*
of the pylons secret, comes forth fire their, flame their against thee,

àm - tu - k *nerȧu* *àat* *ḥetep-s* *ḥer* *χat - k* *Āpepi* *χeft* *en*
devours thee fear great, rests it upon body thy, O Apepi enemy of

Rā *àm - k* *nāi* *àm - k* *śaȧs* 13. *àm - k* *χeper*
Rā. Not thou mayest come, not thou mayest pass, not thou mayest become,

àm - k *θes* *per* *ba* *er - ek* *ḥer* *Àmentiu* *àuk* *en*
not to thee may rise to come soul to thee out of those in Àmenti. Art thou to

nesert *ṭep - re - f* *per* *bȧak* *Ḥeru* *erek* *ḥer* *Àbtiu*
the flame of utterance his, comes the hawk of Horus to thee out of the Àbtiu.

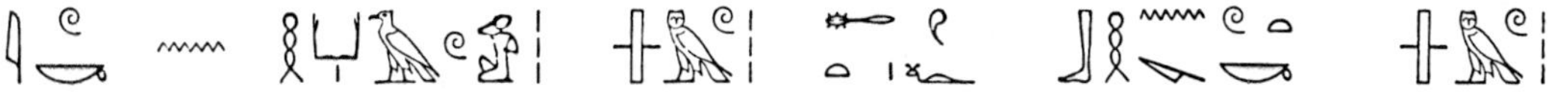

àuk en *ḥekau* *àmu* *χat - f* *beḥen - tuk* *àmu*

Art thou to the words of power within body his, cut in pieces thee those who are in

14.

keràut - *sen* *ṭebu* - *sen* *śesert* - *sen* *erek* *śāiṭ* -

shrine their, accomplish they purposes their upon thee: slay

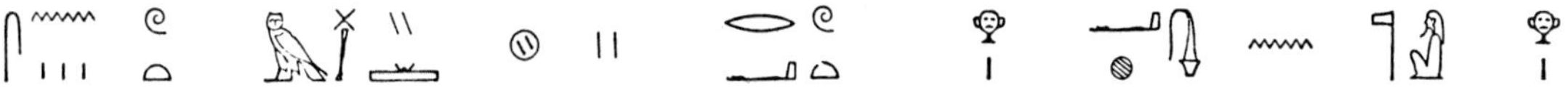

sen - *tu* *em* *nem* *sep* *sen* *erṭātu* *ḥer* *āχ* *en* *neter* *ḥer*

they thee a second time, twice. Placed art thou upon the brazier of the god upon

āχu *ent* *àmu* *uat'et* *àu* *χebt* *en* *àqṭi* *en* *Rā*

the altar which consumes the emerald at the cavern of the rowers of Rā

15.

àu *nemmat* *en* *Teḥuti* *seśep* *neter* *nebt* . . . . *sen* *àm* - *k*

at the block of Thoth. Receives god [great] every . . . . their from thee.

ḥetep *àb* - *sen* *ḥer* *àru* *śāiṭ* - *k* *Āpepi* *χeft* *en* *Rā*

Rests heart their upon doing slaughter thy, O Apepi, enemy of Rā.

ḥa - *k* *ḥem* - *tu* *ṭep-k* *àu* *ta* *àu* *seḥetem*

Back to thee, retreat to thee. Head thy to the earth, are destroyed

mest'eru-k *śep* - *k* *temi* - *tu* *àn* *un* - *nek* *àn* *un* *tut* - *k*

ears thy, blinded art thou, annihilated art thou, not mayest be thou, not may be image thy,

16.

àn *un* *àru* - *k* *àn* *ī* - *k* *àu* *Rā* *em* *pet* - *f* *àu*

not may be attribute thy, not mayest come thou to Rā in two heavens his. Is

Rā en pet - f semātχeru - f erek un set - k ertāt em
Rā in two heavens his, triumphs he over thee, may be tail thy placed in

re - k uśā - k mesq - k t'es-k tebteb- [k] her
mouth thy, mayest bite thou skin thy self thy, mayest be hacked in pieces [thou] upon

χuau en neteru en 17. *paut neteru āat àmu Ànnu*
the altar of the gods, of the cycle of the gods great in Heliopolis.

auk χer-tu seχer - tu seχer - sen - tu per set'ebu per
Art thou fallen, overthrown, overthrow they thee, come forth disasters, comes forth

heh - sen erek en χet sebehu - sen erek em śet
flame their against thee out of the fire, cry out they to thee out of the flame,

hrà - sen erek em nebàt - sen 18. *smāmut erek em*
face their against thee from flame their, clashing against thee

. . . śesau en tes amem - sen - tu her qeb - k ter -
knives of flint, burn they thee upon folds thy, destroy

sen - tu em śāit - sen àm āāiu - sen ter - tu mesu
they thee with knives their in hands their. Destroy thee the children

Heru hekau - sen āq - sen àm - k 19. *χut - sen χeper*
of Horus, curses their enter they into thee. Powers their become

sen erek ḥekau - tu ḥer māu ḥekau - tu em
they against thee, cursed art thou upon the water (?) . . . . . , cursed art thou in

χeperu - k nebt ȧri - nek em unnut-k tui bȧn ȧm - k
becomings thy all [which] made hast thou in hour thy that evil. Not shalt thou

ṭebṭeb ȧu sekti neteru 20. *em seḥak Sebȧu*
make attack upon the *sekti* boat of the gods. Back thou, Sebau,

seḥetem ba - k ȧuk beḥen - tu ȧuk seḥerȧu - tu ȧu
destroyed is soul thy, art thou cut in pieces, thou, driven back art thou from

neter ṭep ȧuk śenti-tu ȧm-k ȧuk seχer - tu
the divine bark, art thou cursed, annihilation to thee, art thou overthrown,

ȧm - tu maa Rā ḥa - k Sebȧu tem erek śeseru
eats thee the eye of Rā. Back thou Sebau, an end to thee! The attacks

21. *en Ḥeru erṭāt em fent-k ȧhai ṭer Āpepi*
of Horus are made upon nose thy, O destroyed is Āpepi!

seχem Rā em χefti - f ȧm - tu χut tui em
Obtains mastery Rā over enemies his. Devours thee eye that in

ren-s pui en ȧmi ȧm - s ȧm-k sām - s ȧm-k
name its that of "Ami," [Flame] eats it into thee, devours it thee

em ḥekau 22. *ṭepre - sen χep - nes - tu mit - k en*
by magical words and utterances their, slays it thee, kill thee

sen χer - sen - tu χesef - sen - tu seχem - sen - tu šep-k
they, cast down they thee, repulse they thee, master they thee, make vomit they thee.

tem - tu ḥem - tu beḥen - tu paut neteru āat àmu
End to thee, back to thee. Cut in pieces thee the cycle of the gods great who are in

Ȧnnu sesunnu uru 23. *āšt tekau mer pā*
Heliopolis, seize [thee] the great ones who multiply the sparks deadly of the flame.

àuk en heh en àmu ren - s tem - nes - tu Āpepi
Art thou to the flames of those who are in name its, makes an end it of thee Āpepi,

χesef - nes - tu em per - k bàn χet erek ušā - s àuf - k
repulses it thee in exit thy evil. Flame to thee, bites into it flesh thy,

àru-s-tu em sesfi ubti 24. *ba - k sesunnu-χet-s ḳesu - k*
does it for thee with fire burning soul thy, consumes it bones thy,

āt - k maa Ḥeru maa Rā àri - s er - ek erṭāt Sut
limbs thy, the flaming eye of Horus, the eye of Rā works it against thee. Places Sut

māb-f em ṭep-k àu - nek maàu (?) *meres ba Bast*
spear his in head thy, is to thee the cat of Meres, the soul of Bast

nebt *śāiṭ* *ḥetep-f* *ḥer* *senf - k* 25. *χet* *àrek* *ḥer* *uat - k* *nebt*
lady of slaughter, reposes he upon blood thy: fire therefore upon ways thy all.

nàk - entu *Peχit* *nesert - s* *nesert* *ur* *nebt* *śāiṭ*
Does evil to thee Peχit, flames she flame great, lady of slaughter,

ḥent *tekau* *neḥem - s* *àuf - k* *nàk - s* *ba - k*
mistress of the spark, removes she flesh thy, injures she soul thy,

ubti - entu *nebàt* 26. *Āpepi* *χeft* *en* *Rā* *àmu - tu* *àmu*
burns up thee the flame, O Āpepi enemy of Rā. Devour thee those who are in

keràut *paut* *neteru* *āat* *ḥetep* *uàa* *tem - k*
the shrine, the cycle of the gods great in front of the boat, that not thou

χeper *àn* *χeper-k* *neqem-k* *st'eràu - k*
mayest become, not mayest become thou, be destruction to thee, mayest be prostrate thou,

àn *nehàs-k* *seχer-entu* *Rā* *er* *neḥeḥ* *àn* *uaḥ-k* *em*
not mayest awake thou, overthrows thee Rā for ever! Not mayest be placed thou in

Column XXXI.

1. *pet* *àn* *un-k* *em* *ta* *àuk* *sekti - k - tu* *en* *ṭes* *pui*
heaven, not mayest rise thou in earth, art thou hacked art thou by knife that

àai *śāiṭ - tu* *em* *nem* *sep* *sen* *χer* *àrek* *em* *tes* *en*
great, slaughtered art thou a second time. fall then by the knife of

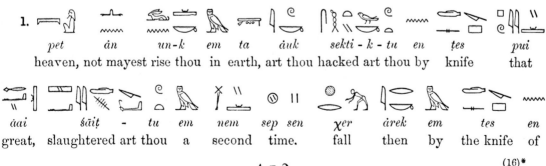

neter àu ḥati ḥer ṭep-k māb en qenti - k māb en
the god. May be the net upon head thy, the dagger in stomach thy, the daggers of

2.
Rā men em tut - k χer - tu en at - k ṭu
Rā stuck into form thy. Overthrown art thou at moment thy evil,

ubti - tu en at ent Ḥeru àu neter per - f er Sebàu
burnt up art thou at moment of Horus. The god comes forth he against the Sebau,

àu seχer Āpepi àu ḥrà - k er nemmàt tui ent āt
is overthrown Āpepi, is face thy at block that of the place

3.
peḳas Rā seḥetem - tu àm - s er neḥeḥ t'etta àn
where spits Rā, destroyed art thou by it for ever and ever. Not

benben - k àn tata - k àn χeper t'ai -
may be emission to thee, not may be erection to thee, not may become male offspring

k àn ruṭ suḥt - k beḥen-tu neteru per em maa Ḥeru
thy, not be strong egg thy, cut in pieces thee the gods coming from the eye of Horus,

4.
ḥeḥ - tu χer - tu seχer - tu Rā Ḥeru χuti per māb em
departed art thou, fallen thou, overthrows thee Rā Harmachis, comes dagger in

ā - f erek t'a śeser - f erek χeper-k em
hand his against thee, comes successful design (?) his against thee, becomest thou

tem *un* *tem* *ȧrek* *Āpepi* *χeft* *en* *Rā* *sep* *fṭu* *ȧn*
not being, end therefore Āpepi enemy of Rā. Times four. Not

χeper-k *ȧn* *χeper* *ba - k* *ȧn* *χeper-k* *ȧn* *χeper*
mayest become thou, not may become soul thy; not mayest become thou, not may become

5. *t'et - k* *ȧn* *χeper-k* *ȧn* *χeper* *mesu-k* *ȧn* *χeper-k*
body thy; not mayest become thou, not may become children thy; not mayest become thou,

ȧn *χeper* *āāiu - k* *ȧn* *χeper - k* *ȧn* *χeper* *ḥāu - k* *ȧn*
not may become hands thy; not mayest become thou, not may become limbs thy; not

χeper-k *ȧn* *χeper* *ḳesu-k* *ȧn* *χeper-k* *ȧn* *χeper*
mayest become thou, not may become bones thy; not mayest become thou, not may become

ḥekau-k *ȧn* *χeper-k* *ȧn* *χeper* *re - k* 6. *ȧn*
words of power thy; not mayest become thou, not may become mouth thy; not

χeper-k *ȧn* *χeper* *qaȧu - k* *ȧn* *χeper-k* *ȧn* *χeper*
mayest become thou, not may become form thy; not mayest become thou, not may become

ȧru - k *ȧn* *χeper-k* *ȧn* *χeper* *χeperu - k* *ȧn*
attribute thy; not mayest become thou, not may become becomings thy; not

χeper-k *ȧn* *χeper* *ȧnememu - k* *ȧn* *χeper-k* *ȧn*
mayest become thou, not may become hair thy; not mayest become thou, not

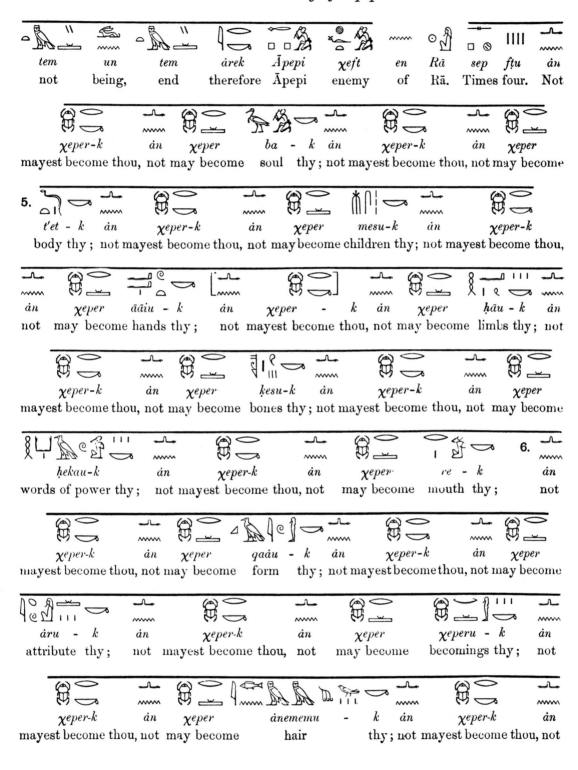

χeper *qer-k* *àn* *χeper-k* 7. *àn* *χeper* *metu-k*[a] *àn*
may become belongings thy; not mayest become thou, not may become emission thy; not

χeper *pautet-k* *àn* *χeper-k* *àn* *χeper* *àuset-k* *àn*
may become substance thy; not mayest become thou, not may become seat thy; not

χeper-k *àn* *χeper* *às-k* *àn* *χeper-k* *àn* *χeper*
mayest become thou, not may become tomb thy; not mayest become thou, not may become

tephut-k *àn* *χeper-k* *àn* *χeper* *māḥat-k* *àn* *χeper-k*
cavern thy; not mayest become thou, not may become chamber thy; not mayest become [thou]

8. *àn* *χeper* *uàt-k* *àn* *χeper-k* *àn* *χeper* *sep-k* *àn*
not may become paths thy; not mayest become thou, not may become times thy; not

χeper-k *àn* *χeper* *θesàs-k* *àn* *χeper-k* *àn*
mayest become thou, not may become speeches thy; not mayest become thou, not

χeper *āq-k* *àn* *χeper-k* *àn* *χeper* *šem-ek* *àn*
may become entrance thy; not mayest become thou, not may become advance thy; not

χeperek *àn* *χeper* 9. *χenṭ-k* *àn* *χeper-k* *àn* *χeper*
mayest become thou, not may become stridings thy; not mayest become thou, not may become

nāi-k *àn* *χeper-k* *àn* *χeper* *ḥems-k* *àn* *χeper-k*
coming thy; not mayest become thou, not may become sitting thy; not mayest become thou,

[a] The words *àn χeper-k* appear to be omitted after *metu-k*.

ȧn χeper ruṭ - k ȧn χeper-k ȧn χeper t'et - k ȧn
not may become growing thy ; not mayest become thou, not may become body thy ; not

χeper-k ȧn χeper bu nebt un-nek 10. *ȧm Āpepi*
mayest become thou, not may become luck any where art thou there, Āpepi

χeft en Rā mit - k sep sen aqa - k aqa ren - k
enemy of Rā. Die thou, die thou, lost art thou, lost is name thy.

ḳanen ȧbeḥu - k θetef t' . . . tu - k šep - k ȧn
May fail teeth thy, may be scattered . . . . thy, be blind thou, not

qemḥu - k χer ḥer ḥrȧ - k seχer - tu 11. *sep sen ṭer - tu*
see thou. Fall upon face thy, overthrown art thou, twice, destroyed art thou,

sep sen tem - tu sep sen mā tes sep sen šāiṭ sep sen
twice, an end to thee, twice, by the knife, twice, the sword twice,

beḥentu sep sen ḥesq - tu sep sen useḥ - tu sep sen šāiṭ
cut in pieces, twice, hacked asunder, twice, sawed, twice. Cut off [is]

ṭep-k em ṭes pui embaḥ Rā hru neb sȧpi - tu - f en
head thy with knife that before Rā day every. Reckons up thee he

Aker seḥem - f ḳesu - f 12. *χet erek seχer - entu Rā*
Aker, turns back he bones his. Retreat to thee, overthrows thee Rā

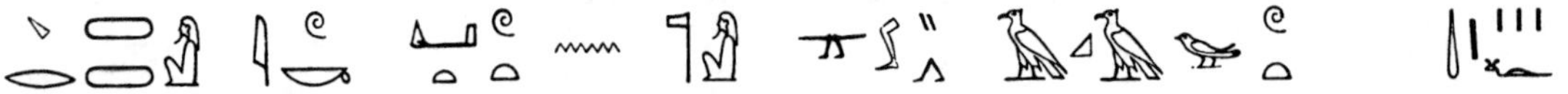

Ḥeru χuti ȧuk ṭāt - tu en neter mes aqa - tu t'eṭtuf

Harmachis. Art thou given to the god bringing destruction to thee. Says he,

māb Ḥeru erṭāt em ȧpt - k āu ṭep-k er neḥb - k ȧu

“Daggers of Horus are placed in head thy cutting head thy from neck thy, is

ba - k χer ȧn χebit - k seḥetem em neter nemmat

soul thy fallen, not [may be] shade thy, destroyed art thou at divine block.

13.

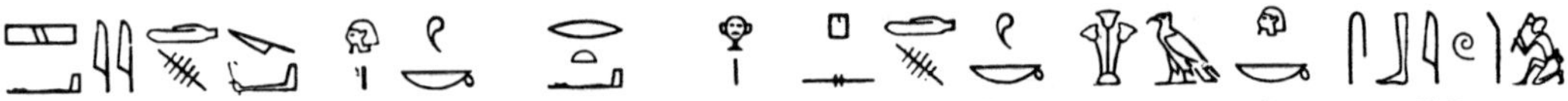

šāiṭ ṭep - k erṭāt ḥer pesṭ - k ḥa - k Sebȧu

Cut off is head thy and placed upon back thy; back to thee, O Sebȧu

χeft en Rā ȧuk beḥentu em per - k bȧn ȧm - tu

enemy of Rā. Art thou cut in pieces at coming forth thy evil, eats thee

χuṭ Ḥeru qeqa - s ȧm - k ȧu ḥetep ȧbtu s heh-s erek

the eye of Horus, bites it into thee. Is resting heart its, flame its against thee,

14.

nebȧt - s erek χet ḥem Āpepi em ret - k tui

fire its against thee. Back retreat Āpepi with foot thy that

bȧn fa paut neteru ḥrȧ - sen erek peḳaȧs - sen

evil. Lifts up the cycle of the gods face their against thee, spit they

nebȧt - sen em mat - k χet erek mer nesert seχem - s

flame their in eye thy, flame against thee, horrible flame, masters it

ȧm - k 15.[a] *ḥu - nes - tu* *t'afi - nes-tu* *ȧuk* *en* *heh - s* *en*
thee, drives it thee, burns it thee. Art thou to flame its

ȧmu *re - s* *beḥen - tu-s* *ḥem* *maa - k* *ȧn* *Rā* *šep - tu*
which is in mouth his, cuts in pieces thee it, turning back eyes thy. Says Rā, "Blinds thee

Ḥeru *em* *uȧa - f* *seχem* *ȧm - k* *ḥāt - k* *ȧru - s*
Horus from boat his, mastering thee and throat thy, makes it

šāiṭ - k *tes* *erek* *aq* 16. *- f* *en* *āt - k* *ȧn*
slaughter thy. Knife to thee, destroys it limbs thy, not

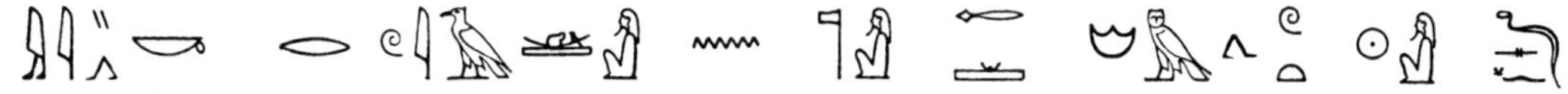

ī - k *er* *uȧa* *en* *neter* *āa* *ḥem - tu* *Rā* *t'esef*
mayest come thou to the boat of god great, turns back thee Rā himself.

ȧuk *er* *nemmat* *ḥrȧ - k* *eres* *seχer - tu* *neteru* *ȧmu*
Art thou to the block, face thy upon it, overthrow thee gods who are in

kerȧut - f *seχer - nes-tu* *šerȧ* *ȧrek* 17. *ȧṭḥeḥ - tu* *mest'er-k*
shrine his, overthrows it thee, walled up art thou, lackest thou ears thy.

seχer-tu *Ȧuset* *em* *ḥekau - s* *šetbu - s* *re - k* *neḥem - s*
Overthrows thee Isis with words of power her, breaks she mouth thy, removes she

mest'eru-k *ȧn* *ṭāt - s - nek* *Rā* *ȧu* *ḥeḥ* *sep sen t'etta* *māb - f*
ears thy, not gives she to thee Rā for ever, for ever and ever and ever. Spear his

[a] There appears to be an erasure here.

tui *ḥem* *em* *àuf - k* *ḳer* *àrek* 18. *χer* *àrek*
that turns back into limbs thy, silence to thee, stabbings to thee,

mit - k *àn* *ānχ - k* *seχer - tu* *Àuset* *Nebt - ḥet* *tut - sen*
die thou, not live thou. Overthrow thee Isis and Nephthys, together they

ḥem - sen *at - k* *χet* *ḥem* *θes* *rer* *šep - k*
turn back they crocodile thy; go back, turn, on the other hand be blind thou,

tem - tu *θes* *rer* *seḥetem* *ba - k* *àn* *ānχ-k*
an end to thee; on the other hand, destroyed [is] soul thy, not live thou

19. *àu* *ḥeḥ* *t'etta* *ḥem* *at - k* *χenp* *peḥti-k* *nesert* *šet*
for ever and ever. Goes back moment thy, takes away strength thy flame of fire

em *t'et - k* *χet* *àrek* *sesunnu - s* *t'et - k* *sesefi - s* *ḳesu - k*
from body thy. Fire to thee, grips it body thy, burns it bones thy;

nebàt *per - tu* *ubti - s* *ba - k* *em* *sā - s* 20. *χat - k*
flame [when] comest forth thou burns it soul thy, chews it body thy,

sesunnu - tu *Àpt - s - ur* *nebàt - s* *àu* *ḥāu - k* *ān - tu* *àu* *nemmat - k*
seizes thee Apt - s - ur, flames she against limbs thy, goest back thou to block thy.

qemam *en* *Rā* *šāiṭ - tu* *Teḥuti* *em* *ḥekau - f*
Made has Rā to kill thee Thoth with words of magic his.

ȧn ī - k er uāa 21. *en Rā seḥem - tu Rā t'esef*
Not comest thou to the boat of Rā, turns back thee Rā himself.

ȧuf reχ ȧri - nek nebt ṭu šet erek qemāu
He knows what done hast thou all evil, flame is upon thee of those in the south,

seχem-s ȧm - k ȧn neter Sept Ānqet utut ȧru erek
masters it thee, says divine Sothis Anqet decreeing what is done to thee.

χet erek en meḥtiu seχem-s ȧm - k ȧn Uat'it 22. *nebt*
Flame is upon thee of those in the north, masters it thee, says Uatit lady of

Pe Ṭepā utut ȧru erek χet erek em Ȧmentiu
Pe and Tep decreeing what is done to thee. Flame is upon thee of those in the west,

ȧn Ḳesun nebt Ȧmentiu utut ȧru erek χet erek
says Ḳesun lord of those in Ȧmenti decreeing what is done to thee. Flame is upon thee

Ȧbtiu seχem - s ȧm - k ȧn Sept nebt Ȧbtiu utut
of those in the east, masters it thee, says Sept lord of those in the east decreeing

ȧru erek 23. *ȧn un-nek em ȧuset - k nebt enti ȧuk ȧm*
what is done to thee. Not mayest rise thou in place thy all which art thou there.

ȧs erek seχem - s ȧm-k ȧuk en χet tui ent maa Rā
Now for thee, masters it thee, art thou to flame that of the eye of Rā,

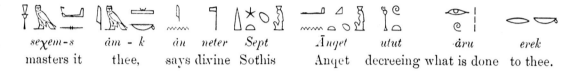

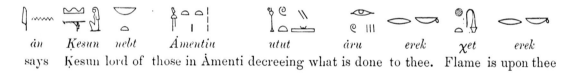

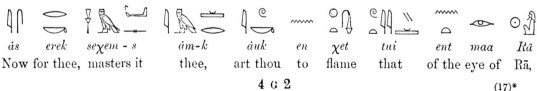

utut - s heh - s erek em ren - s pui en Uat'it
decrees it flame its against thee in name its that of Uat'it,

àm - s àm - k em ren - s pui **24.** *en Àmi*
eats it into thee in name its that of Àmi,

seχem - s àm - k em ren - s pui en Seχet χut - s
masters it thee in name its that of Seχet, flames it

àm - k em ren - s pui en χut mit - k en nesert
against thee in name its that of Flame. Slays thee the flame

χet šep - k erek maa Ḥeru seχem - nes-tu **25.** *neḥem - s*
of fire, blinds thee therefore the eye of Horus, masters it thee, removes it

āāiu - k tet - s rettu-k utut set'ebu - k àn Rā χeper ṭu
two hands thy, carries away it feet thy decreeing disasters thy. Says Rā, "Become evil

àm - k àn Ḥeru àru šāiṭ àm - k qaàs - tu
in thee." Says Horus, "Be made slaughter of thee." Be fettered thou,

netet - tu χer - tu tet ba - k er χebit - k
be bound thou, be overthrown thou. Be carried away soul thy from shade thy,

26. *senḥu ṭep - k ki t'eṭ sená ṭep - k šāiṭ*
be fettered head thy, otherwise said, cut off head thy, be smashed

ḳesu - k *ḥu* *àuf - k* *àu* *ḥāu - k* *setenemem* *ba - k*
bones thy, be dragged off flesh thy from limbs thy, be turned back soul thy

er *χebit - k* *χem* *t'et - k* *àn* *un - nek* *erṭāt - entu* *en*
from shade thy, be brought to nought body thy, not mayest rise thou. Seized art thou by

šet *st'eràu* *mer* *senb - tu* 27. *χer - tu* *en*
the fire, prostrated, brought to nought, turned back thou, overthrown thou by

ṭenṭen *en* *ārāt - f* *uśā - nes - tu* *en* *heh* *en*
the might of uræi his. Chews up it thee the fire of

re - sen *àuk* *en* *šet* *χet* *nebàt - s* *àm - k* *tekau - s*
mouth their. Art thou to the fire, the fire blazes it in thee, sparkles it

àm - k *seḥetem* *s*
in thee, destroys it

Column XXXII.

1. *ba - k* *em* *neter* *nemmat* *paut* *neteru* *āat*
soul thy at the divine block; the cycle of the gods great

χār - sen *erek* *em* *enen* *pu* *àrit* *en* *em* *āāiu - k*
rage they against thee by reason of that, to wit, work which is in hands thy.

ḥur - tu *Àmen* *em* *àpit - f* *semā - nef* *āb - f* *em*
Enfeebles thee Àmen in Apts his, digs he horn his in

χabu - k ȧn Ȧuset utut śerȧt 2. *uat - k se - s*
neck thy, says Isis decreeing to be stopped ways thy, son her

Ḥeru χenȧ - f ren - k ȧn Ṭāfnet t'eṭ stef māu erek
Horus shuts up he name thy. Speaks Tefnut, saying, "Be turned water from thee,

sesunnu ḥer māu per - nek ȧm - f Ṭāt Shu māb - f
be seized on the water comest forth thou from it. Places Shu spear his

ȧm - k herp - k ȧn bes - k Āpepi χeft 3. *en Rā*
in thee, be drowned thou, not pass thou Āpepi enemy of Rā.

ṭep-k Āpepi sep ftu ṭep - ten χeft neb en P-āa ānχ
Be spit upon thou Āpepi. Times four. Be spit upon ye enemy every of P-āa, life,

ut'a senb em mit em ānχ
strength, health, in death in life.

śāt en seχer Āpepi
Book of overthrowing Āpepi.

t'eṭtu ȧ Rā ȧ Ȧtmu ȧ χeperȧ ȧ Shu
Say, "O Rā, O Ȧtmu, O χepera, O Shu,

ȧ Ṭāfnet ȧ Seb 4. *ȧ Nut ȧ Ȧusar ȧ Ḥeru ȧ*
O Tefnut, O Seb, O Nut, O Osiris, O Horus, O

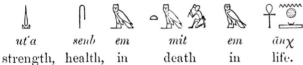

Ȧuset ȧ Nebt-ḥet ȧ Śu ȧ Ṭāfnet ȧ Ḥu ȧ
Isis, O Nephthys, O Shu O Tefnut, O Hu, O

Sau ȧ Ḥeru nebt Kakem ȧ Ḥiku ka en Rā
Sau, O Horus, lord of Kaqem, O Hiku the genius of Rā,

ī en P-āa χer - ten ṭā-f nesert ȧu Āpepi 5. *neḥem - f*
comes P-āa to you, gives he flame against Āpepi, removes he

" . . . . . . en Qeṭṭu ṭā-f reśā em uāa en ḥeḥ aqeṭi
. . . . . . of Qettu, gives he delight to the boat of millions of years. Rowers of

Rā ȧb-sen em ahai em χennu en kerȧut - f baiu
Rā hearts their are in exultation within shrine his, the souls

neteru ḥetep em χut - f neteru ȧmu - s ṭāt - nef ȧau
of the gods rest in horizon his, the gods in it give to him adorations,

6. *ȧu Rā em χent ḥet mesq Ḥeru per ḥer ȧa - f*
is Rā at the head of Het-meseq, Horus comes forth upon stand his.

mātχeru Rā er Āpepi sep fṭu mātχeru P-āa er χeft - f sep fṭu
Triumphs Rā over Āpepi. Times four. Triumphs P-āa over enemy his. Times four."

ket śāt ent seχer Āpepi t'eṭṭu ȧ ret neb set neb
Another book of overthrowing Āpepi. Say, "O man every, woman every,

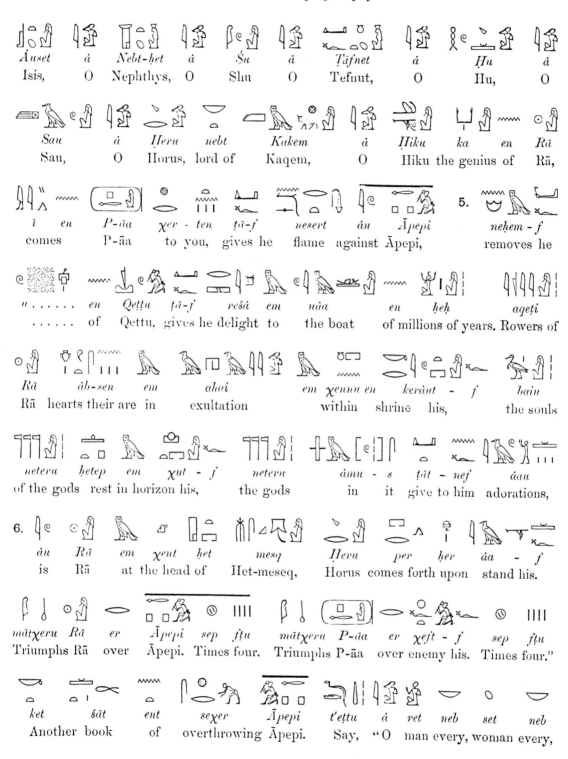

7.

mit neb hamemu neb āba - reu ṭebu - sen en ḥa
dead person every, unborn person every, whatsoever, if accomplish they evil

P-āa ȧ neteru t'ai - sen ȧm - f un-nef em ḥrȧ - ten
for P-āa, may the gods do wrong they to him. May be he in face your

em neter āa nebt pet un nesu - f neb em sebeḥu en
like a god great lord of heaven! May be tongue his all for crying out to

Nebȧu χeft t'a - k ḥer pet ta em meḥu māu
Nebȧu when travellest thou over the two heavens and earth with fulness of breezes

8. *em seḥetem Rā χeft - f ȧuf em ȧputi er Ȧnnu*
in destroying Rā enemies his. Is he a messenger to Ȧnnu

er seḥetep ȧb en Ȧtmu ḥnā t'at'anut-su-f er erṭāt Ȧnnu
to propitiate the heart of Atmu and Powers his, to place Ȧnnu

qemā Ȧnnu meḥt em reśȧ un - nef em ḥrȧ - ten em Ȧbṭ
southern and Ȧnnu northern in delight. May be he in face your like the *Ȧbtu* fish

9. *em nub χeri uȧa en Rā sentˌ - nef χefti neb*
of gold under the boat of Rā. Terrifies he enemies all

en Rā ṭā - f peḥti en en ȧb en Ḥeru set χerui
of Rā, gives he might to the heart of Horus smashing the enemies

en Rā ṭāt reśȧ em ȧb en Ḥeru ṭāt ḥem em
of Rā giving delight in the heart of Horus, placing the rudder in

uȧa āa ȧb en Rā ḥetep 10. *em kerȧut - f*
the boat of the great of heart, of Rā reposing in shrine his;

seḥetem - nef χerui nebt ȧu māāṭ em neteru ȧbu
destroys he enemies all. Is the Māāt boat in strength of heart,

sektet em ḥetep ki t'eṭ em māāu māt χnem - nes en
the *Sektet* boat in peace, otherwise said, in winds of straightness. Unites to it

neb - s Ḥeset em ȧhai ȧu Rā em māket - f
lord its Ḥeset in exultation. Is Rā in protection his,

māket ba 11. *P-āa māket Rā entuf māket - f*
protecting the soul of P-āa, protects Rā him, protects he

su er ret neb set neb mit neb hamemu neb āba reu
him against man every, woman every, dead person every, unborn person every whatsoever.

ȧn Rā χetem - nef re neb t'eṭtu er P-āa em t'eṭtu nebt ṭu
Says Rā shuts he mouth every speaking against P-āa with words any bad.

śep - f ḥrȧ - k maa-nef ȧu nebt ȧri - sen χet nebt 12. *eref bȧn*
Blinds he face thy, looks he at everyone do they things any to him evil and

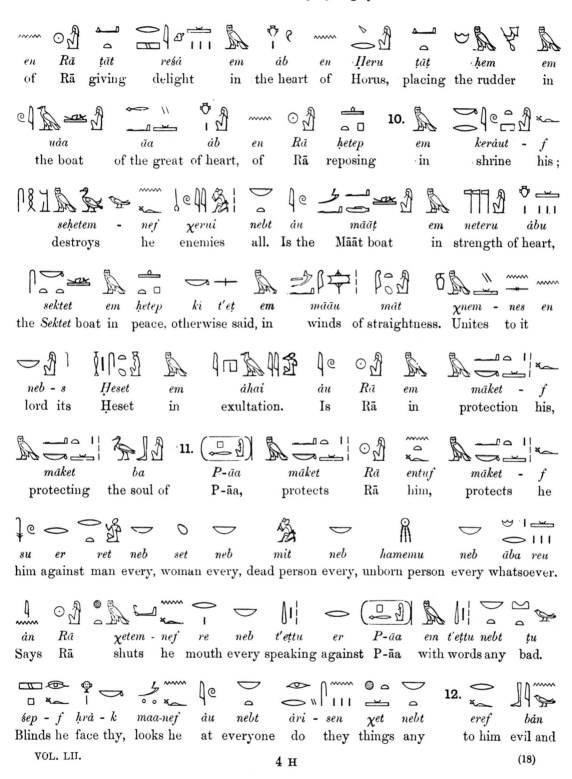

ṭu un - nef re en P-āa ānχ ut'a senb er ret neb
wicked. Opens he mouth of P-āa, life, strength, health, against man every,

set neb mit neb hamemu neb āba reu T'ettu re pen
woman every, dead person every, unborn person every whatsoever. Said is chapter this

χeft Rā ḥer θeset net . . . . er seneχeχ su em ānχ šāt
when Rā is for . . . . to make long life to him in life. The book of

Neb - er - t'er ren - s
Neb - er - t'er name its.

īu - f pu
Gone out has it.

13. *na ren en Āpepi enti ȧn unen - sen*
The names of Āpepi which not shall be they.

14. *Āpepi χer em nešeṭ*
Apepi, fiend. Bristling with terror.

15. *Āpepi χer ṭuṭu*
Apepi, fiend, Doubly evil one.

16. *Āpepi χer ḥau ḥrȧ.*
Apepi, fiend, Backward of Face.

17. *Āpepi χer hemhemti*
Apepi, fiend, Roarer.

18. *Āpepi χer Qeṭṭu*
Apepi, fiend, Evil-doer.

19. *Āpepi χer Qerner*
Apepi, fiend, Qerner.

20. *Āpepi* *χer* *Iubani*
Āpepi, fiend, Iubani.

21. *Āpepi* *χer* *Āmam*
Āpepi, fiend, Devourer.

22. *Āpepi* *χer* *āb - taiu*
Āpepi, fiend, Adversary of the world.

23. *Āpepi* *χer* *sāaṭ - ta*
Āpepi, fiend, Eclipser of the earth.

24. *Āpepi* *χer* *χermuti.*
Āpepi, fiend. χermuti.

25. *Āpepi* *χer* *Kenememti*
Āpepi, fiend, Monkey (?).

26. *Āpepi* *χer* *Śeta*
Āpepi, fiend. Tortoise.

27. *Āpepi* *χer* *Serem-taiu (?)*
Āpepi, fiend. Serem-taui.

28. *Āpepi* *χer* *seχem - ḥrā*
Āpepi, fiend. Strong-face.

29. *Āpepi* *χer* *Unti*
Āpepi, fiend, Unti.

30. *Āpepi* *χer* *Karāu - ememti.*
Āpepi, fiend, Karau-ememti.

31. *Āpepi* *χer* *χesef* *ḥrā*
Āpepi, fiend, Repulsive of face.

32. *Āpepi* *χer* *Sebaa*
Āpepi, fiend, Devil

ent *Sebaa*
of devils.

33. *Āpepi* *χer* *χak - āb*
Āpepi, fiend, Rebel.

34. *Āpepi* *χer* *χan - re - ....*
Āpepi, fiend, χan - re ....

uāa *ki* *t'eṭ* *χa ....*
uāa, otherwise said, χa ....

35. *Āpepi* *χer* *Nāi*
Āpepi, fiend, Nāi.

(18)*

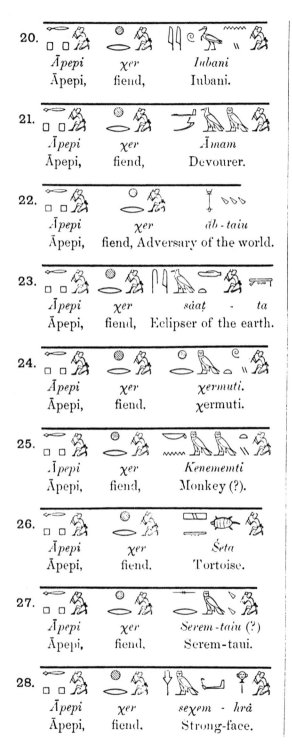

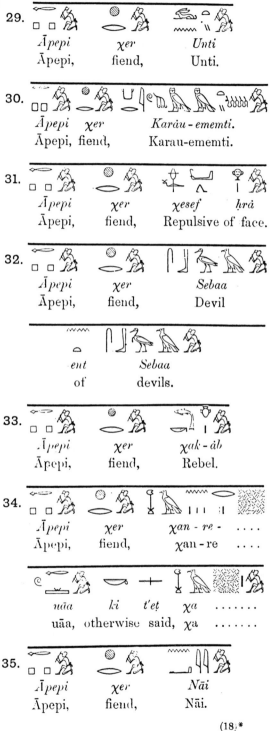

36. *Āpepi* *χer* *Ām.*
Āpepi, fiend, Ām.

37. *Āpepi* *χer* *Turre - pa* (?)
Āpepi, fiend, Turre-pa (?).

38. *Āpepi* *χer* *Iubau*
Āpepi, fiend, Iubau.

39. *Āpepi* *χer* *Uai*
Āpepi, fiend, Uai.

40. *Āpepi* *χer* *χarebuṭu*
Āpepi fiend, fourfold χarebuṭu.

41. *Āpepi* *χer* *Sau*
Āpepi, fiend, Sau.

42. *Āpepi* *χer* *Beteśu*
Āpepi, fiend, Beteśu.

43. *na nāuu en ta neset enti àu àru ḥer śuu nemaut*
The writings of the envelopes which are made upon papyrus new, and

seχertu
thrown and

44. *erṭāt ḥer śet àru χertu uā ḥefi àu set - tuf*
placed upon the fire. Is made now one worm being tail his

em re seχer - f er
in the mouth, throw down him

45. *χeri māṭennu - f ḥer*
having knife his in

atit - f em t'eṭ Āpepi χer Betet
back his, saying, "Āpepi, fiend, Betet."

46. *àri ki*
Make another

śetat t'eṭtu pu àrit en ki tut en χefti ftu em
mystery of words, to wit, make other images of enemies four with

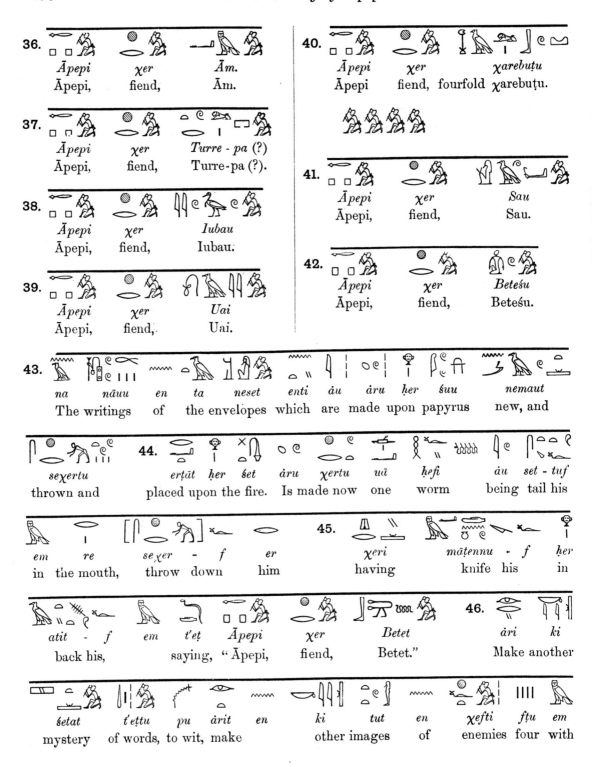

ḥrȧ en . . . . 47. *senḥu netet āāui - sen en*
the face of . . . . bind and tie hands their

ḥa - sen mes beteś pu ȧri ki
behind them, [and call them] "Children of inertness," to wit. Make another

48. *ḥefi em ḥrȧ en maȧu ḥrȧ - f χeri*
worm with the face of a cat, face his having

māṭennu - f em t'eṭ Hemhem 49. *ȧri ki em*
knife its, saying, "Roarer." Make another with

ḥrȧ en . . . . . . er χeri māṭennu - f em t'eṭ Āat - qar
the face of a . . . . . . having knife its, saying, "Āa - qar-

Uaba 50. *ȧri ki em ḥrȧ en aṭ er χeri māṭennu - f*
Uaba." Make another with the face of a crocodile having knife its,

em t'eṭ Haunā - ȧru ḥer ḥrȧ ȧru ki 51. *tut en χeft*
saying, Haunā - ȧru - ḥer - ḥrȧ. Make another image of the enemy

em ḥrȧ en apṭ er χeri māṭennu - f em t'eṭ
with the face of a duck having knife its saying,

Unti ȧru ki 52. *maȧu ḥet'ti senḥu netet*
Unti." Make another [with the face of] cat white tie and bind it

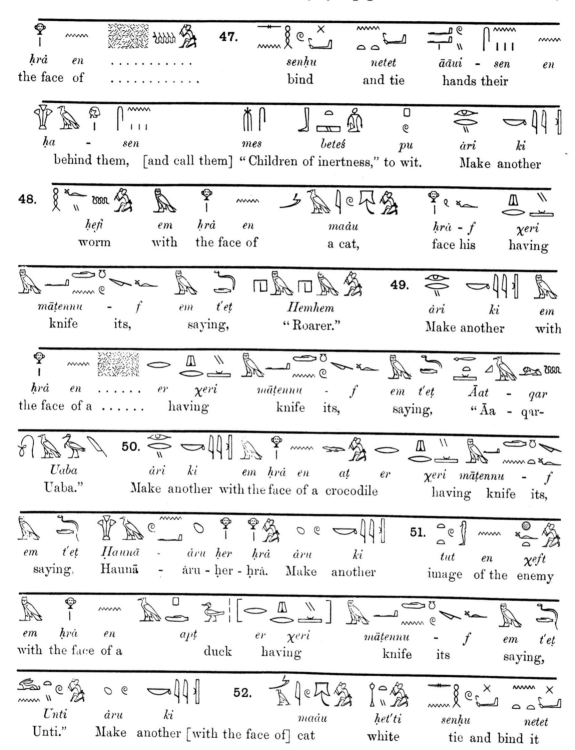

53.

mātennu - f em t'eṭ Āpepi χer àru ki tut en

[having] knife its, saying, "Āpepi the enemy." Make other images of

χeft ftu em ḥrà en apṭ netet em āāui - sen ret - sen

the enemies four with the faces of a duck, tie hands their and feet their

54.
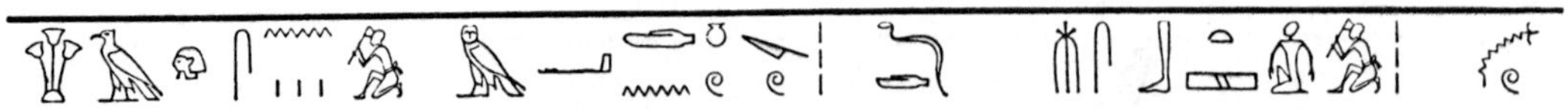

ḥa - sen māṭennu t'eṭ mesu betés pu

behind them, [faces their having] knives [their] saying "Children of inertness," to wit.

Column XXXIII.

1.

ṭuau Rā ḥer-sa enen t'eṭṭu à àtf nebt neteru

A hymn of praise to Rā after this. Say, "Hail, father, lord of the gods,

2.

ur en paut neteru āat pautti ḥetep en neteru

mighty one of the cycle of the gods great, matter primeval of the gods,

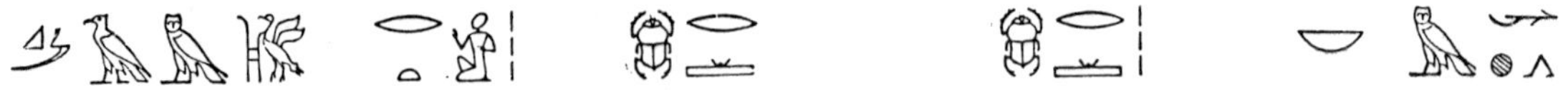

qemam ret χeper χeperu neb emχet

creator of men, evolver of evolutions all after

3.

χeper - f nuk se - k àb - k em māāt netrà

was evolved he. I am son thy, heart thy in very truth, strength of

àb pui pu per em šetat - k seχut χeper - sen

heart that, to wit, coming forth from mystery thy, commemorating becomings their

4.

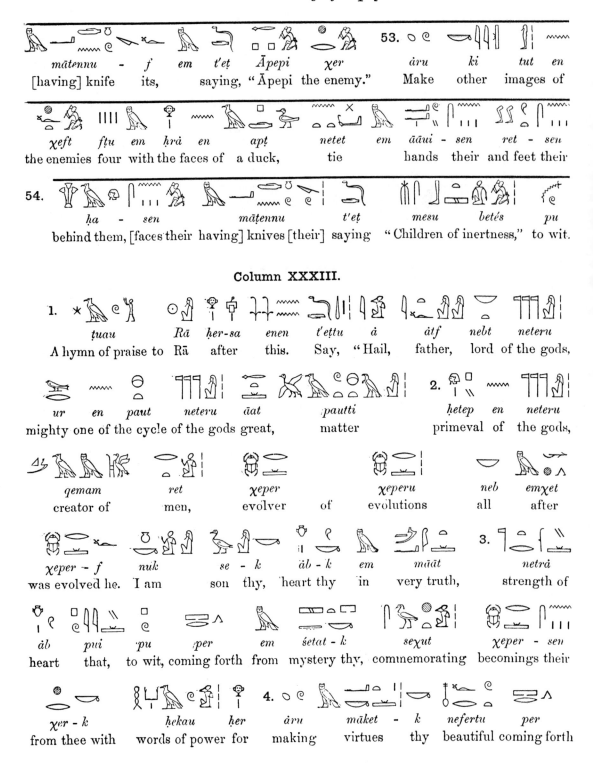

χer - k ḥekau ḥer àru māket - k nefertu per

from thee with words of power for making virtues thy beautiful coming forth *em re - à nuk menχet seχeru māāi māi Rā maa-*

from mouth my. I am perfect with {wisdom / plans}. Come, O Rā, look

5. *ktu em maa - k ḥesu - k ḥer àru - à seχer - à nek*

thou with two eyes thy, be pleased thou at what done have I. Overthrown have I for thee

Āpepi em at - f seḥetem - à 6. *su emχennu en χebut-f*

Āpepi at moment his, destroyed have I him within cavern his.

àu Ḥeru maa χer χet - f ḥer ḥesq tep nu χefti - k

Horus of two eyes has staff his to cut off the head of enemy thy,

Menḥi 7. *χer tes - f ur šāiṭ - f ṭepu Sebàu - k*

Menhi having knife his mighty, cuts off he the heads of fiends thy;

àmi nesert sennu - χet - s 8. *ba - f em nemmat - f àu*

devours the flame, shooting fire its into soul his on block his. Is

ba - k em resà sep sen t'a - nef ḥer em māāu nefer

soul thy in joy, in joy, Sails over it the sky with winds fair,

māāi 9. *māi maa - k em mat - k ḥer àri - à em*

come, O look thou with eye thy at what done have I with

ḥāu en Āpepi . . . .[a] *χefti ànebtet - f* 10. *sam*

the limbs of Āpepi . . . . the enemy. Walled up is he, perished

[a] I cannot transcribe the hieratic character which follows here.

χa - f *ḥetem* *em* *Aā* - *peḳa* *pet - k* *men*
has body his destroyed from Aa - Peḳa and two heavens thy; safe are

nut - k *ḳer* *ṭeṭṭeṭ - tu* 11. *āṭet - tu* *senb - tu* *renp - tu* *sep sen*
towns thy having stability. Firm art thou, strong art thou, growest thou, twice,

uben - tu *sep sen* *pesṭ - tu* *sep sen* *hru* *neb* *χā - k* *em* *uȧa*
risest thou, twice, shinest thou, twice, day every. Risest thou in the boat

12. *ȧb - k* *āu* *meḥ* *ȧb - k* *en* *mesu - k* *Āpepi* *pfi* *χeri*
heart thy is joyful, fill heart thy children thy. To Āpepi that enemy,

uamti *en* *ḥau* *ḥrȧ* 13. *ka - nef* *ḥeru - tu* *er - ef*
the serpent of backward face, cries he, "Away with thee," then

ȧri - nef *uauu* *ṭu* *er* *nemmat - f* *uteb* *su* *qennu - f*
making against him cries horrible at block his, changes he, breaks down he

14. *ḥrȧ - f* *hai* *per* *em* *χut* *taui* *em* *neteru* *ȧbu*
face his. Hail, coming forth from the horizon and the lands with strength of heart,

ne'tem *ȧb - k* *Rā* *hru* *neb* *Āpepi* *χer* 15. *en* *χet* *Nekȧu*
rejoices heart thy Rā day every. Āpepi throws down the fire, Nekȧu

mās *en* *χet* *net'emi* *ȧb* *en* *Ȧmen - Rā* *nebt* *nest*
carries off the flame; rejoices the heart of Ȧmen - Rā, lord of the thrones

taui *χent* 16. *Ȧpi* *χeft - f* *χer* *χeri - f*
of the two worlds, at the head of the Ȧpts, enemy his has fallen beneath him.

mātχeru *Rā* *er* *Āpepi* *sep* *fṭu* *mātχeru* *Ȧmen - Rā* [*nebt nest taiu*]
Triumphs Rā against Apepi. Times four. Triumphs Ȧmen - Rā, {[lord of the thrones of the two worlds]}

17. *χent* *Ȧpi* *er* *χeft - f* *sep* *fṭu* *mātχeru* *Ȧtmu* *nebt*
at the head of the Apts against enemy his. Times four. Triumphs Atmu, lord of

Setemet *er* *χeft - f* *sep* *fṭu* *mātχeru* *Teḥuti* 18. *menχet* *ḥekau*
Setemet, against enemy his. Times four. Triumphs Thoth, perfect of enchantments,

nebt *neter* *t'eṭtu* *er* *χeft-f* *sep* *fṭu*"
lord of divine words, against enemy his. Times four.

iu - f *pu.*
Gone out has it.

THE THIRTY-NINTH CHAPTER OF THE BOOK OF THE DEAD.[a]

1.  2.

re en χesef rerek - f em neter-χert ḥa - k

Chapter of repulsing serpent his in the Nether-world. Back thou,

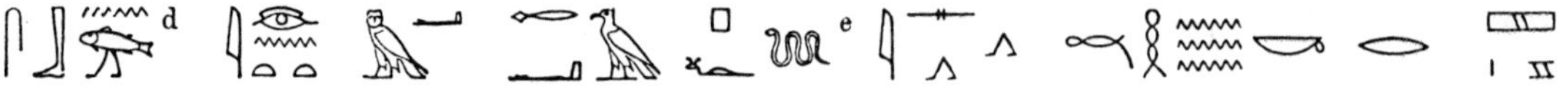

seben àntet mā Āāa - pef àseb meḥ - k er še

depart, retreat, ... baleful worm, withdraw, drowned art thou at the pool of

Nu er bu utut àtef - k àrit šāt - k

Nu, at the place where has commanded father thy to make slaughter thy

---

[a] Naville, *Das Aegyptische Todtenbuch der* XVIII *bis* XX *Dynastie*, t. I, pl. LIII.

[b] The name and titles of Àḥmes for whom this papyrus was written are given as follows :—

àm àuset-a ḥetep en Àmen Mes em neter àri en sab Àḥ-mes suten àm Messhert

[c] *Lb*, *Ba*, 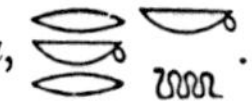. In the variants given here *Pb* = Paris MS. *b*, *Lb* = Leyden MS. *b*, and *Ba* = Berlin MS. *a*.

[d] *Pb* , *Ba* 

[e] *Pb* 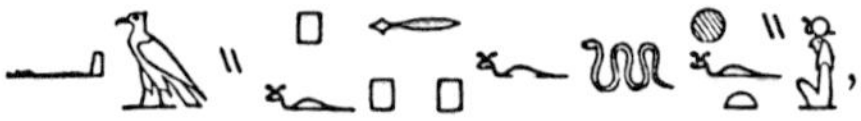, *Ba* 

[f] *Pb* 

àm ḥeru er mesχenet tui ent Rā àmt seṭa - k

there. Depart to place of birth that of Rā in which is terror thy.

nuk Rā àmi seṭa - nef ḥa - k sebai

I am Rā in terror 4. his. Back thou fiend,

em ṭesu seśep - f χer en Rā t'eṭtu - k penā

by the {darts knives} of beams[a] his overthrown has Rā words thy, have reversed

ḥrà - k àn neteru śeṭ ḥāt - k àn maftet uṭet

face thy the gods, has torn out heart 5. thy the lynx (?),[b] has thrown forth

qasuu - k àn ḥeṭeṭet uṭ neken - k àn māāt

fetters thy the scorpion. has shot out destruction thy Māāt,[c]

seχer - s - tu àm - u uat χer seben Āpepi

overthrow they thee those who 6. are in the ways; fall down, depart Āpepi,

χefti en Rā à ruà āṭ em àbet pet ḥer χeru

enemy of Rā. O pass away over the region[d] in the east of the sky at the voice

---

a Lb

b Ba

c Lb

d Ba

qerȧ *nehem-nehem* 7. *un* *sebau*[a] *χut* *ḥetep - ā*

of the thunder-cloud roaring! Opens the gates of the horizon immediately

Rā *per - f* *ḳeḥu* *em* *nespu* *ȧri - ȧ* *ȧb - k* *sep* *sen*

Rā, comes forth he (*i.e.*, Āpepi) ruined in fragments. Made have I heart thy, times two,

Rā *ȧri - ȧ* *nefer* *sep* *sen* *ȧri - ȧ* *em* *ḥetep* 8. *Rā* *ȧri* *hai*[b]

Rā; worked have I well, times two; worked have I in peace Rā; making to advance

ennuḥ - k *Rā* *ȧu* *Āpepi* *χer* *senḥti - k*[c] *qasu* *en*

ropes thy Rā. Is Āpepi overthrown, tie thee and fetter

neteru *resu* *meḥta* *ȧmenta* 9. *ȧbta* *qasu - sen* *ȧm - f*

the gods southern, northern, western, eastern, set fetters they round him,

seχer *en* *su* *Rekes*[d] *qasu* *en* *su* *Ḥertit* (?)[e] *ḥetep* *Rā*

overthrows him Rekes, fettters him Ḥertit (?). Sets Rā,

sep *sen* *sut'a* *Rā* *em* 10. *ḥetep* *Āpepi* *χer* *ha* *Āpepi*

times two, strengthens himself Rā in peace. Āpepi is overthrown, departs Āpepi

---

a Ba

b Pb, Lb

c Lb

d Pb, Lb

e Pb

χefti *en* *Rā* *ur* *ṭept* - *nek* *er* *ṭept* *tuia* *ḥer āb*

enemy of Rā. Greater is taste thy than taste that which is in

ḥeṭeṭet *ur* *ārit* - *nes* *erek* 11. *merθā* - *nes* *χer* - *s* *t'etta*

the scorpion, mightily has been made it for thee; dead for it are courses its for ever.

ān *ben* - *k* *ān* *ṭa* - *k* *Āpepi*

Not may there be erection to thee, not may there be emission to thee, Āpepi,

χefti *en* *Rā* *seχeseƒ* *ḥrā* - *k* *mesṭeṭu* *Rā* *maa* - *nek*

enemy of Rā who repulses face thy, O hater of Rā when sees [he] thee.

12. *ḥa* - *k* *ṭen* *ṭep* *ṭes* *ḥrā* *sennu* *ṭep*

Back thou, smashed is head [thy], gashed is face [thy], carried off is head [thy]

emmā *uat* *t'ent'en* *ṭep* - *k* *āmi* *ta* - *ƒ* *seṭ* *ḳesu* - *k*

among the ways, broken in is head thy in land his, smashed are bones thy,

beḥ[en] *āt* - *k* *sāp* - *ƒ* - *tu* *Nekker* *Āpepi*

hacked in pieces are limbs thy, condemned has he thee Nekker, O Āpepi,

---

[a] *Pb* [b] *Lb* [c] *Pb*

[d] *Pb* [e] *Pb* [f] *Pb* adds [g] *Pb*

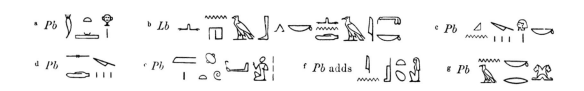

χefti en Rā qeṭet - k [a] *àpepet - k ḥen sep sen* [b] *ḥetep - k*
enemy of Rā, sailors thy, green food thy, necessaries [thy], offered to thee

àm ḥennu - k àm 14. *seχepχep sep sen er pa seχep*
there, provided for thee there. The advance to the house, the advance

àrit-k er pa seχep nefer àn per set'ebu neb
which makest thou to the house is advance good; not may come forth disaster any

ṭu em re-k er-à em àritu-k er - à nuk Set [c]
evil from mouth thy against me in working thy for me. I am Set

šeṭ χennu 15. *qerà* [d] *em χennu χut*
letting loose the storm clouds and the thunder-cloud within the horizon

ent pet mà Net'eb [e] *àb-f pu à àn Temu θesu*
of heaven like Neteb heart his to wit. O, says Atmu, "Make strong (lift up)

ḥràu - θen menfitu Rā χesef-nà 16. *Nent'ā* [f] *em t'at'anutsu à*
faces your soldiers (?) of Rā, repulsed have I Nent'ā by the Powers." O, says

---

[a] *Pb* ..., *Lb* ...

[b] *Pb* ... [c] *Pb* ...

[d] *Pb* ... [e] *Pb* ..., *Lb* ... [f] *Lb* ...

Seb smen-ten ȧmu nest-sen em ḥer-ȧbu uȧa

Seb, "Prepare ye those who are in seats their within the boat of

χeperȧ seśep uat-ten[a] 17. *mesqet-θen ṭāṭāiu-en-ten ḥer*

χeperȧ, take ways your and weapons your, put them ye in

āāiu-θen ȧt[b] *Ḥet-Ḥeru*[c] *seśep nesut-ten i Nut māi*

hands your." O, says Hathor, "Take ye armour your." O, says Nut, "Come

χesef-f-n 18. *t'ā pui śesi ȧm karȧ-f*

and repulse him will we destroying one that, following him who is in shrine his,

t'a-f su em uāāiu Neb-er-t'er ȧti χesef-f ȧ

goes forth he (*i.e.*, Rā) to him alone (?) Neb-er-t'er, without repulse is he." O, say

neteru ȧpen ȧmu 19. *paut-sen rer*[d] *śe em māf-ket*

gods these who are in cycle their going round the lakes of emerald,

māā āāa tuau-n neḥem-n āā karȧ

"Come mighty one, adore we, deliver we the great one of the shrine,

---

[a] *Pb*

[b] *Lb*

[c] *Pb*

[d] *Pb*

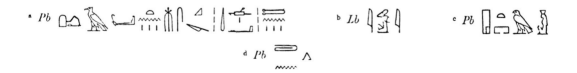

per *en* *paut* *neteru* *ȧm-f* 20. *ȧri - nef* *χut*

cometh forth the substance of the gods from him. Are made for him commemorations,

ṭāṭāu - nef *ȧau* *smȧ* *su* *er* *ten* *ḥnā* *it* *en*

are given to him shouts of acclamation, addressed is he by you and praised." "Hail" says

Nut *er* *net'em* *pef* *ȧn*[a] *ȧmu* *neteru* 21. *per - f*

Nut to Sweet one that. Say those who are among the gods, "Comes forth he,

qem-f *uat* *ȧri-f* *ḥaqet* *em* *neteru* *senehep-f* *χent*[b]

finds he the way, maketh he captives among the gods, drives away evil he from

Nut *āḥā* *Seb* *ȧ* *neru* . . . . . . *ȧu* *paut* *neteru*

Nut, stands up Seb." Hail victorious one! Is the cycle of the gods

22. *em*[c] *teḳas* . . . *Ḥet-Ḥeru* *saṭu* *mātχeru* *Rā* *er* *Āpepi*

marching along, is Hathor trembling. Triumphs Rā against Āpepi.

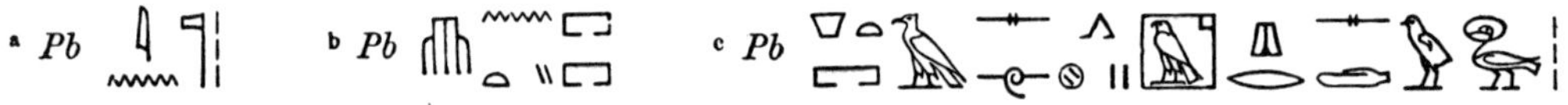

[a] *Pb* [b] *Pb* [c] *Pb*

CPSIA information can be obtained
at www.ICGtesting.com
Printed in the USA
LVOW09s2045090518
576568LV00017BA/381/P